"*Understanding Digital Cinema* is an impressive compilation of information covering both the complex technical and operational aspects of Digital Cinema. The book brings together the collective insight of some of the field's most knowledgeable experts. It is the single most comprehensive book ever written on the topic."

—Brad Hunt
Sr. VP, Chief Technology Officer
Motion Picture Association of America, Inc.

"*Understanding Digital Cinema* is a book that inspires professionalism and instills a sense of meaning for the present and future career of the reader. Finally, a book that really shows how the supply chain of Digital Cinema works. Through an effective and easy-to-follow structure, this book translates the complex patterns of Digital Cinema into practical insights and guidelines to help Professionals. This book is a company's most important asset for the roll-out of Digital Cinema."

—Dr. Angelo D'Alessio
President
MIC – Moving Image Center

"Digital cinema represents a revolutionary change in the delivery and presentation of entertainment in movie theatres. The same technology has been in place for 100 years and is about to undergo a major transition. This book details in an easy-to-read way the technical and business issues facing this transition from some of the many pioneers leading this change."

—Douglas Darrow
Business Manager
Commercial Entertainment
Texas Instruments

Understanding Digital Cinema

A Professional Handbook

Charles S. Swartz, Editor
Entertainment Technology Center
University of Southern California

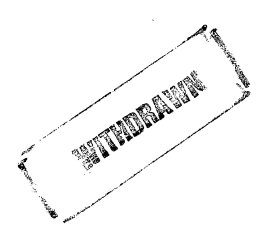

ELSEVIER

AMSTERDAM • BOSTON • HEIDELBERG • LONDON
NEW YORK • OXFORD • PARIS • SAN DIEGO
SAN FRANCISCO • SINGAPORE • SYDNEY • TOKYO
Focal Press is an imprint of Elsevier

Focal
Press

Focal Press is an imprint of Elsevier
200 Wheeler Road, Burlington, MA 01803, USA
Linacre House, Jordan Hill, Oxford OX2 8DP, UK

Library of Congress Cataloging-in-Publication Data
Application submitted

British Library Cataloguing-in-Publication Data
A catalogue record for this book is available from the British Library.

ISBN: 0-240-80617-4

For information on all Focal Press publications

visit our website at www.books.elsevier.com

04 05 06 07 08 09 10 9 8 7 6 5 4 3 2 1

Printed in the United States of America

Contents

Foreword

How New Technology Has Shaped Motion Pictures: A Short History

Richard P. Crudo, ASC
President, American Society of Cinematographers

In 1978 I was a college student whose after-school job was as an assistant cameraman for a documentary/newsreel cinematographer based in my home town of New York City. I loved what I was doing and saw it as the first step on the road to someday becoming a shooter myself. Our work was done in 16mm film format, generally for network television presentation under the auspices of such programs as CBS News' *60 Minutes*. One afternoon my boss and I were dispatched to the Plaza Hotel to photograph an interview with a visiting European dignitary. Upon arrival at the appointed suite, we were met by a second camera crew whose purpose was to simultaneously cover correspondent Mike Wallace's angle and thus help speed things along.

Never mind that the subject before our lens was to be the Italian Prime Minister. The initial thing I noticed about the busy situation was that my counterpart on the "B" camera—Phil—was an uncommon character for our line of employment. As a group, assistant camerapeople at that level tended to be of the young, go-getter variety. Phil looked nothing like me. He was much older, close to retirement, in fact, and had a hard, grizzled air about him. Though he moved with assurance as he unpacked his cases, there was no doubt he would have preferred to be spending his time some other way. On top of that, the burning stump of a cheap cigar dangled from the corner of his mouth. Suffice to say no one had the nerve to tell him to put it out, even among the rare company of our foreign statesman and his entourage.

After an unremarkable shoot during which we exposed what seemed like several miles of Eastman Kodak 7254 negative, Phil and I found ourselves back downstairs on East 59th Street loading the gear into our cars. I had given him a wide berth as the cameras rolled because it was plain that he was infinitely more experienced, and I respected him for that. But I was still one of those eager go-getters. Before we went our separate ways, I couldn't resist asking if he had any advice. Phil slammed the trunk hard and turned to utter his only complete sentence in the eight hours I'd known him. Oddly, his tone was gentle. "Kid, what you're trying to do right now is like trying to become a blacksmith at the time the automobile was invented."

With that, he hung his head and walked away. I never saw him again.

Talk about dashing someone's dreams. In retrospect, this should not have been unexpected. I could sense the greater significance of what he was telling me. The threat of our beloved photochemical process being replaced by video, or some other electronic medium was breathing down everyone's neck. This turn of events would mark the end to a way of life I had already become deeply attached to. No jobs. No opportunities. Worst of all, no hope.

My choices at that moment were clear. One would have had me retreating to the fabled Oak Room inside the Plaza, ordering a double vodka and figuring out a new career path. The other was more sensible and truer to heart. Rather than let the prospect of circumstances that might or might not occur within the industry intimidate me, I chose then and there to welcome new technologies as they came. This didn't just mean embracing them regardless of form. My rejection of easy cynicism also held a nod in Phil's direction. Picturing myself in the company of the many cinematographers I admired, my endorsement would go only to those items that helped me do my job *better*.

Allowing that Phil spoke from some shred of fatherly concern, I'm thankful I had the wherewithal to not heed his veiled suggestion. Twenty-five years later, I see that I was driven by something much more profound than ignorance of the hard road I might be facing if I'd elected to stay the course. Instead, as with so much of the story that relates technology and its effect on the moving image, what motivated my decision came down to something drawn from the opposite side of the brain. It came down to passion.

The idea that emotions and machines are in some way intertwined is not an unusual one. What is unique is that the tools that help put a film together come to life only in creative hands. This is where many so-called experts continue to go wrong in their approach to the subject. They forget that technology is the means to an end, not the end itself. Without an initial, passionate impulse to translate an idea—a *feeling*—into concrete form, that state-of-the-art equipment on display at the rental house, laboratory, or post facility amounts to nothing more than a fascinating conglomeration of metal, plastic, rubber, and glass.

In a similar vein, every so often the industry gets caught up in a frenzy that finds us trying to reduce complex situations to a rote phrase. Lately, for example, it seems all we're hearing is that we're living in a time of "great change." The truth is that we're always living in a time of great change. On the heels of this are two questions: "How does change affect what we do?" and "What role does creative passion occupy in the process?" By trade, cinematographers are both artists and scientists. As a member of their ranks I can attest that the answers are found in hundreds of examples from the rich history of our profession. What follows are a representative few.

Keep in mind that today images are created for the cinema through what is essentially the same set of procedures that brought them to light 100 years ago. For the most part, only the hardware has evolved and in slow, steady increments at that. Along the way, a pattern has emerged that has yet to flag in its predictability. Whenever something fresh appears on the scene, there is a misguided tendency among filmmakers to believe that "new" automatically equates with "improved." The device or method is then overused for a time—misused, actually—until its proper application is found. Most recently, the emergence of digital technology has been noted as "revolutionary." For this to be true, the essence of how and why movies are made would need to have been changed. This hasn't happened. The ball that represents the kinds of tools we use has merely been pushed a bit farther up the field. And in keeping with that, it has no doubt been best for cinematography that to date it has never been subject to a single event of catastrophic technical upheaval.

If only that were true for the rest of the industry.

Short of the sudden appearance of some on-call hologram-based system in which lifelike representations of performers act out a story in real space and in real time, there's no way for us to imagine the impact talking films had when they arrived in theatres in late 1927. Until then movies existed as a purely visual medium, distinct in their popularity and universal in their ability to communicate. Literally overnight, sync-sound erased a pan-cultural language from the face of the earth. Actors and directors were the first to feel the repercussions, often in sad or tragic ways. Cinematographers, on the other hand, weathered the shift in the most ironic of fashions. Everything about their art and craft changed in an instant, yet all of it remained the same.

One immutable fact that helped smooth the transition was that they had already established a long habit of being at the forefront of technological advancement. Beginning in the 1880s with Thomas Edison's research assistant, W.K.L. Dickson (in some corners acknowledged as the "first" cameraman), virtually every one of the early cinematographers was also known as an inventor, a builder, a tinkerer, always reaching for the next new thing. Whenever the current state of affairs conspired against handy realization of an on-screen effect, the solution came from hours of experimentation in one of their garages or at basement workbenches. The result of this habitual striving not only brought better physical experiences to audiences, it expanded film's possibilities and helped define the medium. What's even more amazing is that these men followed no road map. They made it all up as they went along. Should there be any doubt as to the momentous nature of their achievements, consider the not atypical example of Johann Gottlob Wilhelm "Billy" Bitzer (1872–1944).

Best known for his 16-year collaboration with legendary director D.W. Griffith, Bitzer's contribution to motion pictures cannot be overstated. Prior to that time, while working alone as both director and cameraman, many of the aesthetic innovations that grew from his prodigious development and application of technology remain part of our daily convention. In addition to photographing what is believed to be the first movie under artificial light, *The Jeffries-Sharkey Fight of 1899,* Bitzer's short recording of actor Joseph Jefferson in *Rip Van Winkle* (1903) contains the first known use of the close-up. Later, he became expert in filming dramatic chase sequences and was regularly stringing together scenes that used wide establishing shots immediately followed by close shots. Though it's impossible to separate his other ideas from those encouraged by Griffith, during their time together Bitzer invented many new ways of moving the camera. He also originated split-screen photography, perfected the in-camera fade and dissolve, built special filters and lenses that enabled soft focus work and invented the device that allowed for iris-in/iris-out effects, which entered the grammar of film as transition tools. At the same time, he also contributed to the development of three-point lighting by being the first cinematographer to employ backlight.

Despite his genius, Bitzer never became a rich man. In fact, well into the 1920s, at a point during which the Bell & Howell Model 2709 had become accepted as the standard production camera, he stuck with his old Pathe— and was often ridiculed for it. This little cruelty goes to the crux of the issue. Bitzer understood that the tool itself meant nothing without the inspiration and intellect that found ways to use it, to make it sing. Even at that early stage, technology was shaped as a conduit to personal expression. Whether or not today's audiences realize it, their debt to him will continue as long as motion pictures exist.

Bitzer was hardly alone in his pursuits. Indeed, the 1919 merging of New York's Cinema Camera Club with the Static Club of Los Angeles to form the American Society of Cinematographers (ASC) heralded a major event in the evolution of the screen image. For the first time, cameramen joined together as a group with the specific purpose of elevating standards for what they did. Guided by the motto "Loyalty, Progress, Artistry," such pioneering cinematographer/inventors as Karl Brown, Linwood Dunn, Karl Freund, Tony Gaudio, Arthur Miller, Jackson Rose, Charles Rosher, John Seitz, Leon Shamroy, and Karl Struss made their own outstanding contributions to the growth of visual storytelling. In unison with the Society of Motion Picture Engineers (the appearance of television would later spark their reformation as the SMPTE) and the Academy of Motion Picture Arts and Sciences (AMPAS), the ASC has been party to almost every improvement in emulsion, lighting, camera, lens, laboratory, and projection. The work of all three organizations still goes on.

The Mazda Tests of 1928 offer further insight as to what this sort of cooperation signified. Between January and March of that year, suppliers, studio executives, scientists and members of SMPE, AMPAS, and ASC all joined together to carry out a series of studies to determine the effect of incandescent (tungsten) lighting on panchromatic film. Prior to this time, arc and mercury-vapor lamps served as the main lighting sources on the majority of Hollywood sets, but as the General Electric Company began to step up emphasis on their incandescent "Mazda" units, cinematographers saw a way to expand creativity while helping producers cut costs and increase efficiency. Incandescents, though not common, had been around for decades but the crudeness of their fixtures led to unreliable performance. Another goal of these tests then became the discovery of information that would lead to solid standards across a broad spectrum of technical and manufacturing processes.

The eight-week effort was massive. On a set constructed within the confines of a specially designated Warner Bros. stage, 40 ASC cameramen exposed nearly 800 hours of negative. All the leading figures of the time clamored to be involved. Among the service firms contributing to the tests were General Electric, Mole Richardson, Bell & Howell, Eastman Kodak, DuPont, and Agfa. Even make-up specialist Max Factor had a stake in the outcome.

In terms of substance, the set that was photographed for the Mazda Tests was of a type commonly seen in silent films throughout the 1920s. With its fireplace, piano, plush chairs, ornate tables, fine woodwork, and high ceiling, it was essentially a mock-up of a rich man's home. Detailed records were kept for each lighting unit as to how and where it was employed. Closely related to these were notes on exposure and laboratory processes. No item was left to chance.

The ASC took the lead in analyzing some 450,000 feet of raw footage and supervised its editing down to a viewer-friendly 8-reel configuration. The results obtained from screenings held at the Hollywood Chamber of Commerce clearly showed that the consortium of suppliers, enablers and creators was on the right track. Incandescent lighting was deemed superior to all other forms of illumination for motion pictures and was immediately marked as the industry standard. In addition to being convenient and clean, it was economical. More important to cinematographers, tungsten sources were consistent. Over time, they became so dependable that they are still the main choice for use in the majority of filming situations.

This sea change did not go unnoticed on the screen. After the Mazda findings, the widespread deployment of incandescents and panchromatic negative led to a somewhat more diffuse style of photography. Cinematographers' aesthetics had begun to expand, but part of this was due to the different characteristics of the units themselves. The older arc and mercury-vapor lamps produced a light that was harder and more brutally defined on surfaces. Softening the quality of that light to a point where taste was pleased while exposure requirements were met called for great effort on part of the cameraman. Although capable of delivering a sharp-edged beam under the right circumstances, the tungsten filament substantially modified the game. With its inherently gentler throw, less work was needed to achieve a diffuse look. In likely response to the visual texture of the era's most successful films, a trend toward soft lighting then took hold. Though it would be several years before the approach assumed its rightful place in the cinematographer's toolbox, this instance illustrates one of the least known examples of how evolving mechanics affected this mechanical art form and vice versa.

That motion pictures moved so quickly to a point where the Mazda Tests were necessary is no surprise, yet there's something much more reso-nant to be noted beyond a minor (and relatively transient) shift in photo-graphic style. Besides showing the first recognition of the need for industrywide standards, the organization and execution of the Mazda Tests created a template for advancement so invaluable that it remains in place to this day. As part of the progression that began with the work of Bitzer and the other pioneers, the notion of economic feasibility was set in stone. Transparency to an audience also took on a primary role, guaranteeing the best possible effect onscreen while condemning radical departures to failure. But a third factor trumped all as far as cinematographers were concerned. Rather than allow manufacturers to dictate improvements on a presumptu-ous and speculative timeline, the Mazda Tests showed that cameramen could drive the effort through their own creative demands. Newly charged by the industry as "guardians of the image," cinematographers thereafter enforced an unwritten code that until the late 1970s went largely unchallenged. By causing technologists to think as end-users, artistic passion gained a subtle yet intractable stake. The acid test for widespread approval was summed up in reply to a basic question: *Does it help us do our job better?* In today's foggy environment the answers continue to make themselves plain. The introduc-tion of improved high-speed negative stocks would qualify. Repurposing an ENG camera as a cine camera would not.

This little truth is by no means intended as a knock against the current wave of innovations. To the contrary, digital technology is the future of motion picture imaging. But there has lately been a disconnect with regard to whether some of these tools actually help us create more freely and effec-tively. The chief failure among suppliers has been the refusal to acknowledge that photochemical science and electronics exist in two separate and distinct physical realms. They only appear to do the same thing. During this hybrid stage in which a variety of elements overlap, we need to guard against losing a quality of audience experience whose value is matched only by its mar-velous intangibility. Issues of taste and artistic sensitivity dominate here, and rightly so. Without them there would be no reference for the passion that has underpinned all our significant progress. But to ensure the transition reaches its full potential—that everyone involved actually does gain something worthwhile—digital technologists would do well to remember the history that's brought us this far.

Giving the Mazda model its due, this means the highest possible photochemical standard must continue to be seen as the minimum point from which to grow on all fronts. Along with improvements in such areas as dynamic range, resolution, color space, black levels, and archival potency, a standard of quantifiable repeatability that will last over the long term must also be established on the electronic side. Without the option to measure for consistent results from start to finish, the artist is forced to deal in random possibility, and that's untenable. Cameras need to be made smaller, lighter, and more robust, free of cables and other encumbrances that limit their mobility. Other items, such as the optical viewfinder, would be welcomed additions. Chip size, as it relates to depth of field, must also be addressed. Then, as higher benchmarks are inevitably achieved in each area, these same technicians must respond to the needs of the artist and be ready to leap forward yet again.

If all this sounds daunting, it's really not. The good news is that images created and delivered through the best of what digital technology offers right now most likely represent the worst of what an audience will ever see. A successful balance has existed for over 75 years among those with an interest in furthering the ways and means by which movies are made and exhibited. Sidestepping that framework of checks and balances, or worse, tossing it away in the interest of narrow, short-term gain, will leave us with something no amount of passion will be able to salvage.

Whatever the future holds, some things are forever certain. Writers will still need to dream up wonderful new stories. Producers will gather the people and resources that make everything possible. Directors will direct, actors will act. Cinematographers will continue to compose their shots, light them, and use their expertise on the set and in post. Audiences, on the other hand, will be under no such obligation to fill our theatres.

The ethic of Bitzer and those like him guaranteed a level of excellence that not only kept them coming, but created a limitless archive of precious images.

Now, more than ever, it's incumbent upon us to remain faithful in their wake.

1 Introduction

Charles S. Swartz
Entertainment Technology Center
University of Southern California

The process of distributing and exhibiting a motion picture has changed little, in its essence, since the Lumière brothers presented the first motion picture to an audience in 1895. Using a negative, positive 35mm film prints are exposed and developed, and then shipped to theatres, where the images are projected onto the screen. This analog photochemical process is capable of producing screen images of great beauty and expressive power, but in practice the moviegoer's experience is too often degraded by the wear and tear of the mechanical process, which can result in worn, scratched, and dirty prints. The process of manufacturing and shipping prints is also costly; the film industry globally spends more than $1B annually. Recently the industry's attention has turned to digital technology and its potential application to distribution and exhibition, because distributing digital files would theoretically yield great benefits in terms of image clarity and quality, lower cost, greater security, and more flexibility in the cinema.

This Handbook is devoted to an examination and explanation of this new process and the issues that arise in designing it.

Terms

Digital Cinema describes the packaging, distribution, and exhibition of motion pictures in digital form. This term does not specify how those motion pictures are originated, produced, and finished. For the foreseeable future, movies will be shot using mostly film but also digital cameras, edited using a variety of digital (and rarely, analog) devices, and post produced in a variety of ways—depending on issues of capability, flexibility, and cost.

However movies are created, they can flow into a Digital Cinema pipeline. So while this book does not deal with the merits of film versus digital cinematography per se, the decisions made in production, post production, and mastering profoundly affect the way the *Digital Cinema Package* (DCP) is created, so those decisions and the resulting implications are discussed throughout.

The terms *motion picture, movie,* and *film* are used interchangeably in this book to describe the completed work, not the medium in which it is originated or distributed.

Why Do We Need Digital Cinema?

Digital Cinema is at a crossroads. Current trials have demonstrated that today's interim process of digital mastering, distribution, and display in the theatre can create a presentation that moviegoers find compelling, especially when compared to an ordinary release print after multiple showings. At the same time, technology demonstrations provide a window into the future through which we can see a Digital Cinema that equals or even exceeds the quality of a first generation print (an *answer print*).

But obstacles lie ahead that cloud that vision unless they are addressed: we need global interoperable standards; we need a system that enables mastering to a single color reference, with assurance that the images in the theatre will look exactly as creative decision-makers intend, regardless of the projection technology in place; and we need a scalable and extensible deployment that will encourage theatre owners to adopt the system and not penalize them as quality improves.

ADVANTAGES AND CHALLENGES OF DIGITAL TECHNOLOGY FOR MOTION PICTURES

Advantages and Opportunities

Why use digital technology? Its advantages fall into four main areas:

1. *Copying*: In the digital domain, we can copy without deterioration, because every copy is a perfect clone of the original.

2. *Changing:* We can easily transform shape and color, with much more precision than in the photochemical world of film. And we can seamlessly composite elements from both original cinematography and *computer-generated imagery* (CGI).

3. *Controlling:* Digital technology enables us to make the motion picture much more secure from pirates, allowing us to encrypt the digital file and then decrypt it in the theatre—by validated users only—with the appropriate keys.

4. *Delivering:* Digital permits non-physical delivery to the viewer, e.g., Digital Cinema and Video-on-Demand. There is no need to manufacture copies unless desired.

What Opportunities Are Enabled by Digital Technology?

First, a high-quality digital master can preserve creative intent and ensure consistent presentation quality because all versions of the motion picture, including those for the home, can be extracted from this master with minimal adjustment. That saves money as well.

Second, motion pictures are called show *business* for a reason, and dollars will always loom large in any decision to change such a major system. Digital Cinema could enormously reduce the cost of prints and shipping. According to the Motion Picture Association, which tracks costs from the seven major studios and their subsidiaries, the studios collectively spent more than $631 million on prints in 2003 in North America (excluding French-speaking Canada).[1] Add independents and foreign releases in the United States, plus all print distribution internationally, and *Screen Digest* estimates that well over $1 billion is spent annually worldwide on prints and shipping.[2] That's a powerful motivator for change in any studio executive's eye.

Third, independent filmmakers and distributors face a challenging road. Reducing their costs of distribution can help create more diversity in the distribution pipeline. However, it is important to remember that prints account for only about 12% of total *P&A* (Prints & Advertising),[3] so marketing is still the biggest battle for independents. To address this problem, many independent filmmakers envision a network of theatres that would feature independent films released and exhibited digitally.

---

[1] www.mpaa.org

[2] "Digital Cinema Business Models: The Global Outlook," Chapter 4: "Print Cost Savings" *Screen Digest*, June 2003.

[3] www.mpaa.org

Fourth, digital distribution would provide much more flexibility for both distributors and exhibitors. The single Digital Cinema Package—think of it as a "digital print"—will contain multiple subtitled and dubbed language versions, permitting a single theatre to meet the varied language needs of its audience on different screens. Sellout films could easily be expanded to more screens, provided those companies distributing the low-grossing films agree. And many more versions of trailers could be made, permitting filmmakers to try more varied marketing approaches and to match trailers to the demographics of a particular audience.

There is an additional, perhaps more controversial idea: assuming directors and distributors agree, and given credible enforcement by the exhibitor, an R rated film could run on one screen of a multiplex, while the PG-13 and NC-17 versions run in others.

Fifth, presentation quality improves. Once digital projection can equal film in all respects—and many believe it does already—a higher quality presentation will result because the digital presentation is rock-steady, never dirty or scratched. And the audio is uncompressed, with many more channels available.

In summary, the benefits are:

◆ For the consumer: a heightened experience, with improved presentation and choice.

◆ For the director, producer, and creative team: an improved presentation, with greater assurance their creative choices translate to the screen.

◆ For the distributor: an improved presentation and significant savings on distribution costs.

◆ For the exhibitor: an improved presentation and greater flexibility in scheduling.

Challenges

Although its proponents won't always say so, there are disadvantages of using digital technology for Digital Cinema as well. They fall into four main areas. Digital technology is:

1. *Immature*: This means it is undergoing constant change and improvement. Why cite this as a disadvantage—isn't improvement good? Yes, but

not when it results in shifting sands of uncertainty, preventing manufacturers from introducing new products because of the fear they will rapidly become obsolete. To address this problem, Digital Cinema awaits agreement on standards (a topic discussed later in this chapter).

2. *Expensive:* Digital technology is hardware-intensive, and the knowledge of how to make it work well is in the hands of only a few gurus. The idea of a computer in the projection booth of a theatre gives some experts cause for concern.

3. *Complex:* Digital Cinema requires a seamless integration of hardware and software to work well—or even at all. Furthermore, digital doesn't fail gracefully. With analog image creation, there is a range of failure that cinematographers often exploit to create expressive effects that further the story. Even in the theatre, a degraded image is still viewable. With digital, failure will produce a dark screen.

4. *Impermanent:* Digital is impermanent for two reasons. First, the formats of recording the data are changeable; even the operating systems change over time, sometimes rapidly. Second, the media itself on which the digital data is recorded is vulnerable to deterioration and data loss.

What Issues Result from These Challenges?

First, while film technology is mature, digital technology is continually evolving and improving. A requirement of a Digital Cinema system is interoperability: all the components of the system should be modular so improved versions can still work with existing pieces. This requires standards.

A second issue is economics. What about the cost of converting theatres to digital? Since the overall system for digital distribution has not been agreed on, cost estimates are just that. To get a sense of comparative costs, Chris Cookson, CTO of Warner Bros., has pointed out that if we calculate how frequently a typical theatre changes films and how much is spent on the average print, it costs distributors about $13,000 to service one screen for a year. If Digital Cinema distribution could eliminate 75% of this cost— or roughly $10,000 a year—it would take about 7 years, using a conversion cost of $70,000, to pay for it from the distributors' savings alone. And this estimate does not take into account potential contributions from exhibitors or financial advantages in depreciation gained by a third-party entity. So while the issue of how to pay for the conversion remains to be worked out, it does not appear at this time insurmountable.

Third, what about the system that must be created? This is an enormous challenge as well. For several years, the *Society of Motion Picture and Television Engineers* (SMPTE) has been studying Digital Cinema, and they have embarked on the standards-setting process (see the next section, *Who Is Working to Develop Specifications and Standards?*).

Fourth, security is a vital issue for filmmakers, distributors, and exhibitors alike. A robust security system is a requirement to deter piracy, and it needs to be flexible so that, if it is hacked, it can immediately be changed.

Fifth, where do we set the threshold of quality? Early in its development, some reasoned that as long as digital display is as good as the average release print, it would be good enough, and delaying implementation to define standards for the future would only set back the cause. Others argued that if we are to replace 35mm film, which has served so well for more than 100 years, we should standardize on an even higher-quality threshold than we can achieve today in a first-generation answer print. They reminded us that we may be setting standards for the next 100 years, so Digital Cinema should exceed 35mm film in quality.

The work of *Digital Cinema Initiatives, LLC* (DCI), the seven-studio consortium formed to issue a technical specification, points toward a consensus position between these two earlier viewpoints. DCI has described its consensus as a scalable 2K/4K solution.[4] Detailed explanations of how this scalable solution will work are found in the chapters that follow. The important point is that this path will both encourage rapid deployment today and at the same time drive presentation quality improvements for the future.

Finally, none of the theatre installations will matter—indeed, they will certainly not occur—if there are no motion pictures released in digital format. Doug Darrow of Texas Instruments, maker of the DLP Cinema chip that is in all today's projectors in theatres, observes that since the release of *Star Wars: Episode II* the number of digital theatres has tripled, whereas the number of digital releases has barely doubled. A substantial base of digital theatres and a substantial flow of digital releases must go hand in hand.

What steps can be taken to create this future scenario? First, DCI has issued its final performance specifications as version 5.0. Second, all the work described must move forward to build a distribution infrastructure.

---

[4] www.dcimovies.com

Finally, filmmakers themselves can help by insisting on a digital release for their pictures along with the conventional film release.

WHO IS WORKING TO DEVELOP SPECIFICATIONS AND STANDARDS?

A number of groups and organizations are addressing the issues of creating specifications and standards for Digital Cinema.

1. *SMPTE.* In 1999, SMPTE created a technology committee for Digital Cinema, called DC28.[5] SMPTE committee work is done by volunteers as individuals, some employed at companies who may or may not be interested parties and some freelance consultants and interested observers. For its first 4 years of existence, the chair of DC28 was Curt Behlmer, who played a key role in early Digital Cinema installations and now chairs the *Digital Cinema Providers Group* (DCPG).[6] The current chair is Wendy Aylsworth, Vice President, Technology, Warner Bros. For more information on DC28 goals, see the Appendix.

2. *DCI.* DCI was created in March 2002, as a joint venture of Disney, Fox, MGM, Paramount, Sony Pictures Entertainment, Universal, and Warner Bros. Studios.[7] Led by Chuck Goldwater, CEO, and Walt Ordway, CTO, DCI's primary purpose is to establish and document voluntary specifications for an open architecture for Digital Cinema that ensures a uniform and high level of technical performance, reliability, and quality control. The Introduction to the final version of the specifications, with permission of DCI, states as follows:

   A number of significant technology developments have occurred in the past years that have enabled the electronic playback and display of feature films at a level of quality approaching that of 35mm film release prints. These technology developments include: the introduction of high-resolution film scanners, digital image compression, high-speed data networking and storage, and advanced digital projection.

---

[5] For information about how to become a Participant or Observer in DC28 activities, see www.smpte.org/engineering_committees/. For information about obtaining existing SMPTE Standards, see smpte.org/smpte_store/standards/

[6] dcpg.com/

[7] www.dcimovies.com

The combination of these digital technologies has allowed many impressive demonstrations of what is now being called "Digital Cinema." These demonstrations, however, have not incorporated all of the components necessary for a broad-based commercially viable Digital Cinema system. These demonstrations have created a great deal of discussion and confusion around defining the quality levels, system specifications, and the engineering standards necessary for implementing a comprehensive Digital Cinema system.

Digital Cinema Initiatives, LLC (DCI) is the entity created by seven major studios: Disney, Fox, Metro Goldwyn Mayer, Paramount Pictures, Sony Pictures Entertainment, Universal Studios, and Warner Brothers. The primary purpose of DCI is to establish uniform specifications for Digital Cinema. These DCI member companies believe that the introduction of Digital Cinema has the potential for providing real benefits to theatre audiences, theatre owners, filmmakers and distributors. DCI was created, recognizing that these benefits could not be fully realized without industry-wide standards that all parties involved in the practice of Digital Cinema can be confident that their products and services are interoperable and compatible with the products and services of all industry participants. The studios further believe that digital film exhibition will significantly improve the movie-going experience for the public.

3. *ASC.* The American Society of Cinematographers was founded in 1919 for the main purpose of advancing the art of narrative filmmaking. There are some 215 cinematographers and visual effects artists in the organization today and another 135 associate members who work in allied sectors of the industry. Its current President is Richard Crudo, ASC (see Foreword). In May 2003, it formed the ASC Technology Committee, chaired by Curtis Clark, ASC, with the goal to "recommend standards and practices for emerging technologies that affect the art and craft of filmmaking." The committee includes more than 50 cinematographers and technology thought leaders from all sectors of the industry. In September 2003, ASC, under the auspices of the Technology Committee, and DCI announced plans to produce *Standardized Evaluation Material* (StEM) for evaluating the performance of digital projectors and other elements of Digital Cinema systems.[8] The StEM was shot in August 2003 and mastered over the following six months. It has been used extensively by DCI and ASC for testing in the Digital Cinema Laboratory (see point 6 that follows) and shown at numerous conferences, including the NAB 2004 Digital Cinema Summit, Cinema Expo 2004, and the 2004 Naples Cinematography Forum.[9]

---

[8] dcimovies.com/press/09-24-03.tt2

[9] For details about how the StEM was produced and mastered, as well as information about how copies of the StEM can be obtained for non-commercial purposes, see www.dcimovies.com.

4. *MPAA*. The Motion Picture Association of America (MPAA) and its international counterpart, the Motion Picture Association (MPA), serve as the voices and advocates of the American motion picture, home video, and television industries. Founded in 1922 as the trade association of the American film industry, the MPAA has broadened its mandate over the years to reflect the diversity of an expanding industry. Its members are the seven major studios. In August 2000, under the leadership of its CTO Brad Hunt, the MPAA issued "Goals for Digital Cinema," listing ten goals "critical to the successful implementation of a Digital Cinema system that provides real benefits to all stakeholders."[10]

5. *NATO*. The National Association of Theatre Owners is the largest exhibition trade organization in the world, representing more than 26,000 movie screens in all 50 states and in more than 20 countries worldwide. Its membership includes the largest cinema chains in the world and hundreds of independent theatre owners as well.[11] NATO's president, John Fithian, has spoken many times on the important issues surrounding Digital Cinema from the exhibitor point of view.[12] NATO's "Digital Cinema User Requirements" is discussed in Chapter 10 and appears on the website of MKPE Consulting,[13] NATO's Digital Cinema consultant.

6. *Entertainment Technology Center at USC (ETC-USC)*. The Entertainment Technology Center was founded in 1993 as an Organized Research Unit of the University of Southern California's School of Cinema-Television, with the mission to help understand the impact of new technologies on the entertainment industry.[14] Its executive sponsors include all seven major studios, LucasFilm, and several leading technology companies. In 1999, ETC-USC created the Digital Cinema Forum, which produced the concept of creating a neutral laboratory for the testing and evaluation of

---

[10] mpaa.org/dcinema/

[11] www.natoonline.org/

[12] For example, see his speech at the Digital Cinema 2001 Conference, hosted by the National Institute of Standards and Technology at www.infocusmag.com/presidents.htm, and his letter co-authored with his European counterpart, Jan van Dommelen, President of UNIC, at www.natoonline.org/.

[13] www.mkpe.com/articles/

[14] www.etcenter.org

Digital Cinema products and solutions. In October 2000, with the support of NATO and MPAA, the *Digital Cinema Laboratory* (DCL) opened in the historic Hollywood Pacific Theatre. With the most up-to-date film and digital projection and sound, the DCL serves as a test bed for demonstrations and evaluation as well as a high-quality screening venue. In December 2002, DCI announced the Lab as the official site to test Digital Cinema technologies and to work with DCI to establish uniform, open, and voluntary standards for digital movie release that will be scalable into the future. ETC-USC also works with international organizations and consortia to promote greater understanding of Digital Cinema.

7. *ISO.* ISO, the International Organization for Standardization, is a network of national standards institutes from 148 countries working in partnership with international organizations, governments, industry, business and consumer representatives. ISO was founded in 1947 and has its headquarters in Geneva, Switzerland.[15] ISO Technical Committee ISO/TC 36-Cinematography had its first meeting in 1952 in New York. SMPTE serves as Secretariat through the American National Standards Institute (ANSI). The current Chairman and Secretary is Mr. C.V. Girod, P.E., the SMPTE Director of Engineering. The scope of ISO/TC 36 is standardization of definitions, dimensions, methods of measurement and test, and performance characteristics relating to materials and apparatus used in silent and sound motion picture photography; in sound recording and reproduction related thereto; in the installation and characteristics of projection and sound reproduction equipment; in laboratory work; and in standards relating to sound and picture films used in television.

8. *EDCF.* The European Digital Cinema Forum was formed in Stockholm in June 2001 to promote the creation of a technical and business framework for the harmonious introduction of Digital Cinema in all its forms in Europe.[16] Made up of three modules—Technical, Commercial, and Content—it is led by a Management Committee whose current President is Åse Kleveland, Director General of the Swedish Film Institute. Because of its wide-ranging activities in Europe and liaison with SMPTE and other groups, its website is a rich source of information of Digital Cinema developments.

---

[15] www.iso.org/
[16] www.digitalcinema-europe.com/pages/objectives.html

9. *DTB@NFT.* June 2003 saw the launch of the Digital Test Bed at the National Film Theatre in its premiere cinema complex on London's South Bank.[17] The National Film Theatre is a renowned part of the British Film Institute (BFI), established in 1933 to promote greater understanding, appreciation, and access to film and television culture. Established by the Department of Trade and Industry (DTI) in conjunction with BFI, the DTB@NFT is the main UK and European facility for exploring the digital distribution and exhibition of film. Its aim is to act as a neutral research laboratory in the search of universal standards and compatible technology solutions. The Test Bed hosts seminars, training sessions, interactive forums, and special demonstrations.

10. *MIC.* The *Moving Image Center* was established in Italy in 2003 by Angelo D'Alessio.[18] Its key goals are to analyze and study Digital Cinema and advanced media technologies, and their applications and business models, and to prepare tools and methodologies for the education and training of teachers and professional people. The MIC will comprise multiple laboratories, devoted to asset management, content security, audio, mastering, assessment of quality, and the preservation of digital content. In addition to the Italian Center of Excellence that will be an integral part of this effort, it plans to pursue the concept of an International Center of Excellence, with a desire to connect its work with that of the Entertainment Technology Center and others worldwide. The MIC's upcoming projects include "Methodologies and Tools for Education and Training of Professionals Involved in Digital Cinematography" and "Preservation and Management of Digital Cinema Content."

11. *DCCJ.* The Digital Cinema Consortium of Japan is a nonprofit organization formed to contribute to the promotion of culture and art through the development, test, evaluation, and standardization of very high-quality Digital Cinema formats and related infrastructure.[19] Its Board of Directors is headed by Chief Director Tomonori Aoyama, Professor in the Department of Information and Communication Engineering, Graduate School of Information Science and Technology of the University of Tokyo. DCCJ has organized demonstrations of the

---

[17] www.bfi.org.uk/features/dtb/
[18] *angelo.dalessio@infinito.it*
[19] www12.ocn.ne.jp/~d-cinema/index2.htm

NTT-built 4K Digital Cinema projector, using the JVC D-ILA chip, in Japan, Europe, and the United States.

12. *CST.* The Commission Supérieure Technique de l'Image et du Son (CST) is a French regulatory body established by legislation. The CST has the authority to set and enforce the design standards for Cinema Auditoria.[20]

More information about the international organizations above, as well as numerous additional initiatives, can be found in Chapter 11, International Perspectives.

Goals of This Handbook

Because Digital Cinema is currently in a nascent state, this Handbook cannot present a final view of a settled topic. Its goals instead are to present a snapshot of the present and a vision of the future. Both of these goals are bounded by continually evolving technology and business developments. But if "the best is the enemy of the good," then it follows that waiting until all questions are answered would provide no information and guidance during this crucial formative period when readers most need exactly that.

Furthermore, the fluid nature of current developments inevitably can result in differing views about a given topic. While each chapter focuses on a specific area of the proposed Digital Cinema process, authors' views do not always mesh. But from these differing views, which at times may even clash, will come the standards we all seek.

While this Handbook is designed to meet the needs of the technical reader, my hope is that those new to the field can read the Introduction to each chapter and gain an understanding of the fundamental issues.

---

[20] www.cst.fr/

From the birth of the movies until 1916, dozens of film formats and sizes existed and no standards prevailed.[21] In 1916, SMPE (the original organization name before Television added the "T") standardized 4-perfora-tion 35mm film as its first task. Since that date, this single system has acted as an umbrella for significant and continuous improvements in emulsions, lenses, cameras, and processes—all of which serve to enhance presentation quality. In the same way, Digital Cinema requires a system design based on interoperable standards globally deployed and at the same time flexibly capable of improvement as technology permits. Only in this way will the promise of Digital Cinema be achieved.

Acknowledgments

My interest in motion pictures began as an undergraduate at Yale. Jacques Guicharnaud, Professor of French and a lifelong filmmaker and critic, agreed to oversee my senior essay in History, the Arts, and Letters. I wrote about Orson Welles' *Citizen Kane*, and I was thereafter forever hooked on film. Bernard Kantor, then Dean of the USC School of Cinema-Television, pro-vided a scholarship and continuing encouragement for my graduate study in production. And through winning the Warner Scholarship, I had the good fortune of working at Warner Bros. for 3½ years, where writer-producer Jim Barnett was a mentor and always stimulating colleague.

During the years I was designing the professional education courses in digital media at UCLA Extension, Dick Stumpf was my patient and frequent breakfast companion, spending many hours educating the educator. A long-time SMPTE leader and studio executive, he continues in retirement to share his enthusiasm and wisdom with the Entertainment Technology Center at USC.

The true value of this book resides in the contributions of the respec-tive contributors, who have each taken on the challenge of explaining a topic that is at this moment fluid, a task not unlike nailing down mercury. My thanks to Richard Crudo, Leon Silverman, Charles Poynton, Chris Carey, Bob Lambert, Bill Kinder, Glenn Kennel, Peter Symes, Robert

---

[21] See "Inventing Entertainment" on the Library of Congress site memory.loc.gov/ammem/edhtml/ edhome.html; "One Hundred Years of Film Sizes," www.gregssandbox.com/gtech/filmsize/filmsize.htm; "The Complete History of the Discovery of Cinematography," www.precinemahistory.net/.

Schumann, David Gray, Darcy Antonellis, Matt Cowan, Loren Nielsen, Michael Karagosian, Peter Wilson, Patrick Von Sychowski and Wendy Aylsworth. I am also grateful to Walt Ordway for his guidance.

The members of the Entertainment Technology Center Executive Board and Technical Advisory Board have encouraged and supported my understanding of Digital Cinema. I want to acknowledge especially Dean Elizabeth Daley, Jerry Pierce, Bob Lambert, Chuck Dages, George Joblove, Andy Setos, Dave Schnuelle, Brad Hunt, Garrett Smith, and Leon Silverman. Lastly, Phil Barlow was my earliest guide through the perplexities of the subject.

Joanne Tracy, Senior Editor at Focal Press, originally proposed this book, and she has provided guidance and insight throughout its development, always with good judgment and good humor.

Finally, my thanks to Stephanie Rothman, my filmmaking and life partner, from whom I have learned so much.

Sherman Oaks, California
June 13, 2004

The New Post Production Workflow: Today and Tomorrow

Leon Silverman
LaserPacific Media Corporation

To many, post production is mysteriously confusing; a black art performed in darkened rooms, which when executed with a high degree of art and skill, literally becomes unknowably transparent in service to the story. Though its importance to the filmmaking process is undeniable, the fashioning of disjointed bits of picture and sound into a finished work is often eschewed as a lesser and certainly lower-paid skill when compared to the highly visible and better-compensated writer, director, or cinematographer. Post production can often help make marginal work better and cement great work as a timeless masterpiece. It is interesting to note that many directors pose for photographs, pictured in front of editing devices or sound mixing consoles, albeit with nary an editor or mixer, their necessary collaborators and oftentimes saviors, in frame.

The rallying cry of "We'll fix it in post," uttered in reverential tones, although usually without much notion of what actually happens in "post," has helped to urge on countless productions or assuage the horror of the best laid plans gone awry. Post production, which encompasses both creative expression and the technical details of the filmmaking, manufacturing and delivery processes, has been undergoing dramatic technological change over the past 20 years. Electronic and digital tools have helped to point the way to increasing numbers of new processes, which not only have changed the creative character of motion pictures, but also are changing the forms and methods from which the cinema of the future will take shape.

The creative and workflow impact of new electronic and digital tools and "toys" that are the hallmark of "the look" of commercials, music videos, digital animation, and visual effects, has also influenced the motion picture post production process as well, altering the practice that has been decidedly film-based since the beginning of cinema. These new evolving tools and methods will help hasten a merging and blurring of film and digital processes, ushering in the era of what might be called "the modern motion picture."

The stage is currently being set for a cinema of the future that may include digital cinematography, will most certainly utilize an increasingly digital post production process, and is destined to be distributed into what the industry is grappling to envision as the Digital Cinema.

The challenge for many working in the industry today, especially for those who have been tapped to lay the technological groundwork for future cinema, is to ensure that an uncompromised, robust, and extensible technical pathway can be built. For film, when considered as technology, in its relative simplicity and its 100-year endurance, is unquestionably quite elegant.

THE TRADITIONAL POST PRODUCTION WORKFLOW

Regardless of technology or terminology, post production usually does not begin "after production" but more accurately is concurrent with production. Typically and traditionally, post production encompasses the process of preparing, editing, and "finishing" both picture and sound as well as creating the intermediate and final elements necessary for distribution.

The process is usually overseen by a group of post production professionals, some who work for the studio and some who work for the producing entity or the film itself. The management hierarchy extends from the studio or production company VP of post production and his or her staff, through line producers, producers, associate producers, post production supervisors, post production coordinators, editors, assistant editors, and the various people associated with the "vendor community" of laboratory and sound. These relationships are sometimes strained when creative, financial, or scheduling needs clash as the editors, who are often aligned with the creative filmmakers, find themselves in the middle of a tug of war.

The complexity of the post production process is little understood in most studio executive suites and indeed by many producers and production managers, who are responsible for creating post production schedules and budgets and sometimes have precious little knowledge of the intricacies and nuances of the process. The pressure to shave costs and time from a film can often result in the squeezing of post production, as production or *above the line* (story rights, script, actors, director, and producer) costs and issues are oftentimes sacrosanct.

Certain recent developments put an even greater strain on the process of completing motion pictures: the need to create a big splash in a short time at the box office, the fear of piracy, which has contributed to the acceleration of worldwide distribution, as well as the requirement to ready video delivery elements for earlier *windows* (phases of distribution on different formats). The impending need for Digital Cinema elements will further articulate new post production methods that might help to meet the challenges and pressures of today's motion picture delivery needs.

To begin to discuss how these technological and marketplace changes might affect these processes, we must first outline the traditional post production workflow.

Dailies

It all begins with *dailies*, the process by which yesterday's footage is readied for viewing by the creative filmmakers and studio as well as editing. So-called because it happens every day, the importance and timeliness of this step that feeds and enables the post production process can be even better understood when referred to by its name outside of the US: *rushes*. Dailies inform the filmmaking process by enabling the various disciplines involved in motion picture production to gauge the progress of a film.

The film shot during each production day is delivered to the film laboratory where it is processed overnight (except for Saturday and sometimes Friday nights when most labs are closed). For dailies that will be screened on film, commonly referred to as the *workpicture*, the processed negative is *broken down* or separated in the lab into "*A*" and "*B*" negative. The "*A*" negative, or *circle takes*, includes the takes the director wishes to have printed for viewing and editing. The director asks for them to be circled, or marked as "good," on the camera report that is delivered with the film to the lab.

The "B" negative is vaulted at the lab in case the director or editor later wishes to see an *outtake* printed. The "A" negative then heads to the *timing* department. The dailies *timer* will evaluate the negative film's exposure and determine the proper *timing lights* that need to be applied to the film for it to be properly printed.

Film Timing

The primary tool of the film timer is a device rarely called by its official name, the color analyzer. Instead, it is almost universally known by the name of the company, *Hazeltine*, that designed and made the most commonly used analyzer, sometimes even when the analyzer is made by different company. The Hazeltine made its way into the industry in the 1960s and was hailed as a significant development. As a foreshadowing of the importance of utilizing electronic display and color calibration technology for film, the Hazeltine is a precursor to both the modern *telecine* (a device used in television to transfer film to video) and the digital color timing systems that dominate our industry today.

Named for Professor Alan Hazeltine, who in 1923 invented a new, more easily tunable circuit that became widely used in the broadcast, medical, and photographic industries, the Hazeltine company went on to become a major defense contractor and developed significant technology for radar, mine detection, and electronic defense systems. The analyzer represented a show business dalliance for Hazeltine, which nevertheless ended up winning an Academy Award for its efforts.

The color analyzer is an electronic device that displays the film (similar to a crude telecine) on a monitor and provides timers with the ability to alter the image using values of red, green, and blue and *density* (which simplistically can be thought of as contrast). It is set to a reference called the *LAD* (Lab Aim Density), a standard means to control color and density in the timing process, whose purpose is to calibrate the analyzer so that by changing the values of color and contrast, these characteristics can also be altered in the film print. The LAD contains an image of a woman's face, which helps to establish a flesh tone reference, as well as red, green, blue, and various shades of black and gray patches that serve as a visual reference for the experienced timer. Unlike a telecine, which can display a *WYSIWYG* (what you see is what you get) rendition of a scene for a video transfer, a color analyzer's image is not as visually intuitive in relation to the end result.

Some refer to the process of printing the negative each day as *one light dailies*. This refers to the notion that the timer determines the proper *printing light*—values of red, green, and blue and density—and applies this one light to the entire camera roll for printing. The more accurate description of the dailies timing process might be *best light dailies*. The timer creates a timing value for each unique lighting setup and determines the best light for printing the scene. Cinematographers want to know their printing lights in order to verify that they are exposing the film correctly relative to their own expectations. This is an important reference and calibration tool for them to understand how the exposure of the film correlates to their understanding of their goals when shooting it.

Printing

Once timed, the film is sent to the printing department where it is printed at the lights that the timer has determined. From the printer, the film is usually viewed on a high-speed projector by a representative of the lab. This *lab contact* will communicate with the cinematographer about what he or she saw in the cinematography, commenting on exposure and other issues with the film. The lab contact might order a retiming and reprinting of certain takes if it is felt that they are not accurate representations of the look of the film. All of this activity happens during the wee hours of the morning in time for the assistant editor to pick up the resulting print as early as possible to begin the process of syncing the sound with this silent film workpicture.

Production Sound

The sound that was recorded during production makes its way overnight on a separate path from the film. In the past, the most common method had been to transfer the production sound to 35mm film, which is coated with a magnetic surface, called *mag*. The assistant editor then uses a *synchronizer* to synchronize the mag with the workpicture. This is accomplished by aligning the exact film frame where the slate's *clapper stick* closes with the sound of the closed clapper on the mag. When no sticks were used, the assistant editor must create sync manually by aligning the actor's spoken words with his or her moving lips, or some other reference in the frame. *Syncing dailies* has always been one of the most important tasks of the assistant editor.

Once picture and sound are in sync, both are *coded* by a machine that prints the same series of *code numbers* along the edge of each roll of picture and sound. These code numbers are logged by the assistant editor after dailies screening, so that once a shot is cut into a scene, and the clapper reference is lost, the picture and sound can always be easily aligned.

While 35mm picture and mag *double system* (meaning the sound and picture are not on the same element) is still a common way of screening dailies, there has been recent interest in the use of new technology to eliminate the need and expense of mag film. Digital devices on sets and film production locations have largely replaced analog sound recording. Some editors feel that transferring digital sound to a magnetically coated analog piece of film is anachronistic and have begun to utilize what is being referred to as *magless* dailies. There are a number of schemes to accomplish this task. Some transfer sound to computer drives, CDs, or DVDs, or new digital sound playback units, but there is no universally accepted method of syncing film with digital files. It is increasingly common that digital sound is introduced directly into nonlinear edit systems during the initial editing process so that this high quality digital sound can be made available for subsequent post production sound steps.

Using Dailies

Filmmakers traditionally view dailies during lunch or dinner breaks, and every effort is made to ensure that they are prepared in time. Dailies screenings typically are a collaborative and communal event, with the various departments watching them to judge how yesterday's footage compared with expectations or, in the case of the editor, how it might cut with other footage. It is not uncommon for an editor to suggest to a director that other angles or takes might be necessary for a scene to play or cut better.

The amount of footage that is shot each day obviously plays a large role in the dailies process. While there is no such thing as a typical motion picture, the average non-action motion picture today might shoot for 50 to 60 days and expose about 1.5 to 2 hours of negative film each day. From that negative, the circle takes amount to 1 to 1.5 hours of footage. On scenes that involve action or the use of multiple cameras, the amount of footage can grow almost exponentially. Large action films or certain big budget motion pictures can sometimes shoot 4 to 5 hours of negative and print 2.5 to 4 hours of footage each day. The sheer volume of film makes it very difficult to screen all of the dailies. Sometimes the material is viewed at high speed or saved for weekends or nights, or sometimes only the footage from a certain camera is viewed. Obviously, the editor must view all of the footage in order to know the full range of choices.

On most films, the filmmakers see the dailies first before releasing the film to the studio or production company. Some influential filmmakers limit what a studio is allowed to see by creating a *select* reel of only certain chosen scenes that have been approved by the filmmakers for studio dailies screening.

Although new processes for viewing dailies in high-definition video are increasingly being considered, dailies are still primarily screened from a film workpicture, even though the edit room today is invariably working on a digital edit system. The most common method of getting the film workpicture into a digital form for editorial is to transfer the workpicture and the track that was synced by the edit room onto videotape and sometimes onto edit system-compatible hard drives.

In addition, videotape copies of dailies or DVDs are sometimes circulated to studio executives and the filmmakers. One of the issues that this chapter will later explore is this growing interest in transferring dailies for feature films to high-definition video and utilizing digital projection technology to screen dailies.

Editing and the Role of the Cutting Room

The editor is responsible for assembling the footage each day during production using the dailies prepared in the form most appropriate to the editing technology employed. The goal of most cutting rooms is to be *up to camera*. This means that the editor has screened and *cut* (edited) as much of the current footage as has been shot to the extent possible, given the fact that scenes and locations are shot out of order. On big pictures with a lot of footage this can be very challenging. As we mentioned earlier, simply screening the sheer volume of material that can be shot on a big picture can be a daunting task, let alone fashioning it into a cohesive story.

The editor usually has a number of assistants who perform various technical and organizational tasks. The assistants typically deal with the physical tracking of film and electronic elements as well as cataloging the footage so that it can be conformed when the creative editing is completed. In addition, the assistants are usually responsible for dealing with the lab and other vendors, as well as for coordinating the scheduling of various finishing tasks on the picture. The editor and his or her team also play a crucial role (along with the post production supervisor and the studio post production department, which are sometimes one and the same) for overseeing the creation of all the necessary delivery elements.

Even though many assistants are on a time-honored apprenticeship path to becoming creative film editors, the cutting room is increasingly a technically sophisticated and complex environment. The introduction of electronic and digital technology to the cutting room has created a conflict between the need for extremely technical, computer-savvy assistants and the desire for the next generation of creative editors. Many of today's editors who currently use very sophisticated digital editing technology started their careers physically cutting film. It is very common for these editors to delegate the more technical tasks to their assistants.

With the advent of new editing technology, a future editor who may possess a high degree of creativity ability but is not a computer geek may not be able to rise through the apprenticeship/assistant process, which more and more emphasizes technical skills over creative ability. Hopefully, future editors who today grow up with digital editing tools such as Final Cut and Avid Express literally in their bedrooms may be able to hone enough of their creative and technical skills to enter the craft, even if they are more artistic than technical.

Editors themselves see their primary role as an integral creative participant in the film making process. The editor, who is often hired by the director, usually works alone with the film through the production process. With his or her personal insight and experience as well as the knowledge of the director's vision of the film, the editor fashions the *editor's cut* (or *first cut*) to present to the director soon after the completion of photography. Never refer to the editor's version as a rough cut, which is considered highly derogatory and demeaning to the craft of editing. In fact, today's editors' versions are not rough in any sense of the word, as most editors spend a great deal of time cutting *temp* (temporary) sound effects and music, to the point that they would appear to be finished, polished works to many.

Once the production is complete, the director works with the editor to refine the cut. The director, as a contractual right of the Director's Guild of America contract, is given 10 weeks to work with the editor to create his or her version of the film, called the *director's cut*. Also during this step in the post production process, visual effects are finalized and cut into the film as it nears completion. As the director's cut progresses, versions of the film will be conformed and screened. Some directors obtain through negotiations the sole right to view these screenings and to invite others of their choosing, who may or may not include representatives of the studio (until they are ready or the 10-week period has passed).

Preview Screenings

Once the director has either finished his or her version or approves it, studio executives will screen the film. The film is then shown to recruited audiences in marketing test *preview* screenings. These preview screenings are usually conducted by a third party market research company that will give the studio marketing department feedback about how test audiences responded to various aspects of the film.

These preview screenings are traditionally double system—a film workpicture and a separate 35mm sound track—although some magless systems have been used as well. Theatres selected for previews, however, normally have only one projector to show *release prints*, where the audio track is physically on the same film with the picture, called *single system*. So the studio post production department must arrange for the necessary audio technology to be delivered to the theatre for the preview screening, which is usually the mag machine or the magless system, and the theatre's existing film projector is usually employed for picture. In addition, representatives of Dolby Laboratories usually participate in setting up the sound that will be played for the preview audience. The sound utilized in a preview is usually a preliminary mix of the film referred to as a *temp mix*.

Preview screenings are usually held in typical suburban cineplexes, in locations such as Orange County or the Valley suburbs in southern California or in New Jersey on the east coast. The reason for this is that the studio wants test market audiences who represent a broader cross section of opinion and input than might be found in "hip" urban environments such as Los Angeles or Manhattan. Sometimes a studio will preview a picture out of town if it is worried about how it might literally "play in Peoria." The feedback from previews usually results in changes being made to the picture, even to the extent that parts of films are re-shot. Most studio films will have at least one preview, with the typical number being two. Where the studio feels there is a lot riding on the results of the preview, three or more previews may be scheduled.

Once the previews are completed, the picture can be finalized, or *locked,* and the process of *cutting the negative* (conforming the negative to the final workpicture) begins. At the same time, the sound post production work can also begin in earnest. The preview process is becoming increasingly impacted by technology, especially Digital Cinema technology. There is a growing trend to use digital projectors and not the film workpicture for previews. This trend will be explored in greater depth later in the section *Digital Preview and Potential Cost Savings* found later in this chapter.

Visual Effects / Opticals

Visual effects (*VFX*) are as much a part of the production process as post production. Many types of visual effects involve directly photographing elements, such as miniatures, models, puppets, or actors, sometimes on blue or green painted stages, that will later be combined with other live action or computer-generated elements to complete a visual effects shot.

Visual effects originated as photographic or optical solutions, hence *opticals.* Traditionally, opticals such as matte painting, titles, composites, fades, dissolves, variable speed effects, reverse action, blow-ups, and shot repositioning have been accomplished in a film environment using film cameras and special optical stands. Over the past 10 years, however, visual effects have increasingly become computer generated, with 3-D animation and compositing technology virtually eliminating certain types of film-based opticals and visual effects. While film opticals are still common today for dissolves, fades, and titles, the move to digital post production of entire films will some day make the film optical process a thing of the past.

Today, even films that are not primarily visual effects films take advantage of the new digital toolkit. Techniques such as crowd enhancement, where people are literally copied and pasted so that a couple of extras can be made to look like a cast of thousands, have become commonplace. So have virtual extensions on buildings or the painting out of signs, telephone poles, wires or other objects in films whose historical setting did not include what was seen by the camera and should not be seen by the audience.

The sophistication of visual effects technique both from an artistic and technical point of view has elevated the importance of the *visual effects supervisor*, who participates in both the production and post production processes. Sometimes working with the cinematographer and sometimes directing his or her own photographic unit, the visual effects supervisor directs the creation of photographic foreground or background elements that will then be combined in post production digital compositing with other live action or computer-generated elements. The visual effects supervisor must also coordinate with the editorial team so that the shots to be created are of the right length and character to intercut with existing footage.

It is not uncommon for a large visual effects film to have many hundreds of individual shots subcontracted out to multiple visual effects vendors, depending on their field of expertise or the need to create many shots within the tight time frame of a film's schedule. The final approval of visual effects shots is exacting and usually maddeningly "last minute."

The cinema of the future will increasingly be composed of digital elements as the technology itself and the visual effects community continues to push the envelope to satisfy the desires of an audience which has come to take sophisticated photo-realistic visual effects for granted.

Conform and Negative Cutting

During the process of making a film, whether edited using film-based or digital edit systems, it is very difficult to get the full impact of the film by viewing it on the relatively small screen of the edit system itself.

Since most films today are edited digitally as opposed to the traditional physical cutting and splicing of the film workpicture, a separate conform cutting room is utilized. A team of assistant editors works alongside today's digital editing system. By using the edit system's *edit decision list* (EDL) or *cut list*, the assistant will conform the film workpicture by physically cutting and splicing it to prepare the version for screening. When necessary, the edit room may need to order *reprints* of scenes that have been cut in one version, but are now extended in another. This is necessary because when making a physical splice in film, one frame is usually lost on either side of the splice.

By the time the picture is ready to screen for studio or preview audiences, because of the cutting and re-cutting of the workpicture, it usually shows signs of dirt, scratches, and other marks of its constant handling through the editorial process.

One of the most important jobs of the assistant editor is to keep track of the film, its relationship to sound rolls, the original camera reel of a particular scene and take, and the other information that will be necessary to quickly find the film and prepare it for conform. Referred to as the *code book* in the past, this paper journal has for the most part been replaced by both electronic databases kept in the edit system and frequently as a separate database file maintained by the assistant.

Once the picture is locked, the final conformed workpicture is prepared for delivery to the *negative cutter*. The negative cutter, who has one of the most exacting jobs in the filmmaking process, is responsible for matching the original camera negative to the now conformed workpicture. The negative is first separated, or *broken down,* into individual scenes and takes so that each scene is easier to find. The negative cutter begins the process of assembling the negative by utilizing code book information that designates the *key numbers* imprinted (at the factory) on the edge of the negative film every foot or 16 frames, and then in the dailies process at the lab printed through to the workpicture. The negative cutter consults the list provided by the edit room that designates a scene/take and a specific key number entry point of the cut. Once this piece of film is found, the negative cutter locates the precise frame to cut by locating the correct key number. The list will designate a key number plus a certain number of frames as the in-point or *head* of the cut as well as a key number plus a certain number of frames as the out-point or *tail* of the cut.

Using the workpicture as a visual reference, the negative cutter verifies that the number in the list, the image on the workpicture, and the image on the negative are all identical before a cut is made. Because cutting the film destroys the frame adjacent to the head and tail, great care has to be taken to ensure accuracy. Although mistakes do sometimes happen, the negative cutting profession prides itself on its steady hands, steady nerves, and its incredible track record of accuracy. This is definitely not a job for the shaky of hand or of confidence!

Cutting the negative usually takes about a week. The negative cutter usually does not splice the film. This is more commonly done at the lab using devices that can create a very smooth splice. The goal is a cut that is joined with a minimum of excessive thickness at the splice point. If the splicing is not done carefully, a thick splice might cause a noticeable disturbance or jump as it passes through film printers or scanners.

Final Color Timing

Once spliced, the film can now be prepared for the final film release. One of the most critically important as well as most creative steps in the motion picture process, color timing is where the final *look* of the film is created. During production the cinematographer has lit, exposed, and sometimes processed the film in a certain way. During dailies, the dailies timer has provided a dailies film print that represents the best light for each particular shot or scene. But now that the film is cut together, there is another opportunity to adjust the color: first, to make the color within each sequence consistent from shot to shot, since consecutive shots in a sequence are often filmed on different days; and second, to creatively apply a color palette and look to the film that will further help to illustrate the story and set the mood.

The timer will, after meeting with the director and cinematographer, time the picture using the color analyzer to set the timing lights. Through timing, making a print, screening the film for the filmmakers' reaction, and then going back to make the necessary changes, film color correction proceeds through an iterative process. Because the filmmakers cannot make changes directly while viewing the film, changes are noted, re-timed, and then a new print is made, usually overnight. The early prints that come off are sometimes referred to as Hazeltine prints. They are usually discarded in the process, but they can sometimes be used as a picture reference in the sound post production which is usually concurrent with timing. While every film is different, it typically takes about two weeks to get the final print, called the *answer print*, approved by the filmmakers. The answer print contains the results of the final timing of the cut negative.

Traditionally, the final timing is accomplished by collaboration between the director, the cinematographer, and the *final timer* in the lab. The timer who helps guide this process is highly regarded and certainly holds the most highly paid and respected position in the hierarchy of technicians in a film laboratory. Usually the final timer has come up through the ranks in the lab, starting in the film lab equivalent of the mailroom in jobs such as film vault, negative make-up, splicing and then sometimes apprenticing to a more seasoned timer. In some labs, these apprentices are called *timing pooches*, literally dogging the traditionally manual procedure of noting the timing values of particular scenes and making sure that this information is transferred to the subsequent print. Their first official timing position might be to time dailies, sometimes for many years, before they are qualified to be a final timer of motion pictures.

This long apprenticeship process is in stark contrast to the relatively short training received by most *colorists* (the video equivalent of the film timer). For the most part, colorists, who have achieved a nearly cult-like status in the world of digital timing, do not have the deep understanding of film, lab process, or color theory that film timers learn over their many years of apprenticeship and experience. Yet their salaries can reach many times that of the highest paid film timer (as much as half a million dollars a year or more!) Many film timers are chagrined at how the cult of the colorist has begun to overshadow the lab's most respected creative technicians. Some film timers have become colorists, but for the most part, the digital timers are young video "computer heads," who came up through the video facility equivalent of the mailroom—tape vault, tape operator, and dailies colorist—before landing the big money opportunity in commercials or feature film *mastering* for video or DVD release.

While the timing process in the lab has become increasingly electronic with computers employed to note timing values and sometimes to carry timing information from dailies, the creative, technical, and physical limitations of film timing have led to the significant interest in the notion of digitally timing motion pictures. It seems that the role of the film lab timer is destined to diminish over time as the interest in new digital timing technology and methods supplants the traditional film timing process.

Intermediate Elements and Release Printing

Except for the answer print, the original cut negative is usually not used to make *release prints* for distribution to theatres. Such use could damage irretrievably what is the most pristine version of the film record. Even if major damage were avoided, the process of high-speed printing required for release prints would inevitably produce wear and tear. So it is necessary to produce one or more *duplicate* (or *dupe*) *negatives*.

Using the timing values derived from the answer print, intermediate elements are made to protect the negative and serve as the source for the release prints that will be sent directly to theatres.

The first intermediate element, the *interpositive* (IP), is carefully made in direct contact with the cut negative of the picture. In this step, the negative is printed onto a specially formulated very fine grain film stock. The interpositive is referred to as an intermediate element because of its role as the source for the next element in the process—the *internegative* (IN). The IP is printed with the answer print timing values so that the timing will flow through to the subsequent steps in the process. An IP is usually printed on a *wet gate* printer, a special device in which the film is immersed during the printing process in a chemical liquid that has the same refractive quality as the base of the negative film. If there are scratches on the film's base layer, this liquid fills in the scratches and reduces their apparent visibility on the print (see Figure 2.1).

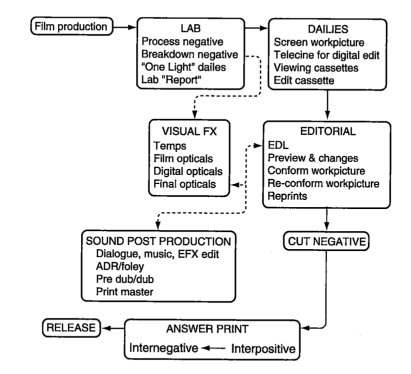

FIGURE 2.1   Intermediate elements workflow.

Even though the IP is a positive element, it is not designed and cannot be used for direct viewing or projection because it is printed on negative film stock. From this timed IP, the IN (the next intermediate element) is made, either as *direct contact* or *optical* print.

In contact printing, the source (the element from which a duplicate will be made) is positioned *in contact* with the raw unexposed film stock in an elaborate and tightly controlled threading path. The calibration and alignment of the printer is critical, as excess movement or lack of calibration can affect the quality of the duplicate element. The printer incorporates illumination that passes first through the source, exposing its image onto the raw unexposed stock, thereby creating the duplicate image. In the case of printing an IN, the positive image of the IP when exposed onto intermediate stock will create a negative image—the internegative (IN) (see Figure 2.2).

The IN can be thought of as a duplicate of the original negative. Because it contains the timing of the answer print, it can now be used as a source for

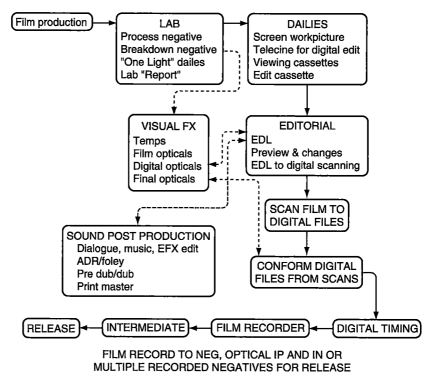

FILM RECORD TO NEG, OPTICAL IP AND IN OR
MULTIPLE RECORDED NEGATIVES FOR RELEASE

FIGURE   Release printing workflow.
2.2

release prints. For large release orders, multiple dupe negs are created as these elements can wear out during the printing process. Generally a single dupe neg can create 800 to 1,000 release prints before it is considered worn.

Sometimes it is necessary to make this IN element as an optical print. One reason this might be necessary stems from the aspect ratio of the original photography. Some widescreen films are shot using a method that is commonly referred to as *Super 35*. Unlike *CinemaScope* (sometimes called simply *Scope*), which utilizes anamorphic lenses to create a wide screen image on the film, Super 35 utilizes spherical or *flat* lenses. Both techniques make use of the entire surface area of the film, although Scope takes the wide-screen image and squeezes it into the negative area, while the wide-screen image of the Super 35 frame must be cropped from within the 35mm frame.

For Super 35, an *optical printer* must be employed to take this cropped wide-screen image and blow it up to fill the entire frame of the IN. An optical printer is essentially a projector and a camera. The lenses and optics of the printer are used to accomplish this process. The impact on quality is an important consideration in deciding to use an optical step in making an intermediate element.

There is an overall concern about the loss in quality (resolution, stability and the increase in film grain) with each successive film duplicate generation. With optical printing, there are additional concerns. The characteristic of the lens in the printer itself also becomes of prime importance and can absolutely affect quality. In addition, with Super 35, it is necessary to enlarge (or *blow up*) a smaller negative area of the original negative (compared to Scope) to fill the full anamorphic frame size. These factors not only have an impact on the quality of the intermediate, but more importantly, also affect the quality of the prints made from this element.

Optical printing is also employed when a film originated in 16mm and a 35mm release is necessary. In that case, the optical blow-up to 35mm usually occurs in the creation of the interpositive element.

One of the factors driving interest in the *digital intermediate* process (the timing of films scanned into a digital post production workflow) comes directly from concern about generational and optical issues in the film process.

Once the film intermediate elements are produced, a check print is made from the IN. This print is used to verify that the answer print timing values are reflected in the prints from the IN. After any timing calibration and screening to give the filmmakers this assurance, release prints can be made.

For film laboratories, release printing has traditionally represented the largest source of their revenue. The typical motion picture release print order today is approximately 3,000 prints, and many more in the case of blockbusters. A major lab using high-speed printers can print and ship this size order in a week.

The number of release prints for a film seems to be constantly rising due to the studio's piracy concerns and current marketing/distribution strategy and box office attendance trends, which seek to emphasize opening weekend results. The interest in simultaneous (or *day and date*) release worldwide has created a need to generate increasingly large numbers of release prints for distribution.

The major labs have built huge worldwide release print capacity in order to react flexibly to shorter turnaround times and to the increasingly larger print orders, especially for the studio's biggest releases. It is not uncommon for a lab to print a large release in several of its worldwide plants.

It is this huge worldwide capacity of high-speed printing that has made the wide release possible. Ironically, it is the lab's highly efficient release print capacity and worldwide infrastructure that the Digital Cinema process seeks to supplant, primarily in the name of release print and shipping cost savings.

Sound Editing and Mixing

To understand the importance of sound to a film, try watching one without it. The dialogue, natural background sounds, sound effects, and music add essential elements to the telling of the story. In recent years the term *sound design* has come to describe the *foreground* use of sound as a storytelling element. This vital part of the post production process begins in earnest as picture editing nears completion. The sound post production is oftentimes scheduled to complete literally a few weeks ahead of the release.

Sound post production is usually thought of as having three distinct components: music, sound effects (or simply *effects*), and dialogue. In fact, on motion picture sound mixing stages (or *dubbing stages*), there are traditionally three mixers whose function is to oversee the mixing of each of these three components that have been brought to the stage after extensive sound editing and preparation. The *lead* mixer is responsible for the most crucial of the elements, the dialogue. There has been a move over the years to consider two mixers, one for backgrounds and sound effects, the other for dialogue and music. This two-mixer configuration, while practiced on some features, is most popular outside of Hollywood, especially in New York. Most major Hollywood films that mix at the top mixing stages usually use three mixers.

Sound post production begins with selecting, or *spotting*, the areas of the film that will be enhanced with music, sound effects, and possibly dialogue replacement. This is usually done from as final, or *locked*, a version of the picture as possible. During this *spotting session*, the supervising sound editor will meet with the director, and usually the editor, watch the picture with them, and discuss the plan for the sound of the film.

During the session, it will be determined how much dialogue replacement is required. Dialogue replacement, also called *looping* or *automated dialogue replacement* (ADR), is necessary to account for line readings that the director feels can be improved or for technical issues such as live background sounds that interfere with the clear understanding of dialogue (for example, an airplane passing over during the scene). The supervising editor prepares a *spotting sheet* of the lines that need to be re-recorded, listing the time needed for each character so that the actors can be scheduled for their ADR sessions. These lines are often recorded in different cities because of an actor's current work commitments, and sometimes actors' schedules require that ADR be done before the picture is locked. In recent years, a number of technological ADR advances have been employed, such as mobile ADR studios and high-speed telecommunications connections, which link studios in different cities to record the actor's lines.

A similar spotting session is held with the composer, including the *music editor*, a job function both technical and creative. The music editor *cuts in* (or *lays in*) each musical *cue*, or section, often contributing creative ideas about when to use a music cue and when not to. It is common for the composer to see earlier unfinished versions of the film. This allows the composer to begin composing general themes and prepare for the types of scenes that will need to be scored. The composer is anxious to get final timings of scenes as soon as possible because the music score must typically be composed and recorded within a 4-week period of time.

During the picture editing, the editor will request temporary (*temp*) sound effects from the supervising sound editor. The supervising sound editor will select (*pull*) these effects from a library for the picture editor, which will help make the film in process more realistic and believable. Due to the increased use of digital edit systems, the editor can deliver digital sound files from the edit system to help the sound effects process along by giving sound editors *in-sync* effects taken from production sound recording. These effects, along with others that the supervisor or the sound effects editor may choose, will be prepared for the eventual mix of the film.

Sound editors usually take on a single task such as dialogue editing, which involves assembling a complete dialogue track from the original sound that was recorded on the set. The dialogue editor will smooth out the dialogue track, eliminating lip smacks or other extraneous sounds so that the dialogue is more intelligible. The editor will prepare the dialogue with *handles* (extra frames of sound before and after words) so that during the sound mixing process, the mixer will have greater flexibility on how the dialogue can be mixed (for example, when multiple characters speak at once). Generally speaking, a dialogue editor can cut between 5 and 7 minutes of dialogue in one day.

Once the scope of the sound task is known, the supervising sound editor will divide the task of editing sound among a group of sound editors. Typically the sound post production will take 6 weeks from the locked picture to the completion of a finished mix, although on a large feature it will often take 6 weeks to do the final mix alone. During this "race to the finish" time period, all of the following steps must take place: the sound editing, ADR, music composition and scoring, *Foley* (the physical re-creation of specific sound effects), *pre-dubs* (preparatory mixes of music, dialogue, and effects) and the final mix. It is a hectic time in which all the final elements must come together to create the finished picture.

What makes this time even more harried is that sometimes the director makes picture changes during the sound editing or even on the mixing stage itself. The editors and assistants need to be able to react immediately to these changes by re-cutting the affected scenes and re-conforming the affected reels, providing either newly conformed workpicture or electronic viewing copies from the edit system for viewing the changed picture during the sound post process.

Digital sound technology, in music and sound effects creation, composing, as well as editing and mixing, has now become standard in the creation of the finished soundtrack. This new digital sound workflow is about to be joined by the increasing digital picture workflow due to new tools, creative approaches and new digital distribution opportunities.

THE MODERN MOTION PICTURE—THE NEW DIGITAL WORKFLOW

In considering the future of theatrical motion pictures, especially as it relates to what we in the early part of the 21st century are thinking of increasingly as Digital Cinema, it is important to note that this transition has been underway for more than 20 years. The worldwide computer and telecommunications revolution, as in so many other industries, has also provided our industry with a pathway to the evolution of cinema, in both creation and distribution.

Nonlinear Editing and the Birth of the Digital Workflow

Beginning in the early 1980s, the industry's toolkit has increasingly been filled with new tools that have emulated and extended the existing film process. The most important of these tools is the *nonlinear editing* (NLE) device, which set the stage for a totally new approach to post production.

The first of these devices—the legendary EditDroid (built by George Lucas's R&D team), the Ediflex, the Montage Picture Processor (a word processor for pictures), and the BHP (Bell & Howell Products) TouchVision— allowed film to be cut electronically in a very different way from the video editing devices of their day.

These new edit systems differed from both traditional film editing and video editing. Unlike film, which is physically cut and spliced together, they allowed non-destructive editing. Unlike video, where the first edit must be re-recorded to a new tape, and each successive edit re-recorded onto this new tape in a linear fashion, a cut could be made in any part of a scene or take. These early nonlinear devices were not digital, but rather electronic, using multiple copies on analog videotape or laser disc, which allowed for the illusion of *random access*, as the first cut was played from one tape or laser disc, the next from another, and so on. If a change needed to be made, the device would just play it another way. Nothing was ever physically cut or copied until someone wanted a copy, which was then output to tape.

Although imperfect and often cumbersome and clunky (the Montage had 18 Betamax VCRs and the Ediflex had 12 VHS VTRs, which noisily clattered as they switched from tape to tape to give the illusion of seamless play), these early devices pointed to a new way to edit film. The ability to attempt an edit without having to worry about losing frames at a splice point was both liberating and maddening, as the endless variations of potential edit points could lead editors and directors in circles. Film editing, with its very cerebral planning of what will flow together, based on the immutable fact of a physical edit, was being challenged by an electronic upstart in which one could try out multiple edits in the same amount of time it would take to splice, undo a splice, and re-do an edit. Hailed by the early sales proponents of these devices as time and cost savers, electronic editing delivered neither. The cost was many times that of the film-based editing tools of the day, and hardly anybody saved time when those as yet unseen, endless variations were just a few clicks of the keyboard and one more edit away. This is the electronic editing equivalent of Parkinson's Law, which states that "work expands to fill the time allotted!" However, these new tools, as immature as they were, seemed tremendously attractive to a creative community that saw them as potentially powerful extensions of their creativity.

These new film editing tools were at the heart of the new methods that swept television post production introduced by Pacific Video's (which became LaserPacific) Electronic Laboratory process in 1984. The Electronic Laboratory spelled out a workflow that began with the scanning of film from negative on a telecine, transferred as best light, edited on a nonlinear edit system, conformed electronically, and then color-timed shot-to-shot and scene-to-scene on an electronic color correction system. This workflow, which was analogous to the film process, provided a new range of flexibility and quality. These imperfect but powerful new electronic nonlinear editing tools, the image enhancement associated with the transfer of film directly from the negative, and the practice of tape-to-tape color correction on new, more powerful electronic timing tools than were available in film, soon won many converts (see Figure 2.3).

For example, in 1984, 80% of prime time television programs were shot on film and 20% on videotape. Of the 80%, all but one show was edited on film. The exception was *Fame LA* whose editor was experienced in the linear video offline techniques of the day. By 1989, as a direct result of the impact of the Electronic Laboratory approach, of the 80% of television that was still shot on film, all but one show used electronic post production techniques. The last film holdout, steadfastly defiant and indifferent to these new ways, was the long-running Universal hit *Murder She Wrote*. In a short 5-year time span, film post production for television ceased, overtaken by a new electronic workflow that offered a new creative flexibility that was undeniable.

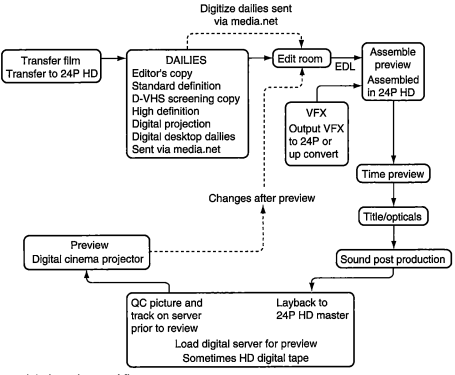

FIGURE

2.3

Digital preview workflow.

While the picture editing revolution was decidedly *electronic*, sound editing workflow was the first to become *digital*. Experiments with a digital sound effects library at the sound post production company Nieman-Tiller presaged the work that was to see the first fully realized end-to-end sound editing and assembly process in 1989. That system, introduced by Pacific Video and created by a company called Cybermation (later to become Waveframe), was the result of collaboration between Chuck Grindstaff, an aerospace signal processing engineer; his father, well-known film sound editor Doug Grindstaff; and Pacific Video and its President, Emory Cohen (who had hired Doug Grindstaff to help it enter the sound post production business).

This system was the digital equivalent of the physical splicing and preparation of magnetic film sound tracks. Like the early electronic picture editing tools, this system helped lead the way to the now virtually ubiquitous digital sound post production workflow. Sound was the industry's first digital process for a simple reason: in digitized form, sound's smaller file size and storage requirements made it more practical for the era's relatively limited computer processing and storage technology.

Digital technology for pictures had begun to influence certain broadcast and post production applications beginning in the late 1970s in the form of new digital signal processing tools. Introduced by NEC by the now generic acronym DVE (*digital video effects*), these first digital tools took analog images and digitized them to resize an image within another (*picture in picture*) and move an image off the screen. Soon spinning digital cubes, page turns, and all manners of ways to fly images on and off a video screen became the rage in "video post production." Even though the Montage Picture Processor used digitized images as the picture reference in its electronic edit system, it was not until 1989 when the first practical digital edit systems premiered. That year at the National Association of Broadcasters (NAB) Convention and Exhibition, attendees marveled at a true digital edit system from EMC^2, which was acknowledged as a "hit of the show." Also, in a small corner in the back of the hall, a small Massachusetts-based company called Avid Technologies showed their approach as well.

Enabled by digital compression technology that allowed video images to be digitized at rates appropriate to the storage and computer power of the era, these new edit systems were not embraced by Hollywood at first. Because of the limitations of compressed image quality, which made it very difficult to actually see if dialog was in sync, and storage limitations that prohibited storing footage for a full reel, digital edit tools were destined to cut their teeth on short form projects such as commercials.

Soon rapid advances in digital compression image quality, along with computer processing and storage, helped to create a market for some evolved edit tools such as digital versions of the Montage and Ediflex. In addition, new edit systems such as the UK-built Lightworks, and early desktop tools such as the Media 100 appeared. But by 1992, Avid held the lion's share of the nonlinear edit market, displacing at that point many of these second- and third-generation nonlinear edit devices.

It is important to note that while a handful of motion pictures experimented with new edit tools, the electronic and digital post production revolution at first was decidedly a television phenomenon. Theatrical motion pictures did not embrace these tools for a variety of reasons. Traditional film editing devices such as the KEM simply displayed better images than these new edit systems. Negative to first-generation print presented a higher resolution than even the finished release prints. Although the workpicture through cutting and handling becomes a bit beat up, scratched and dirty, the undeniable quality of the film image represented a very compelling reason to continue physically cutting film for movies. Having a film print made it possible to screen the picture in a theatrical environment on a big screen, which enabled the creative team to determine how it would play there by viewing it in the proper scope and scale just not possible on a video or computer monitor.

Many also felt that these tools were more geared to television than motion pictures. Editors and directors looked at the screens of electronic edit devices as low-quality televisions and felt that their art and the time-honored editing craft was somehow degraded if practiced in the TV way. In addition, the methods needed for creating proper lists and guidance for negative cutters were not initially developed for these tools. But eventually the power and flexibility of these new nonlinear digital editing systems became too attractive to ignore. The Lightworks edit system in particular featured the same film shuttle control as the KEM, which many film editors found friendly. The team from Avid took great pains to listen to editors and build features and capabilities based on their input. By the mid-1990s the majority of features was edited digitally, and by the end of the millennium the transition to digital editing was virtually complete. Avid's dominance of the edit system market for both television and features was so complete that it was a very rare exception if a Lightworks or a Media 100 was used on a project. Apple's Final Cut Pro promises to be the first new edit system to be seriously considered for features, although the few highly publicized films cut on the system are still very much the exception to Avid's continued rule.

By 2000, even though feature films were using electronic edit systems, virtually all motion pictures also continued to screen film dailies, as well as to conform the film workpicture to the digital cut. Now there were two edit rooms—one digital, one film—and the edit crew and budget grew to accommodate this structure. This budget and labor allowance became a true testament to the power of these new digital tools because once most directors and editors experienced their impact there was no turning back. One of the most notable exceptions to the complete digital transition is Steven Spielberg and his long-time collaborator and editor Michael Kahn, who prefer to physically cut film for what they feel are important creative considerations.

The Evolution of the New Workflow: on the Path to the Modern Motion Picture

As we envision the era of digital distribution of motion pictures, the post production process is undergoing significant and dramatic change. The Electronic Laboratory workflow that was once the domain of television is increasingly becoming a model for feature films as well. At the heart of this transition is the interest in *digital preview* and the promise of a complete end-to-end digital workflow.

Possible cost savings initially drove much of the interest in using high-definition post production workflow and digital projection for motion picture previews. But in practice, the quality of the images and the potential for time savings have also impressed many studios, producers, directors, and even cinematographers, who usually prefer to see film images.

In 1999, with LaserPacific's introduction of the 24P high-definition laboratory workflow concept, the industry quickly adopted high-definition post production at the same 24 fps frame rate as film. During that same time, companies such as Texas Instruments and JVC began showing new digital projection devices that were beginning to reproduce images more cinematically than existing video projectors.

Through the solicited input of the cinematography and technical community, these projector manufacturers began to become more knowledgeable and responsive to the needs and quality expectations of Hollywood's creative professionals. Texas Instruments, in particular, went out of its way to understand how the nuances of color, contrast, dynamic range, and resolution in film might be emulated in its digital projectors. Through a series of side-by-side digital and film projection comparison demonstrations (particularly in the Entertainment Technology Center's Digital Cinema Laboratory), they gained valuable feedback about how to create digitally projected images that were trustworthy.

One of the most important issues relating to the adoption of digital post production and Digital Cinema workflows and techniques has been the long-standing role of film as a predictable reference point for filmmakers. While that may seem self-evident, most cinematographers learn how different film emulsions, exposures, lighting characteristics, color timing, lab processes, and print stock affect the look of dailies or the finished film. This knowledge serves as the cinematographer's reference for the calibration of his or her work.

In a digital process such as a telecine film transfer, a colorist has the ability to alter the look of the digital transfer almost infinitely. Displaying the digitally transferred image on a digital projector can create an unnerving array of variables for a cinematographer whose expectations and career have relied on understanding his or her work in a film system, where the lab's film printer lights can impart valuable information about exposure and validate that the cinematographer accomplished what he or she set out to do.

This issue of how cinematographers and other creative film professionals will calibrate their work and expectations continues to be one of the major challenges of the new digital workflow. That being said, the adoption of digital preview is a significant step toward a complete end-to-end approach that will at some point help to define the modern motion picture as one with an increasingly accepted and trusted digital process.

Digital Preview and Potential Cost Savings

The continuing advances in digital projection technology have made it practical to display large-screen, high-quality cinematic digital images to preview audiences at the same local cinemas that currently house film previews. New, next-generation, high-quality, highly portable projectors also have made it possible for high-definition dailies to be screened on location and in studio screening rooms as part of this new motion picture post production process that results in a digital preview master.

The potential savings that drive the interest in digital preview screenings come from a number of areas. Many films that are previewing digitally reduce costs by reducing the film daily print and reprints. Most films using the preview process continue to print certain selected takes when there is a question of calibration or "how it will look on film." Some films are shot in Super 35 3 Perf (exposing either a 2.35:1 or 1.85:1 aspect ratio over 3 film perforations instead of 4). This results in a 25% savings in both film negative stock and processing. Printing any amount of film in 3 Perf is not very practical as there are few 3 Perf-capable film projectors to use for viewing. Additional savings also result by totally eliminating the daily print. The interest in 3 Perf is also related to the interest in using new digital intermediate finishing methods, since many are shooting 3 Perf as a trade-off for the costs of digital conform and digital color timing for release. In addition, with digital preview the film-conform cutting room (space, equipment, personnel, and overtime) can also be eliminated. Furthermore, there can be a reduction of costs associated with creating temp opticals for preview.

Opticals and visual effects are one of the key reasons the digital preview process began. For films that have a significant number of incomplete VFX shots or opticals, a digital preview allows the VFX and optical teams to continue working on *finals* while temps are completed in a high-definition video environment or output from digital files to HD, without having to create *film outs* (film recorded from the digital data) of digital shots.

Digital Preview Workflow

Films can be previewed digitally by transferring a cut film workpicture to a digital master, with opticals, titles, and subsequent versions conformed digitally. Many who first realized the benefits of the digital preview used this process.

A second method involves outputting the current version of the cut directly from the edit system and *upconverting* (*electronically transcoding*) *standard definition* images to high definition for preview. Depending on the image quality of the edit system, this can result in a projected image of acceptable to marginal quality. Some studios and directors accept this marginal quality by comparing the process favorably to the workpicture, which at the time of a preview has been handled so extensively that it is certain to show wear and tear. Traditionally, preview screenings are initiated with a proviso to the audience that they have been invited to see a work in progress and should expect the film to look a bit rough.

A third method of previewing a film assembles the standard definition elements from the initial telecine transfer and upconverts this version for digital preview. This method can yield slightly better quality than output from the edit system.

But a fourth method is beginning to define a new workflow for motion pictures: a process whereby film negative is transferred directly to 24P high-definition digital videotape as dailies. This method also yields efficiency in subsequent preview screenings, featuring images significantly more pristine than can be derived from a cut film workpicture (see Figure 2.3).

Using this method, dailies can be screened in high-definition on a variety of devices including CRT monitors, plasma *flat panel displays* (FPDs), or with high-quality digital projectors. In the past, the quality of digital projection, and the corresponding ability to discern critical resolution and contrast, was limited. Directors and cinematographers especially were concerned that these early-generation digital projectors could not adequately convey what had been captured on the film. These new breeds of D-ILA projectors from JVC, as well as projectors featuring the Texas Instruments DLP technology from a variety of manufacturers, represent a significant advancement in digital dailies screening projection technology with unprecedented resolution, contrast, and image quality.

Transfer Negative to 24P High Definition

The film laboratory processes each day's film negative, and if no daily print is needed, the film is usually available for the digital transfer earlier than if it was to be printed and synced on film. This unbroken-down negative is transferred and sunk with the production audio track in a telecine suite to 24P high-definition digital videotape. During this transfer the data needed for the edit system are generated. The color timing of this *digital daily print* is made, based on input from the cinematographer and consultation with the dailies colorist. The communication of this look from the cinematographer to the digital dailies process is a component that is crucial to the success of this approach.

Some cinematographers rely on a relationship with a colorist with whom they have worked in the past and whom they trust. Similar to the bond of trust with a film lab contact, this helps the cinematographer. There are often phone conversations discussing how to interpret the camera report notes or what might have been seen during the transfer. The colorist becomes the eyes of the cinematographer in the transfer of the images to the digital tape for dailies.

Look Management

New tools are evolving for *look management*, a process of communicating the intended look of the picture more directly to the post production process. In 1999, Panavision and Kodak launched a system called PreView, which enabled a cinematographer to better visualize and communicate the result of film emulsion, filters, lab process, and other variables to the director and other collaborators such as the lab or the telecine colorist. The system consisted of a digital still camera, a thermal printer, and a laptop with software that could emulate these processes. While the system garnered significant interest, especially because of the power of the software, the early digital camera and print technology was immature and a bit cumbersome, and the system was not pervasively used. Many cinematographers devised their own methods, often using Adobe Photoshop to create still images that communicated their intended look. These systems too, had drawbacks, as it was difficult to create a print of the exact look on the digital screen. Oftentimes, these stills were sent as computer JPEG files, which itself became problematic because of the lack of calibration between display devices.

Kodak has recently introduced a new approach called the Kodak Look Manager System, which includes display management and calibration as part of the toolkit. The updated software package contains powerful emulation tools that enable the cinematographer to view the color, film stock, filtration, lab, and telecine processes on a calibrated viewing device, which is designed to match another calibrated device at the lab or in telecine. In this way, cinematographers can be assured that the look has been communicated and that all who view it are viewing it in the same way.

In addition to communicating the look to dailies, this tool also promises to actually communicate the intended look directly into the post production process. The vision is to codify the look as a recipe that will create a 3-dimensional *look-up-table* (LUT) that will modify the scanning (either as HD video or data scans) so that the intended look will be created as the image in dailies. The idea is that these LUTs would be traced through the post production process, allowing the look of the film to be created early in the filmmaking process and used to inform the other steps in *look realization*. These new tools, as well as others such as the TrueLight system being marketed by FilmLight, coupled with color management, promise to play a large role in creating a reliable and predictable digital process in the future.

Dailies Screening Copies

From the timed high-definition dailies master, various screening copies are generated. There are many options for high-quality dailies screening.

D-VHS

A new, cost-effective method is now available to screen dailies in high definition. Developed by JVC, *Digital VHS* (D-VHS) is a format that records a
high-definition digital file on a new type of videotape that is the same size as
VHS tape used in conventional VHS players. When this tape is played on a
D-VHS VTR, high-definition images of higher quality than HDTV broadcasts can be displayed on digital projectors or high-definition monitors. This
format has both a consumer and a professional variant. In its professional
mode, it can be used to create a tape that can be played only in specific players, or groups of players, pre-designated for a specific production as a security precaution. In addition to this security feature, the VTR itself can be
locked with a password. The role of security in the digital production
process is an increasingly important issue that the technical and creative
community is struggling to address.

Hard Drive Dailies

There are also a number of different systems that allow the viewing of high-
definition dailies directly from a hard drive. While the quality of the image
(MPEG2 at 25 mb/sec) is identical to D-VHS, the ability to create playlists or
randomly jump from one scene or take to another is of great interest and
utility. In film dailies, it is quite common to high speed through the film,
especially when there is a lot of footage. While D-VHS does have a fast forward function, the ability to create a play list or store all of the dailies at once
is a great attraction of these hard drive dailies systems.

When film dailies are printed, the negative is assembled in the order
of the scene coverage, with all the cameras and the takes arranged in a
meaningful way. In typical video dailies, the negative is transferred in the
order that it was shot, because it is very slow and inconvenient and
requires excessive negative handling to put up and take down camera rolls
so that the transfer has the same *coverage order* (or *script order*) as print
dailies. With a hard drive dailies system, the playlist function can be programmed to emulate this coverage order.

DVD Dailies

Another increasingly common method in which dailies are viewed is on
DVD-R (recordable) discs. Unlike D-VHS or hard drive systems, dailies on

DVD are currently standard definition, albeit much higher quality than the VHS cassette, which still exists as a popular but low-quality method of screening dailies. For the most part, DVD dailies are intended for individual viewing and not the large-screen, high-quality collaborative viewing that is used for the high-definition dailies sources. Many post production facilities provide DVD dailies discs that allow the user to access individual scenes or takes. Some provide additional functionality such as viewing in coverage order.

Digital "Desktop" Dailies and Connectivity

The Internet and other private, high-speed telecommunications networks are also being used to transport dailies and other digital files such as for edit systems or for visual effects. The quality of images and the size of files that can be sent are directly related to the amount of bandwidth and connectivity available to the user.

For the most part, dailies sent and made available over the Internet are standard definition and can have quality ranging from VHS-equivalent to images that exceed DVD. Sometimes called *desktop dailies* because a computer is usually used as the receive station, these dailies can be stored on a computer hard drive and played through a computer monitor, laptop, or television set if the computer is equipped with a graphics card with *video out*.

There are a number of set-top devices that can be used to connect to a DSL or a higher-bandwidth Internet line to serve as the receive or send station for digitally delivered dailies. It is increasingly common for films shot outside of the United States to send or receive dailies or versions of cuts through the Internet, by either posting to a website that can be viewed from an authorized computer or to one of these set-top devices.

Another use of these networks is to send digitized edit system data directly to the cutting room. Post production houses routinely create digitized files for the edit system and can transmit these files directly to the cutting room, assuming sufficient bandwidth and connectivity. In addition, this technology can also be used for creative collaboration sessions. A typical use might enable a remote working session with an editor and a director in different cities. By using a private network or the Internet, the editor can show a cut to a director who can comment and direct changes in real time as they both watch. Dailies using efficient new compression schemes such as MPEG 4 and Windows Media9 may soon result in practical high-definition images sent over telecommunication links. Next-generation blue laser-based DVDs, which can also hold high-definition content, could very well be used in dailies well before their consumer debut, due to current industry effort to define standards and security issues prior to a consumer introduction of the high-definition DVD.

The Edit Room and the Digital Workflow Process

The digital preview process allows the cutting room to start working considerably earlier than with traditional film dailies. There is no need to sync and code the track prior to the transfer. And because the editor's source material comes directly from the negative to a high-definition transfer master, the downconverted standard definition image and sound quality in the edit system are superior to the typical print transfer video dailies.

The editor has a number of options of how the dailies will be digitized into the edit system. Whereas 3/4″ videotape cassettes are still one choice, the poor image and sound quality make them the least desirable source. BetaSP, while a component source, is still an analog format in both picture and track and is prone to tape damage and *dropouts* (momentary loss of image because of uneven magnetic coating on the tape). Edit systems are beginning to be equipped with digital tape decks such as DVCam and DVCPro, which offer a clean digital component picture and digital track from which to digitize into the edit system.

But increasingly, the most desirable choice for the edit system is a direct digitization from the high-definition master to the standard definition edit system file. Many post houses provide a service in which the edit system files are either transferred to portable digital hard drives (typically *IEEE 1394*, sometimes called *FireWire*) or sent directly to the cutting room via a network service provider. The main advantages of digitized edit system files are, first, superior picture quality and, second, that cutting can begin as soon as the edit room receives digitized edit system files. In addition, the sound files are of the same digital quality as what was recorded during production. This means that these files can be used as the source for dialogue editing for the final mix, by merely outputting the editor's digital sound for delivery to the post production sound crew.

Additional significant benefits are derived due to the better image quality in the edit system, so output tapes are far superior to the poor quality tapes that directors and executives have had to put up with for many years.

Preparing Visual Effects for Preview

In the digital preview process, fades, dissolves, freezes, and variable speed effects that are part of the edit decision list are automatically assembled as part of the preview assembly. Other visual effects that are to be part of the preview need to be transferred to 24P high-definition in order to be inserted into the preview assembly. If these visual effects are computer-generated and the visual effects house does not have the capability to transfer to 24P high-definition videotape, there are many methods by which visual effects files can be transferred to high-definition.

Preview Conform / Assembly and Color Timing

Once the film is ready for preview, it is assembled from its high-definition sources to a high-definition master. The film is then color-timed digitally using a digital projector with the same characteristics as the one that will be used in the theatre preview. This is a departure from the model of previewing film, where the workpicture is generally not re-timed. Directors and cinematographers are beginning to use the opportunity of digital preview timing as a way to visualize the final timing of the picture. If the film is to be finished digitally in the digital intermediate process, this early timing session allows the filmmakers to understand how the film might be digitally timed for the final release. As end-to-end systems are developed, it is envisioned that this preview timing will be applied to a subsequent data scan and digital timing for film record or digital cinema.

Once timed, any temp titles for preview will be electronically prepared and inserted into the preview master. During this session, any opticals that were not inserted prior to the assembly or additional opticals such as blow-ups, repositions, or other opticals that can be accomplished in an electronic environment are inserted into the picture.

Temp sound editing and mixing for the preview is done to a video version of the picture derived either from the output of the edit system, from a downconverted copy of the assembled high-definition preview master, or in some cases (as sound stages become equipped) from the high-definition version. The picture is edited and mixed in reels. Once mixed, a final (*print master*) version is created on digital hard disc or digital audio tape to be used to *lay back* (*transfer*) to the 24P high-definition preview master reels.

Building the Preview Element

After sound post production, a high-definition version with the final six track mix is created on D-5 high-definition tape (the *long play version* or *preview master*). This long play version on videotape can be used as a source for the preview, to load a digital server that will play the picture and track during the preview, or for the various tape copies of the film that are ordered for studio marketing or production executives after the preview. The HD D-5 videotape format is usually used because this format can accommodate up to eight tracks of uncompressed digital audio.

Load and QC Server for Digital Preview

A digital server, such as the QuBit made by QuVIS, is a common device used for digital previews. The advantage of using such a server is that these devices store a digitized version plus a back-up version (a *mirror*) that will play instantly if there are any problems with the main digital file. In addition, these devices can be programmed with a playlist so that only the changed reels need to be loaded for subsequent previews. These devices provide very high-quality images and sound and are portable and straightforward to run at the preview. Sometimes, an HD VTR is used to run the picture at previews, but these devices are usually more expensive and do not have an automatic back-up mode.

Once the preview master is created, either on a server or on tape, a complete quality evaluation of the main and back-up picture and sound elements are conducted to verify that the elements are ready for preview. Generally, the layback of the track, the creation of the long play, the loading of the server, and the QC can be done in one day and usually take place the day (and evening) before the scheduled preview.

The Digital Preview at the Theatre

There are certain theatres that have installed digital cinema projection technology that have been used for previews. However, these theatres are generally not in the outlying or suburban areas preferred for previews, so digital projectors are usually brought into an existing film cinema. Digital projectors used for previews can be set up within a few hours. It is common either to use a theatre's view port or to move the existing film projector aside to accommodate the digital projector.

Subsequent Previews

After notes are compiled from a preview, editorial changes are made in the edit system. The changes are then conformed in a second high-definition assembly and any un-timed or changed footage is timed, the server is again loaded with any changed reels, and another QC takes place. The projector and server are brought to the theatre, and if there are any changes from this second preview, the changes are re-conformed and timed before any subsequent previews.

Finishing Films Digitally

The digital preview is only one aspect of the dramatic and radical technological change in motion picture post production. The significant interest in finishing films using digital color timing and then creating film, digital cinema, and electronic delivery versions has touched an undeniable nerve in both the technology and creative community. This process, sometimes referred to as the *digital intermediate, digital film finishing,* or *digital mastering,* has been the focal point of many who look at this new post production workflow as the wave of the future.

There are some who predict that by 2007, it will be only the odd motion picture that will utilize the photochemical process that has defined the film workflow since its inception. There are some who feel that film itself will become threatened as an origination medium as new digital cinematography tools become increasingly powerful and accepted by the creative community. And without a doubt, there are others who feel that film will be part of our industry for many years to come. But there seems to be little doubt that the post production process will become digital and the transition will be as rapid as any technology adoption in motion picture history.

The origins of this digital pathway can be traced to a system of hardware and software developed by Eastman Kodak in the early 1990s. Practical digital film scanners coupled with Kodak's Cineon software allowed negative film to be digitally scanned, manipulated in digital workstations, and then recorded back to film on new digital film recorders. The significance of this systems approach was that the resulting digital images could be recorded back to film in a way that allowed the digital files to be seamlessly intercut with the adjacent film scenes. Cineon enabled digital visual effects on a scale and at a quality level that revolutionized the industry. Theatregoers soon became connoisseurs of extraordinary images of amazing realism and scope. The new digital visual effects industry could quite literally make believable dinosaurs once again walk the earth as audiences eagerly anticipated releases of films that demonstrated this new digital artistic prowess.

In the early 1990s, digital editing devices were just beginning to make their inroads into the motion picture post production process. The early notion of complete digital post production workflow revolved around the very complex computer programming-intensive and almost secret society world of those who practiced the "black art" of visual effects. This was a world of Jolt Cola-imbibing young digital artists, code writers, and a few who made the transition from film opticals and effects to computers.

This digital community, with their powerful new tools and the images they produced, began to redefine the world of opticals and visual effects. Like the other electronic and digital workflow transitions that had taken place in sound, picture editing, and film and television post production, the photochemical optical and visual effects process was quickly becoming anachronistic.

In 1998, filmmaker Gary Ross explored the notion of using this digital visual effects technology to create whole scenes of his acclaimed *Pleasantville* in which color would subtly creep into the black and white world in which much of this film took place. This use of digital technology, and Ross's collaboration with Kodak's Cinesite, raised significant industry awareness of how these new tools might be used for something other than strictly visual effects. However, the model of this workflow was still very much visual effects-oriented, as *Pleasantville*'s digital scenes were still post produced and thought of as so many VFX shots, sort of an extended set of color opticals.

In 2000, the Coen brothers, stimulated by their cinematographer Roger Deakins, enlisted Cinesite's help and expertise to help create an entire film using a digital workflow. The result was the birth of a new digital methodology. The idea was to scan an entire film into digital files and then to use the tools to color-time the full picture in a way that simply was not possible in film timing. *Oh Brother, Where Art Thou?* was essentially entirely a color optical. Using the stylized look of the color-timed files, a Kodak laser film recorder digitally recorded the entire film onto the same intermediate film stock used for the creation of interpositives and internegatives. This digital intermediate element was now essentially a replacement for the cut negative and could be used as the source for the printing elements for release. Originally meant to refer to the physical element that was the result of this digital scanning, color timing, and film recording, the term *digital intermediate* has become a colloquial reference for the entire new digital post production workflow.

The Digital Intermediate

This idea of the digital intermediate, born from visual effects workflow, was almost instantly acknowledged as a significant development. Cinematographers as well as directors hailed an expanded palette enabled by powerful digital color timing tools. The digital intermediate process was further popularized by the entry of EFILM, which had significant expertise in creating film from digital files for visual effects, as well as Technicolor, which made a significant investment in creating a new infrastructure for digital film finishing.

The process essentially consists of scanning the negative, conforming the negative digitally, importing and integrating visual effects elements, color timing, recording the finished timed movie to film, and creating various other delivery elements from the digital files.

In order to begin the digital intermediate process, the negative is scanned on a digital scanner. The early, very slow scanners required 6 seconds or more per frame for 4K resolution (4096×3072 pixels for the full 35mm frame), but the newest ones scan the negative at 2K resolution (2048×1536 pixels for the full 35mm frame) in real time at 24 fps and 4K resolution at 6 fps. Current scanners differ in speed, their ability to hold an image steady in "pin registration," their optical systems, their ability to scan at various resolutions, and their own imaging characteristics.

While those wishing to take advantage of the digital intermediate process have been driven by the flexibility in color timing, the importance of quality considerations also looms large. Much of the industry has focused on resolution as a key and important element in determining quality. An issue of hot debate has been the question of "How many Ks are OK?" with "Ks" referring to the thousands of pixels in the horizontal or vertical dimension that comprise a digital frame. There have been industry scientists, most notably Roger Morton and his team at Eastman Kodak, who have described a film system in which the negative has potential resolution of 6K or more.[1] Others disagree, and claim that the negative through the film print process barely yields 2K resolution.[2] This issue of pixel resolution has also been hotly debated in the context of setting digital cinema standards of quality.

The most common practice today is a workflow in which color timing is done at 2K from files that may have been scanned at 2K, 4K, or 6K and then *down-rezed* or down-converted to 2K resolution. There is a general industry consensus that anticipates a 4K workflow when it becomes practical to do so. Computer processing power, digital storage, and network capacity need to undergo significant improvement in capability and cost effectiveness in order for the industry to move in that direction. Even though 4K is the goal of many in both the creative and technical community for digital cinema, as well for the digital post production process, there are some who feel that today's film lenses and film systems are just not capable of exhibiting moving images with that much resolution. That being said, everyone in the industry wants to be assured that the cinema of the future and the process by which it is made and exhibited are not compromised or hamstrung by setting the quality bar too low.

Initially, the negative for the digital film finishing process needed to be cut in order for it to be scanned. It was cumbersome to scan from unbroken-down camera or lab rolls, as the devices and software that ran them had no easy way to find the needed negative section from the edit decision list. Now, most of the devices and companies that offer these services can scan from the sometimes thousands of camera rolls and find the exact frames that need to be used for the timing and finishing process.

Once scanned, the individual frames need to be assembled into the film exactly as edited so that the film can be timed. If cut negative is scanned, the film is largely intact except for any visual effects shots or opticals, which may need to be inserted or created. If camera reels or uncut negative are scanned, most companies have devised a way to conform these individual files into the assembled picture. The task involves translating an edit decision list that specifies feet and frames, key numbers and time code into a

---

[1] R. Morton, M. Maurer, and C. DuMont, "An Introduction to Aliasing and Sharpening in Digital Motion Picture Systems," *SMPTE Motion Imaging Journal*, May 2003, Vol. 112, No. 5, pp. 161–171; "Relationships between Pixel Count, Aliasing, and Limiting Resolution in Digital Motion Picture Systems," *SMPTE Motion Imaging Journal*, July 2003, Vol. 112, No. 7, pp. 217–224.

[2] V. Baroncini, H. Mahler, and M. Sintas, "The Image Resolution of 35mm Cinema Film in Theatrical Presentation," *SMPTE Motion Imaging Journal*, February/March 2004, Vol. 113, No. 2 & 3, pp. 60–66. But also see R. Morton, A. Cosgrove, and A. Masson, "Letter to the Editor Re: 'The Image Resolution of 35mm Cinema Film in Theatrical Presentation,' " *SMPTE Motion Imaging Journal*, April 2004, Vol. 113, No. 4, p. 102.

conforming list that assembles the 150,000 or more individual digital files into a movie.

One of the most daunting tasks in this new digital workflow is accounting for visual effects shots. Invariably last minute in nature, it is ironic that the visual effects workflow that spawned this new digital post production workflow has had a hard time integrating within it. That is because the digital visual effects workflow was created with film output as its target and cutting the output film into negative as its method. With a complete digital post production workflow, the calibration of scanners, displays, and color management becomes critical. In addition, finding efficient methods of inserting the "bushel baskets" of shots delivered on computer drives, data tape, film for scans, over the Internet, and in file formats different from the other data has made the integration process challenging. Of course, since the entire digital process gives the creative community the impression that anything can be changed instantly, it invariably is. While the tools might allow last-minute iterations and changes, the process of updating all the changes is certainly not currently efficient or painless.

Once conformed, the digital timing process begins (although conforming and changes also take place during the timing process). Timing environments initially resembled the telecine suites that were familiar to the directors and cinematographers who had used video color correction tools for creating commercials or home video releases. Currently more of these environments are being built to simulate theatres, with large screens and digital projection so that the scope of the film can be taken into account during timing. The tools are also evolving as software-based color correction devices, more powerful than today's telecine-type color correction tools, are augmenting hardware color correction. Remember that LUTs have several capabilities: they alter the display device to emulate film, take the digital data to film, alter the data to play on television, and create images for digital cinema. Modeling the complex digital-to-film process so that the images viewed in the digital environment can be delivered on film has become the "secret sauce" that differentiates competitors within the service business. In what only can be described as the "Battle of the LUTs," these proprietary approaches yield a "my LUT is better than your LUT" pitch to potential customers. As there are no standardized approaches to color management in the workflow, many facilities have created "home brew" LUTs.

Color management and look management that allow for consistency and predictability are topics that echo loud in discussions of the new digital workflow. A management process that accounts for different display devices and media and accurately emulates the look of the image in these differing environments is a key goal to both digital motion picture creation and distribution. Digital cinema would simply not be possible without the assurance of color management. The digital post production workflow must include processes whereby images intended for film, digital cinema, and home video distribution can be created and viewed with the assurance that they will be correctly displayed.

Post Production Evolves

Indeed, much of this new digital workflow is evolving as are the roles of industry professionals. The digital timing medium allows directors and cinematographers to extend production beyond the limitations of principal photography. The ability to alter expectations in production, such as knowing that *magic hour* (the time before the sun has risen or after the sun has set, but the sky is bright enough for good tonal rendition) can be achieved in post production with significantly more control than for a crew waiting for the sunrise or the sunset to be "just right." The knowledge that certain parts of a scene might be "lit" in a digital timing environment more efficiently and cost effectively might lead cinematographers to light differently. These emerging powerful tools will allow for new kinds of lighting and looks.

One of the issues that burns the midnight oil in the venerable clubhouse of the American Society of Cinematographers is the question of who will be responsible for creating and utilizing this new palette. In an era when everyone, even amateurs, has access to powerful image manipulation tools such as Photoshop, cinematographers are very concerned that they not play secondary roles to other collaborators in the process. The ascendant colorist who commands attention and remuneration has been a linchpin in many decisions to try these new post production paths. The visual effects supervisor is increasingly playing a role in creating the look and lighting feel of a film. Digitally mastered movies such as *The Lord of the Rings* point to a new type of film in which the cinematographer might photograph a scene in a very straightforward way, but the post production teams of visual effects, colorists, and directors might actually realize the ultimate creative vision.

This evolution of the digital workflow process, directly descendant from the visual effects workflow, might very well diverge into a VFX path and a more production-oriented path. With evolving look management and color management tools, it will be possible to track the creative look intent from the earliest pre-visualizations through the dailies, preview, and final timing process. In this way, all the color and look decisions in production could follow along and inform the post production process of the color choices that were made in dailies and previews. Of course any of these choices could be changed in the film digital mastering for film recording and other distribution. Today's digital intermediate workflow, in which the negative is scanned and the color decisions happen at the end of the process, could be made more efficient if the color workflow and management were part of the process from the beginning.

This new workflow will encompass a process by which many forms of distribution elements will be created. It will surely be influenced by the Digital Cinema specifications being articulated by *Digital Cinema Initiatives* (DCI), the consortium formed and funded by the seven major Hollywood studios, and by standards created by SMPTE (Society of Motion Picture and Television Engineers). At the junction of these new post production pathways, there must be color management that will allow the creative community to take advantage of new digital methods and tools in a transparent and seamless way. This workflow must allow for the creation of 35mm film that will be part of the distribution chain for quite some time as well as ensure that digital elements embodying the creative intent can easily be generated.

An important question the industry needs to address in the new digital era is, with increasing amounts of images no longer represented by physical film but by data and files, how will motion picture elements be archived? The notions of digital archiving and digital asset management, which seem to so easily roll off tongues of vendors, especially at industry technical conferences, are illusory at best. Many industry professionals who are charged with the task of maintaining the libraries and archives of the major studios remain unconvinced that there are good current long-term and deep archive solutions to store digital data. This issue remains high on the list of tasks that need to be accomplished before these new digital ways will be considered robust.

This new post production workflow, which may very well allow filmmakers to exhibit and distribute the most pristine, highest quality cinematic images ever, is still a work in progress. But it is progress itself, and the dedication of countless industry professionals, that feel a calling to create the infrastructure for a future cinema that can be truly worthy of its past.

3 Color in Digital Cinema

Charles Poynton

This chapter outlines issues of color image reproduction and color science that are important to digital cinema. Many of the issues that I will discuss here have technical implications that are beyond the scope of this book. Technical details concerning many of these topics can be found in my book, *Digital Video and HDTV Algorithms and Interfaces*.[1]

"FAITHFUL" AND "PLEASING" REPRODUCTION

The central problem of most applications of digital imaging is to take an original scene, as a viewer might witness it directly, and code it into digital data that can subsequently be decoded and displayed as a faithful reproduction of the scene. Digital image data can easily be modified such that the scene is not faithfully reproduced. Modifications may be unintentional: we hope that a good understanding of image science on the part of system designers will prevent unintentional modifications. On the other hand, modifications may be intentionally applied for artistic purposes. Faithful reproduction is the difficult problem: once that is solved, achieving unfaithful reproduction—presumably to serve an artistic end—is well understood. In consumer photography, equipment and staff at the photo lab make only minimal alterations to the captured image; it is up to the film manufacturer

---

[1]Poynton, Charles, *Digital Video and HDTV Algorithms and Interfaces* (San Francisco: Morgan Kaufmann, 2003).

to determine what is "faithful." (Perhaps a film manufacturer would use the term "pleasing" instead, as pleasing pictures are ultimately what sell imaging products to consumers.) In consumer digital photography, there is no "lab;" all of the technical requirements associated with "faithful" or "pleasing" reproduction must be built into the hardware and the algorithms. In cinema, it is not always necessary for the scene to be captured faithfully. What is important is that the cinematographer's intent is expressed in the projected print that is presented to him or her for approval: the answer print. The expectation at the approval stage is that the answer print will be faithfully reproduced, within a certain tolerance, in the cinema.

FILM

Ultimately—perhaps in 20 years' time—most movies will be originated, processed, distributed, and exhibited in digital form. The film industry is large, traditional, and dependent on craft; many aspects of the workflow used in making movies stem from the processing of film. Many movies today have computer graphics integrated with live action that was captured on film; live action film is often processed to insert digital effects, and even completely synthetic computer-animated films need to be transferred to film for exhibition. To accomplish these tasks, it is necessary to integrate digital technology into the film workflow: preexisting practices must be taken into account. Finally, although some characteristics of film reproduction are undesirable consequences of photochemical processing, some characteristics have their origins in visual perception, and those characteristics we seek to emulate digitally.

Film Workflow

To understand digital cinema, it is helpful to understand the workflow ordinarily used in cinema production and post production (see Figure 3.1).

Live action is normally captured on camera negative film, sometimes called *original camera negative* (OCN). Camera negative film has three emulsion layers and obviously records color. However, the relationship between colors in the scene and colors in the developed negative is not sensible: tones and colors are recorded inverted. For example, red in the scene is

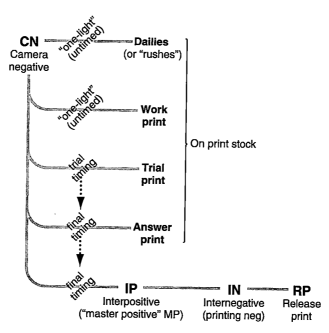

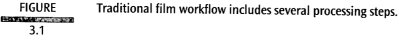

FIGURE

3.1
Traditional film workflow includes several processing steps.

recorded as cyan in the negative, and yellow in the scene is recorded as blue in the negative. The inversion is reversed when camera negative film is printed. Unexposed or lightly exposed (shadow) regions on developed camera negative film have a characteristic orange color. OCN film incorporates colored couplers that develop into an orange mask in unexposed or shadow regions. The orange mask compensates for unwanted absorption of short-wave light by the cyan and magenta dyes.

Captured scenes are printed onto print stock. Prints called *dailies* or *rushes* are viewed by the creative team to ensure that the scene is adequately represented on film while scenery, props, equipment, and personnel are still available in case a re-shoot is necessary. Later on, similarly produced *workprints* may be made for various technical purposes.

Color grading refers to achieving the intended color characteristics subsequent to capturing the original scene. Color grading in film is effected when the OCN is printed onto intermediate film stock to produce an *interpositive* (IP). The IP records positive imagery whose colors are sensible. However, because intermediate stock has a dramatically different transfer function from print stock, the apparent color quality of an IP is poor. The IP is not intended to be directly viewed, however: it is itself printed onto intermediate stock to produce an *internegative* (interneg, IN, printing neg, or dupe neg). Like imagery on camera negative film, the colors on the IN are not sensible until printed onto print stock.

When the movie is ready for distribution, the IN is printed using a high-speed contact printer onto print stock to make release prints that are distributed to the theaters. (The release prints are said to be *struck*.) The IN is spliced into a loop, and release prints are produced in a continuous process. An IN, or printing neg, can be cycled through the printer between 500 and 1000 times before its quality starts to degrade from mechanical wear. At that point, it is replaced by a fresh IN produced from the IP.

Negative film reverses tones and colors. Film material and its associated processing can be designed to reproduce colors correctly without requiring a second printing step. *Reversal* film is used in consumer 35mm slides and in graphic arts (where positive transparencies are preferred to negatives). The reversal process is occasionally used for art films. Though called "reversal" film, this film and its processing paradoxically do not reverse colors! In another paradox, an *IP* is printed onto *negative* film stock! It is best to think of the term *negative* as describing the state of the image, not the intrinsic characteristic of a film stock. Film stock is best described as *camera, intermediate,* or *print* (or in rare cases, *reversal*).

Color Grading in Film

Color quality in film is adjusted during printing by altering the intensities of separate red, green, and blue printing lights. Ordinarily, these colored components are separated by color filters from a single light source. When a skilled craftsperson manipulates the intensity settings during printing to achieve the desired film color reproduction, the process is called *color grading.* In traditional photography, exposure can be controlled by adjusting exposure time. When motion picture film is printed, ordinarily the exposure time is fixed, and exposure is controlled through adjustment of light intensity. Nevertheless, in a historical reference to color photography, color grading is often called *color timing.* When no control is exercised over the relative intensity of the lights, the print is described as *untimed, flat, best light,* or *one light.*

Printing light wavelengths are chosen to minimize the amount of cross talk and, as a secondary goal, to match the peak sensitivities of the print film. The lights are adjustable in exponentially spaced increments called *points*.[2] Applying 40 increments causes printing exposure to be multiplied by 10—that is, one point corresponds to 0.025 density units in the negative. Applying 12 increments causes a doubling of the printing exposure. (If you are familiar with cameras, you might be tempted to call this a *stop;* however, that term is misleading in this context for reasons that will become clear in a moment.) Nominal exposure is achieved at a setting such as 25-25-25 ("25-across"). The usual range of each light is from 0 to 50—that is, printing exposure can be increased by a factor of about four or decreased by a factor of about four from nominal.

The effect of a certain set of printer light settings can be related to the change in exposure at the camera, expressed in *f*-stops, that would achieve an equivalent effect. The relationship is indirect because of the nonlinearity of camera negative film. The gamma of camera negative film is about 0.6. Increasing negative exposure by 1 2/3 stops produces approximately the same effect as halving exposure at the printing stage—that is, subtracting 12 points. Twelve points at printing corresponds to about 1 2/3 stops in scene exposure, so about 7 points correspond to 1 stop of scene exposure.

In the process of color grading, several *trial prints* of each scene are typically made. The cinematographer views each trial print and sends instructions back to the lab concerning the printing lights to be used for the next print. The print whose color is accepted by the cinematographer is called the *answer print.*

The printer lights approved by the cinematographer on the basis of the answer print are applied to print the OCN onto the IP. The IP records positive imagery with sensible color, but as I have mentioned, the color is not visually correct. However, when the IP is printed to an IN, and that IN is in turn printed onto print stock, colors in the release print will closely match those of the answer print.

When *computer-generated imagery* (CGI) is recorded to film, it is ordinarily recorded onto intermediate stock, with exposures proportional to the tristimulus values of the real scene. (Though proportional to the scene, the exposures are much higher than a real scene because intermediate film is

---

[2]A *printer's point* in common language refers to 1/72 of an inch.

much less sensitive than camera film.) Although intermediate stock is used instead of camera negative stock, CGI recorded to film is equivalent in color terms to a camera negative. Such imagery is often referred to as *duplicate negative*, or *dupe neg*, even though nothing was actually duplicated. This approach allows CGI material to be treated for the remainder of the production process identically to the original camera negative. Such material can be spliced into (*intercut* with) original film footage.

DIGITAL CINEMA

In digital cinema, we seek to produce a digital answer print that will be approved by the cinematographer. The goal in distribution and exhibition is then to have the movie exhibited with its color reproduction closely approximating the digital answer print.

    If the tristimulus values of the digital answer print, as approved on a reference projector, are displayed faithfully in the cinema, then the color issues of distribution and exhibition are solved. However, color in digital cinema encompasses more than just distribution and exhibition. We wish to use digital technology in capture and post production; color at those stages is not necessarily the same as the final color. We want the capability of transforming the color values of a digital cinema master into the color range available in alternate release formats, such as broadcast or home video. Finally, we wish the digital cinema master to address the issue of color gamut: we want to enable a path toward wide-gamut capture, post-processing, and exhibition capability so that future movies will have access to a wider color palette than today's movies. (Part of that goal is artistic, and part is commercial: many participants in the movie business seek to retain a strong product differentiation between movies in theatrical exhibition and home theater.) For all of those reasons, we need to delve deeper into color issues, starting with the digital representation of color image data.

Color Space

Because human vision is based on three different kinds of color photoreceptor cells in the retina, three components are necessary and sufficient to describe color. A vision scientist may talk about color values being represented in terms of cone fundamentals—estimates of the outputs of the photoreceptor cells themselves. Color measurements are based on *tristimulus* color values denoted *XYZ*, and derivatives of these, such as chromaticity values (x, y) and perceptually uniform color values $L^*a^*b^*$ (CIE LAB) or $L^*u^*v^*$ (CIE LUV). For image capture and display, it is more practical to deal with color values representing *additive RGB* primaries or nonlinear derivatives of *RGB* such as $R'G'B'$, $Y'C_BC_R$ (or in analog video systems, $Y'P_BP_R$, $Y'UV$, *or* $Y'IQ$). Conventional photography uses *subtractive* color, based on cyan, magenta, and yellow (CMY) dyes.

All of these systems have three components. It is natural for us to create a spatial metaphor for color, relating the three-color component values to three spatial coordinates. We speak of various color representations as being three-dimensional *color spaces*. Colors are described as locations in 3-space; differences between colors are conceptualized—and even computed—as distance.

Historically, the computational inefficiency of color measurement spaces precluded their use for image coding. Color spaces suitable for color measurement (such as *XYZ*, *xyY*, $u'v'Y$, $L^*a^*b^*$, and $L^*u^*v^*$) were distinguished from color spaces suitable for image coding (such as *RGB*, $R'G'B'$, $Y'C_BC_R$, and *CMY*). However, the phenomenal increase in computational performance has made it feasible to directly use color measurement spaces for image coding. One example is Adobe's Photoshop application, which can store graphic arts images in LAB format. Another example is DCI's proposed $X'Y'Z'$ coding for digital cinema images, where the prime of *XYZ* designates that a power function (gamma) has been applied for perceptual uniformity.

Many color spaces historically used for image coding were considered to be device-dependent. For example, in cinema film, the color produced by a particular combination of *CMY* densities depends on the characteristics of the dyes. In many applications, *RGB* is considered to be device-dependent, because of the failure to standardize exactly what colors are associated with pure red, pure green, and pure blue. However, the high degree of accuracy in studio video equipment and rigid conformance to standards mean that studio *RGB* can be considered to be a form of device-independent *RGB* that is optimized for a certain class of devices.

Terminology

Prior to embarking on a description of color image coding, I must introduce five technical terms: *tristimulus value, luminance, relative luminance, lightness*, and *luma*. I use the term *brightness* only in a casual sense, for two reasons. First, as defined by the CIE,[3] brightness is subjective. Second, the brightness scale has no upper bound, but in color image coding it is important to discuss quantities relative to some white reference.

Tristimulus value. *Tristimulus value* quantifies light power weighted by a specific spectral weighting function. Tristimulus values are *linear light* measures, proportional to intensity. (The term *intensity* is generally unsuitable for use in color image coding because it disregards spectral distribution.) In 1931, the CIE standardized a set of three weighting functions $\bar{x}(\lambda)$, $\bar{y}(\lambda)$, and $\bar{z}(\lambda)$ called *color matching functions* (CMFs). Weighting a spectral power distribution by the CIE CMF curves yields tristimulus values *X*, *Y*, and *Z*. These are pronounced "cap-*X*", "cap-*Y*", and "cap-*Z*" (or "big-*XYZ*") to distinguish them from chromaticity values *x* and *y* ("little-*x*", "little-*y*"), which I will introduce later in the section *Perceptual Uniformity*. The *X*, *Y*, and *Z* tristimulus values form a distinguished set; however, *RGB* values proportional to intensity can also qualify as tristimulus values if their spectral composition satisfies a mathematical relationship to *XYZ*: the *RGB* values must be obtainable through a 3×3 linear transform of *XYZ*. Linear-light *RGB* values in digital imaging typically approximate tristimulus values.

Luminance. Tristimulus values ordinarily come in sets of three, as their name suggests. However, the CIE *Y* tristimulus value, known as *luminance*, can stand on its own. The $\bar{y}(\lambda)$ spectral weighting function approximates the spectral sensitivity of the brightness sensation; it is what you'd expect a light meter to read. Absolute luminance has units of candelas per meter squared (cd/m^{-2}, or "nit"). Maximum luminance of a computer monitor may reach 200 cd/m^{-2}; a television display typically has peak luminance of 100 cd/m^{-2}. In the cinema, maximum luminance is typically 40 cd/m^{-2} (equivalent to 14 ftL).

Relative luminance. A white card typically reflects about 90% of the incident illumination. In the original scene, this is called *diffuse white luminance*. In an outdoor, sunlit scene, a diffusely reflecting white card may reach a luminance value of 10,000 cd·m^{-2}. Very few displays can achieve luminance com-

---

[3]Commission Internationale de l'Éclairage: the international body that sets standards for illumination and color.

parable to an outdoor scene, and in any event, such a high luminance is undesirable for imagery to be viewed indoors. Ordinarily, we seek to reproduce luminance values relative to the luminance of a reference or maximum white. We generally seek to display an image in which the *relative luminance* of elements in the scene is approximately reproduced.

Lightness. The characteristics of the human visual system are such that lightness perception is nonlinearly related to physical light intensity (or more generally, to tristimulus values). Vision does not respond equally to the same physical increment of intensity across the whole tone scale from black to white; instead, lightness perception is roughly proportional to the ratio of intensity values. The threshold of lightness perception corresponds to a ratio of luminance values of about 1.01—in other words, an increase of luminance of 1% lies on the threshold of visibility. Lightness is a nonlinear function of luminance that estimates the response of human vision. The standard function is denoted L^* ("L-star"); it is essentially a power function[4] having an exponent of 0.4. L^* has a range from 0 to 100; a difference in L^* values ("delta-L") of unity is taken to lie at the threshold of lightness perception. The usual mid-gray test card has a relative luminance of 18%; this corresponds to an L^* value very close to 50.

Luma. Digital video and HDTV sometimes use $R'G'B'$ coding, but more commonly use $Y'C_BC_R$ color difference coding. The luma component (Y') estimates lightness; the chroma (C_B and C_R) components represent color with lightness removed. Lightness is not computed directly, but approximated as *luma*. Unfortunately, many video engineers and many computer graphics practitioners mistakenly use the term *luminance* to refer to what is properly called—and computed as—luma. For details, see Appendix A, *YUV and luminance considered harmful,* in my book.

ISSUES IN COLOR IMAGE DATA REPRESENTATION

The following issues are central to color representation in digital cinema:

---

[4]The exponent ⅓ appears in the equation for L*; however, a linear segment is inserted near black. The offset and scaling associated with the linear segment cause the function to closely resemble a 0.4-power function across the whole range from black to white.

♦ Perceptual uniformity

♦ Contrast ratio

♦ Metamerism

♦ The necessity of signal processing

♦ Color gamut

♦ Rendering

♦ Specular highlights

I will summarize each of these issues in the following paragraphs and then discuss details of most of these topics in the remaining sections of this chapter.

Perceptual uniformity.   For efficient utilization of digital code values, an image coding system must mimic the lightness perception of vision. Imaging systems rarely use pixel values proportional to intensity; values nonlinearly related to tristimulus values are usually used. Video and HDTV systems use $R'G'B'$ values, where the prime symbols indicate that linear light tristimulus values have been subjected to a nonlinear transfer function, typically resembling a square root. In digital film, code values typically approximate the logarithm of relative luminance.

Contrast ratio.   *Contrast ratio*—or more technically, simultaneous contrast ratio—is the ratio of luminance between the lightest and darkest regions of an original scene or a reproduced image. Contrast ratio is a major determinant of image quality. A dark viewing environment is more demanding of image coding than a light viewing environment. Projected cinema film can deliver to the viewer a contrast ratio approaching 100:1, considerably better than television (about 30:1), which is in turn better than viewing in an office environment (about 15:1). *Sequential contrast ratio* is the ratio of intensity between the lightest and darkest achievable reproduced luminance levels, where these levels need not be displayed simultaneously. The sequential contrast ratio for a given display system is typically much higher than its simultaneous contrast ratio. While high sequential contrast ratio is important, simultaneous contrast ratio is the more important measure.

Metamerism.   To capture an accurate representation of a color in just three components, it is necessary to have carefully chosen spectral sensitivities.

A color measurement instrument such as a *colorimeter* incorporates three spectral filters whose shapes are dictated by CIE standards. It is impractical for a camera designer to construct camera separation filters that adhere strictly to these curves. However, departure from these curves leads to color reproduction that is inaccurate to some extent. Camera *metamerism* refers to the phenomenon by which a pair of spectral stimuli that appear identical to human vision are reported by a camera as having different *RGB* values, or conversely, the phenomenon by which a pair of spectral stimuli that appear different to human vision are reported by a camera as having the same *RGB* values. A camera designer strives to minimize camera metamerism, but engineering compromises are necessary to minimize color reproduction errors while simultaneously achieving high sensitivity and good signal to noise ratio.

The Necessity of Signal Processing.　When James Clerk Maxwell first demonstrated color reproduction around 1861, he used identical red, green, and blue filters for both capture and reconstruction. We now know that this approach reduces color saturation. Reproducing color correctly requires not only suitably chosen camera and display spectral characteristics, but also certain signal processing operations. The reasons for this are complex, but a simple explanation that applies to many image reproduction situations is that spectral overlap of the capture sensitivities, or of the reproduction primaries, causes lack of saturation. Loss of saturation can be compensated by processing linear light *RGB* signals through a 3×3 matrix having diagonal elements fairly close to unity and having small negative numbers off the diagonal (*signal processing*). In photochemical film, a process comparable to matrixing is implemented by DIR couplers (see the section *The Necessity of Signal Processing*).

Color Gamut.　The human visual system can correctly perceive a wide range of colors in the real world. Display systems do not typically offer nearly as wide a range of colors as vision can see. The range of colors available in an image capture, recording, or display system is called its *color gamut.* Various display media and display devices have different gamuts. There is a substantial difference between the color gamut available from typical subtractive color reproduction systems, such as film or offset printing, and the color gamut available from typical electronic display systems such as CRTs, LCDs, PDPs, and DLPs.

Rendering.   It is common for images to be reproduced in viewing environments whose conditions differ substantially from the environments in which the images were captured. The naïve approach to image reproduction is to simply scale the scene tristimulus values to the tristimulus values that achieve the brightest possible white at the display. However, naïve scaling of tristimulus values yields poor image quality: in the usual case that the display white is dramatically less than the scene white, the tone scale appears incorrect, and colors appear desaturated. To achieve the correct image appearance requires modifying the image data as a function of the ambient conditions at scene capture and at viewing. In digital video and HDTV, the characteristics of the assumed viewing environment are incorporated into the transfer function applied at the camera (called *gamma correction*). In desktop computing and computer graphics, a transfer function different from that of video is used owing to the difference in typical viewing conditions. In cinema, the viewing conditions are different again, and yet another transfer characteristic needs to be applied to image data. For image data intended for display in diverse viewing environments, the required alteration of the transfer function needs to take place at display time.

Specular highlights.   Typical scenes contain *specular highlights* that arise from reflections from materials such as glass, chrome, and water. The presence and importance of specular highlights are highly scene dependent, but specular highlights typically far exceed the luminance of diffuse white. Accurately reproducing their relative luminance would require a huge reduction in the luminance of diffuse white and would thereby reduce average luminance. Fortunately, the characteristics of vision are such that convincing reproduction of specular highlights can be achieved even if they are displayed with substantially lower relative luminance values than they had in the scene. Cinematographers control tone scale reproduction to compress the luminance of specular highlights.

Having just briefly summarized the issues of perceptual uniformity, contrast ratio, metamerism, color gamut, signal processing, rendering, and specular highlights, I will now discuss several of these topics in detail.

Perceptual Uniformity

The lightness perception of vision is nonlinearly related to physical intensity: vision cannot distinguish two luminance levels if the ratio between them is less than about 1.01; in other words, the visual threshold for luminance difference is about 1%.

In a cinema-class viewing environment, a few hundred gray tones need to be reproduced; however, these tones are not equally spaced in the physical intensity domain. The problem of inefficient usage of code values is compounded as the number of bits per component increases. Linear light coding with 14 bits per component has 16,384 code values across the range from black to white. Only a few hundred of these codes are perceptually useful.

Linear light coding is necessary in certain applications, such as CGI, where computations must mimic the physical mixing of light. However, in most image coding applications, its lack of perceptual uniformity is highly inefficient. The solution to the inefficiency of linear light coding is to use nonlinear coding, whereby code values are distributed across the tone range from black to white in accordance with lightness perception of human vision. Such coding is referred to as *perceptually uniform*. Two methods of perceptually uniform coding are widely used: *power-law coding* and *logarithmic coding*.

Power-law coding has been used in video systems since the 1940s. It is ubiquitous in today's digital video, MPEG, and HDTV systems, and is very widely used in desktop computer graphics and graphics arts. In power-law coding, the code value for each of the red, green, and blue components is proportional to the corresponding linear light (tristimulus) value raised to a power of approximately 0.5; in other words, each component's code value is roughly proportional to the square root of scene tristimulus value.[5] Eight-bit components were sufficient for studio video in the 1980s and early 1990s, and 8-bit components remain commonplace in desktop computer graphics applications today. However, 10-bit components are now standard for studio video and HDTV. Ten-bit power-law-coded components, as in Rec. 709,[6] have performance comparable to 12-bit linear light components. The high contrast ratio of cinema viewing demands one or two additional bits.

The transmittance of film has traditionally been measured and stated in logarithmic units of optical density. Logarithmic coding, having code values proportional to the optical density of the negative, was established in Kodak's Cineon system in the early 1990s; the system continues to be used in many digital film applications today. Technically, code values are proportional to printing density. Perceptual uniformity is achieved through a

---

[5] In graphic arts, *RGB* values typically represent the 1.8 root of displayed relative reflectance.
[6] ITU-R Rec. BT.709-3, *Basic parameter values for the HDTV standard for the studio and for international programme exchange.*

combination of two factors: a certain degree of perceptual uniformity is imposed by the 0.6 gamma of the negative film; subsequent logarithmic encoding of film transmittance also confers perceptual uniformity.

Some emergent digital cinema cameras implement logarithmic encoding of scene tristimulus values. These log-*RGB* values are not quite comparable to printing densities, because of the absence of film gamma.

No matter what nonlinear coding scheme is used at encoding, it needs to be inverted on image display. In video, the inversion of the camera's gamma correction historically took place at the CRT. In film, the gamma of the negative film is compensated by the gamma of the print film. However, the inversion is deliberately not mathematically perfect, for reasons that I will explain in the section *Rendering*.

The left-hand sketch of Figure 3.2 represents linear-light coding; the right-hand sketch represents log-*RGB* coding. In both cases the end-to-end transfer function is linear. However, the nonlinear coding of the right-hand sketch delivers better performance for image coding schemes having fewer than about 14 bits per component. In a DLP display, perceptually uniform coding is inverted by digital processing of the signal to impose a power function (*inverse gamma*).

The DCI has proposed a coding system for Digital Cinema that directly encodes gamma-corrected CIE *XYZ* values. Perceptual uniformity is

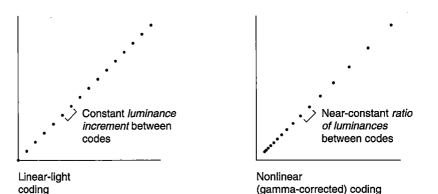

Linear-light
coding

Nonlinear
(gamma-corrected) coding

FIGURE

3.2

End-to-end luminance mapping, from camera luminance to display luminance, needs to be approximately linear. However, the nonlinear lightness sensitivity of human vision makes it highly advantageous to assign code values to luminance levels nonlinearly. The left-hand sketch shows a linear assignment of codes; the right-hand sketch shows a logarithmic assignment. In both cases, luminance end-to-end is reproduced linearly, but the right-hand (nonlinear) scheme exhibits much better performance in any system having fewer than 14 bits per component.

approximated by imposing a power function—having an exponent of 1 2/6, about 0.385—on each of the *XYZ* components. A 2.6 power is applied at decoding. Twelve bits per component suffice for excellent image quality.

Specular Highlights

When an original scene contains no specular highlights, diffuse white can be placed at the top of the coding range. However, in order to capture specular highlights, diffuse white must be placed somewhat lower than the maximum luminance value.

Maximum brightness in the reproduced image is obtained when diffuse white is reproduced at maximum display brightness. In order to reproduce specular highlights at the display, diffuse white needs to be reproduced at a somewhat lower luminance than maximum.

Consider a scene containing a specular highlight whose luminance is four times that of diffuse white. Accurate reproduction of that specular highlight would require reproducing diffuse white at just one-quarter of the display's maximum luminance. Reserving three-quarters of the available luminance range solely to accommodate specular highlights would require a huge reduction in the luminance of reproduced diffuse white and would lead to a dim picture.

Convincing reproduction of specular highlights can be achieved even if they are displayed with substantially lower relative luminance values than they had in the scene. Depending on the nature of the scene, highlight luminance may be reduced by a factor of two, or even four, without causing any visual impairment.

In film, handling of specular highlights is established by the cinematographer during image capture, mainly through control of exposure. (Camera negative film has sufficient dynamic range that highlight handling can be modified in post production.) Film projectors and cinema theaters are sufficiently similar that their display and viewing conditions can be considered to be fixed: an answer print can be approved in a screening theater with confidence that matching release prints will be displayed reasonably accurately in commercial cinemas.

In video and HDTV, the camera operator controls specular highlights by controlling exposure (through the iris) and by adjusting the *gain, knee,* and *slope* controls of the camera's signal processing circuits. For video and

HDTV material, approval is done on a reference monitor in a studio control room. That monitor and that environment represent the ideal for the ultimate consumer of the program. Given the importance of the reference monitor, it may come as a surprise that the transfer function of the reference monitor is not standardized by any organization—SMPTE, EBU, ITU-R, or anyone else. Today's working practices tacitly assume that a reference monitor exhibits a 2.5-power function.

The standard digital video coding range extends to about 109% of reference white: the top 9% of the coding range is available to accommodate specular highlights. Ideally, the display's 2.5-power function would continue through that range. However, continuing the 2.5-power function causes reference white to be displayed at just 80% of maximum display luminance. Many designers of consumer electronics displays consider the corresponding penalty on average luminance to be too severe, and many consumer displays saturate or clip the highlight range to maximize display brightness, as suggested by Figure 3.3.

Cinema projectors are used in very dark viewing environments with dark surrounds. Many movies that have been released digitally in the past several years either have been captured using HDTV technology, or have employed HDTV technology in post production. Signals encoded according to Rec. 709 appear somewhat lacking in contrast and color saturation when

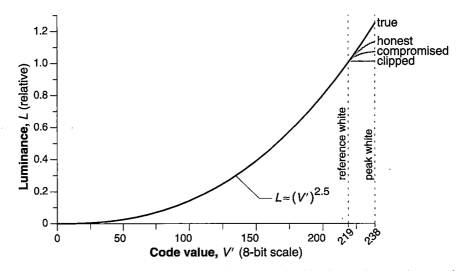

FIGURE

3.3

Highlight handling in consumer display is compromised by the market requirement for high brightness: the higher the brightness that is required for the application, the more severe the saturation (or clipping) near white, and the flatter the image looks.

displayed directly on a linear light display (such as a DLP) using a 2.5-power function in a cinema environment. Better visual performance from HDTV material is achieved, without compromising perceptual uniformity, by using a slightly higher exponent, typically 2.6 (but perhaps as high as 2.7). The 2.6 value has been incorporated into the proposed DCI $X'Y'Z'$ coding scheme.

All of the considerations of specular highlight handling that I have discussed are bypassed in any system—such as the proposed DCI scheme—that has the goal of simply reproducing in the cinema the tristimulus values displayed on a reference projector at the approval stage. However, speculars have to be considered at capture, in post production, and whenever a digital cinema master is transferred to a noncinema display environment.

Rendering

Examine the flowers in a garden at noon on a bright, sunny day. Look at the same garden half an hour after sunset. Physically, the spectra of the flowers have not changed, except by scaling to lower luminance levels. However, the flowers are markedly less colorful after sunset: it is a property of vision that colorfulness decreases as luminance decreases.

Reproduced images are usually viewed at a small fraction, perhaps 1/100 or 1/1000, of the luminance at which they were captured. Daylight illumination of an outdoor scene may cause a white card (diffuse white) to have a luminance of 10,000 candelas per meter squared; however, the reproduction may be limited to a peak white luminance of 100 candelas per meter squared. If reproduced luminance were made proportional to scene luminance, the characteristics of vision would cause the reproduced image to appear less colorful, and lower in contrast, than the original scene.

To reproduce, at a low luminance level contrast and colorfulness comparable to an original scene at a high luminance, we must alter the characteristics of the image. An engineer or physicist might strive to achieve mathematical linearity in an imaging system; however, the required alterations cause reproduced luminance to depart from linearity. The dilemma is this: we can achieve mathematical linearity, or we can achieve correct appearance, but we cannot simultaneously do both! Successful commercial imaging systems sacrifice mathematical linearity to achieve the correct perceptual result. In broad outline, correction is made by applying a power function to scene tristimulus values. The exponent chosen depends upon several factors.

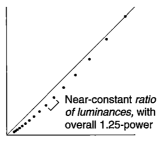

Near-constant *ratio of luminances,* with overall 1.25-power

Nonlinear (gamma-corrected)
coding, with end-to-end power

FIGURE

3.4

An end-to-end power function is necessary to achieve good subjective image quality in a reproduction viewed on a typical display in a typical viewing environment. For video, an end-to-end 1.25 power is appropriate. Due to the dark ambient conditions in cinema, an end-to-end power of 1.5 is suitable. This sketch shows an end-to-end 1.25-power function combined with perceptually uniform coding. The execution of this idea is subtle because perceptual uniformity and rendering are intertwined; nonlinear processing is performed at encoding and at decoding.

CRTs used for television display today have maximum luminance of about 100 cd/m^{-2} and quite good contrast ratio, approaching 100:1. However, television displays are typically viewed in dim environments with dim surrounds. For video, the required end-to-end exponent is approximately 1.25. The luminance of the red, green, or blue primary light produced by a CRT monitor is proportional to voltage (or code value) raised to approximately the 2.5 power. An encoding exponent of about 0.4 would be optimum for perceptual uniformity. Encoding at 0.4 power would be perfectly inverted by the CRT's native 2.5 power; however, that combination would lack the required rendering correction. Instead of encoding at 0.4, a 0.5 power is typically imposed by gamma correction in the camera. The product of 0.5 and the 2.5 power at the display results in the 1.25 end-to-end power appropriate for the viewing conditions typical of television. Figure 3.4 shows the perceptually uniform coding of Figure 3.2 combined with the imposition of an end-to-end 1.25 power.[7]

When television is viewed in a dark environment, such as a home theater, the display gamma should be adjusted slightly higher than 2.5, to perhaps 2.6 or 2.7. Some home theater projectors have gamma values (exponents) in this range.

---

[7]Color rendering is discussed in detail in Giorgianni, Edward J., and T.E. Madden, *Digital Color Management: Encoding Solutions* (Reading, MA: Addison-Wesley, 1998).

Most emergent display devices involve transducers that do not exhibit a 2.5-power function. To suitably reproduce pre-encoded video signals, such a display system must incorporate signal processing to compensate for its native characteristic to produce approximately a 2.5-power relationship between code value and displayed luminance. Because of the perceptual uniformity of video coding, the signal processing causes the display system to respond to code values in a perceptually uniform manner.

For cinema viewing conditions, the end-to-end exponent is approximately 1.5. In film, this relationship is achieved through the combination of the 0.6 gamma typical of camera-negative film and the 2.5 gamma typical of print film. Intermediate IP and IN stages may be involved, but because intermediate stock has roughly unity gamma, the intermediates do not contribute to the end-to-end power function.

As in specular highlight handling, rendering considerations can be ignored in any system that simply reproduces the tristimulus values of the answer print. However, rendering has to be considered at capture, in post production, and whenever digital cinema masters are transferred among different display environments.

The Necessity of Signal Processing

Maxwell made the first color photograph by capturing three exposures of the same scene onto three pieces of photographic material, using different colored filters—red, green, and blue—for the successive exposures. He reproduced the image by optically superimposing the three images, each projected through the corresponding color filter. His results were astonishing and stimulated the development of color photography.

Maxwell used identical filters for capture and reproduction. We now understand that this causes a desaturated reproduction. Achieving correct saturation requires carefully choosing the camera spectral sensitivities and carefully choosing the spectral characteristics of the primary colors used for reproduction—for example, carefully choosing primary spectral power distributions of phosphors in a CRT. But no matter how carefully these spectral characteristics are chosen, in order to reproduce saturation correctly, it is necessary to impose signal processing between capture and reproduction. For an additive RGB system, it is necessary to impose a 3×3 linear matrix. The nine coefficients of the matrix depend on several factors.

In video, 3×3 matrixing is implemented in the signal processing at the front end of the camera, ordinarily just prior to gamma correction. In high-end cameras, the matrix coefficients are adjustable.

In film, the signal processing necessary for accurate color reproduction is achieved through the use of *developer inhibitor releasing* (DIR) couplers, through which development of one emulsion is slowed as a function of the degree of development in a neighboring emulsion. This can be thought of as a form of matrixing implemented in the chemical domain.

COLOR GAMUT

RGB values are not meaningful as accurate descriptions of color unless the color characteristics of the primaries and the white reference are known. The simplest description provides the luminance and chromaticity values of the three primaries and white. If nonlinear coding is used, then the parameters of the nonlinear coding must also be taken into account.

In all color reproduction systems, gamut is a function of luminance. As luminance increases toward white, the available range of chromaticity values in (x, y) or (u', v'), or chroma values in (a^*, b^*) *or* (u^*, v^*) decreases. Color gamut should be considered in 3-space; a 2-dimensional plot is not sufficient to appreciate the luminance dependence. As an example, in Rec. 709 *RGB*, available chromaticity values encompass the entire triangle whose vertices correspond to the primary *chromaticities* at relative luminance up to 0.0722. However, luminance can exceed 0.0722 only through some contribution from red or green, and that precludes displaying pure blue. At luminance values above 0.2126, pure red is unavailable, and at luminance values above 0.7154, pure green is unavailable. As luminance approaches 100%, only a small color range in the vicinity of white is available.

There are many variations of *RGB* coding. Three flavors of *RGB* are particularly important for digital cinema: Rec. 709 *RGB*, DTIM *RGB*, and P7V2 *RGB*.

◆ Rec. 709 *RGB* was first standardized for HDTV. It was subsequently adopted for SDTV and then for desktop computing (there called *sRGB*[8]). Rec. 709 *RGB* has a narrower color gamut than motion picture print film.

[8]IEC 61966-2-1, *Multimedia Systems and Equipment—Colour Measurement and Management. Part 2-1: Colour Management—Default RGB Colour Space—sRGB.*

♦ DTIM *RGB* approximates the native color range available in contemporary DLP Cinema projectors. DTIM almost encompasses film gamut—but not quite.

♦ P7V2 *RGB* is essentially a refinement of DTIM *RGB*; P7V2 has been used to code most digital movies released at the time of this writing. In P7V2, the concept of parametric *RGB* is extended somewhat beyond the additive mixture of *RGB*, to include the luminance and chromaticity values of the secondary colors. The transformed secondary colors and transformed white need not be identical to the sum of the corresponding contributions of the primaries. For example, the output color triple for cyan may be different from the sum of pure green and pure blue.

Parametric RGB refers to describing an *RGB* coding system by the luminance and chromaticity values of its primaries and of its reference white. The parameters of video and HDTV systems have historically been specified in documents! No dynamic interpretation of image data was necessary. In some computer image interchange standards, the parameters of *RGB* coding are carried as metadata in the image files, so the image data reader may have to perform color transformation on the fly. This is computationally expensive and potentially creates challenges in system engineering and workflow.

The subtractive nature of film mixture leads to curved loci of extreme chromaticity values.[9] As in Rec. 709, DTIM, and P7V2, gamut shrinks as luminance increases. Over a fairly wide range of luminance levels — but particularly at low luminance — film covers a wider range of chromaticities than Rec. 709.

CIE *XYZ* values can be transformed into *RGB* through matrix multiplication by a suitable 3×3 matrix. The matrix coefficients depend on the characteristics of the *RGB* used in the coding system. Any color can be described by an all-positive combination of *XYZ*; however, transforming color using this linear algebra approach may result in negative values for one or two components, and perhaps a component value greater than unity, when the color being transformed lies outside the gamut of the particular *RGB* system. Such out-of-gamut colors can be clipped to the nearest realizable color in the system; however, clipping is liable to lead to visible image artifacts.

---

[9]Subtractive color reproduction in film is explained in: Lang, Heinwig, *Colour and Its Reproduction* (Göttingen, Zürich: Muster-Schmidt, 2002).

In practical situations where out-of-gamut colors must be accommo-dated, sophisticated gamut mapping algorithms are used. Gamut mapping usually involves 3-dimensional lookup table interpolation (3-D LUTs).[10]

Image data encoded as additive *RGB* can be transformed to *CMY.* However, the subtractive color mixture of *CMY* is nonlinear because of unwanted absorp-tions. Such conversion—and the opposite conversion, from *CMY* to *RGB*—usu-ally involves 3-D LUT interpolation. These conversions must deal with out-of-gamut colors: some gamut mapping is typically necessary.

CHOICE OF A COLOR CODING SYSTEM

Concerning the choice of primaries, I'll quote Spaulding, Woolfe, and Giorgianni:

Two of the criteria applied that affect the selection of RGB primaries are somewhat con-flicting. First, their chromaticities should define a color gamut sufficiently large to encompass colors likely to be found in real scenes/images. At the same time, their use should result in efficient digital encodings that minimize quantization errors. Increasing the gamut can only be achieved by trading off against correspondingly larger quantization errors. If the primaries are chosen to include the maximum possible chro-maticity gamut (i.e., the entire area within the spectrum locus), a significant fraction of the color space would correspond to imaginary colors located outside that region. Therefore, in any encoding using such a color space, there would be "wasted" code val-ues that would never be used in practice. This would lead to larger quantization errors in the usable part of the color space than would be obtained with different primaries defining a smaller chromaticity gamut. It is therefore desirable to choose primaries with a gamut that is "big enough" but not "too big."[11]

THE DIGITAL INTERMEDIATE

It is now common to have entire movies finished in the digital domain. A scene may originate on film and be scanned into the digital domain; it may

[10]3-D LUT interpolation and various other color transform techniques are detailed in: Sharma, Gaurav, *Digital Color Imaging Handbook* (Boca Raton, FL: CRC Press, 2003).
[11]Spaulding, Kevin E., Geoffrey J. Woolfe and Edward J. Giorgianni, "Reference Input/Output Medium Metric RGB Color Encodings (RIMM/ROMM RGB)," in *Proceedings of PICS 2000 Conference* (March 26-29, 2000, Portland, Oregon), pp. 155-163.

originate at a digital camera; or it may originate as CGI. When finishing is accomplished digitally, a master for digital release can be made. The majority of viewers for many years to come will see the movie on projected film; to accommodate film release, the digital master is typically recorded out to a film master as a "dupe neg" that is printed to release prints in the conventional way.

Experiments have been made to record digital masters directly to IPs, saving one generation of film processing. However, recording directly to IP presents several challenges in image quality and color quality. One major film was recently recorded not to an IP but to an IN from which release prints were struck directly. This method saved two film generations compared to the usual process. Several identical intermediates had to be recorded to enable printing of several thousand release prints.

No firm standards are yet in place for the color data representation of digital intermediates. Several broad classes of systems are evident.

◆ Many digital intermediate systems represent image data in the printing density metric, also referred to as *Cineon printing density* (CPD). All film colors can be represented, but certain HDTV colors cannot. Image data files are usually in either the *DPX* (.dpx) file format, or its close relative, the *Cineon* (.cin) file format. (The DPX file format can accommodate a variety of image coding systems, but it is ordinarily used with CPD.)

◆ Some digital intermediate systems are based directly on video and HDTV coding standards and use HDTV equipment and interfaces. *RGB* coding is limited to HDTV gamut, which fails to accommodate a significant portion of the film gamut. The Rec. 1361 standard specifies a method of using $Y'C_BC_R$ values, conformant with the standard range of signals in HDTV systems, to encode wide-gamut colors. This scheme shows promise in the medium term, because it allows existing $Y'C_BC_R$ HDTV processing and recording equipment to be used. However, this scheme has not yet been deployed.

◆ Some digital intermediate systems are based on video and HDTV equipment and interfaces, where the *RGB* primaries—hence, the *R'G'B'* data values—are reinterpreted as representing wide-gamut colors. Ordinary HDTV processing equipment can be used, but color transforms are necessary for capture and display equipment to correctly portray colors.

◆ Some digital intermediate systems are based on "linear" *RGB* code values stored in file formats such as 16-bit TIFF. The system designer must determine the color characteristics of the *RGB* data and must decide whether the data values are proportional to scene tristimulus values or to reproduction tristimulus values. (These differ according to rendering.)

◆ The emergent OpenEXR file format stores *high-dynamic-range* (HDR) linear light, scene-referred *RGB* image data. Each component is represented as a 16-bit floating-point number comprising a sign bit, a 5-bit exponent, and a 10-bit mantissa (fraction). OpenEXR can't be called a color data metric, because the colorimetric interpretation of the data values isn't defined.

◆ Emergent *log-RGB* systems encode the logarithms of *RGB* scene tristimulus values. The log coding effects good perceptual uniformity; decent results are obtained using 10-bit components. There is a superficial similarity to DPX or Cineon coding: both systems use 10-bit components, and both systems advertise the use of logarithmic coding. However, log-*RGB* files encode scene tristimulus values, where the encoding of DPX and Cineon incorporates the transfer characteristics (including 0.6 gamma) of camera negative film.

THE CHALLENGE OF WIDE-GAMUT REPRODUCTION

At low luminance levels, the chromaticity available from print film covers a much wider range than Rec. 709 RGB. As luminance increases, Rec. 709 has a wider gamut than film in certain regions of color space. This discrepancy in color gamut between film and video must be taken into account when preparing a movie for video release (e.g., broadcast or DVD); color adjustments are necessary. The contrast ratio of video or HDTV display is typically less than the contrast ratio in the cinema; tone scale adjustments are also necessary.

Color adjustments are traditionally made in a color grading pass that takes place during (or shortly after) telecine transfer. Some of the adjustment can be made statically; colors can be desaturated to fit within the Rec. 709 gamut, and the tone scale can be subject to an overall compression. However, the wide tone and color range of film is used by cinematographers as a storytelling element. Indiscriminate compression of the tone and color range may weaken the story. Color and tone adjustments must be made in a manner sensitive to the importance to the story of visual elements in each scene. In the limit, the color and tone adjustments may depend on the plot! A colorist must pay attention to the overall aesthetic of the film and to the dramatic effect that is intended for each scene.

Most people expect the contrast ratio and color gamut of digital cinema exhibition to match the contrast ratio and color gamut of film. Matching additive *RGB* to subtractive *CMY* is technically challenging; however, this problem has been solved for digital cinema projectors that have a DTIM or P7V2 gamut.

Today, digital projection is almost always accomplished using DLP Cinema projectors based on core technology developed by Texas Instruments. Two or three other technologies are in development by other manufacturers. It is very likely that competitive displays will be introduced to the marketplace, and it is very likely that future Digital Cinema displays will have different native color gamuts than today's projectors.

A purely colorimetric mapping between two devices is possible for colors that lie within the gamuts of both devices. By colorimetric, I refer to a computational approach—such as the 3×3 matrix processing that I explained earlier —in which the device data values are computed such that the *XYZ* color values are preserved. I have explained the digital answer print approach to digital cinema, where a movie is approved by creative staff based on screening on a reference projector. Color mapping from the color space of a digital cinema master into the color space of a particular projector is easily accommodated for in-gamut colors: the science of color matching is sufficiently advanced that we can be certain that the same colors will be displayed.

One of the goals of Digital Cinema is to enable migration, in the future, to wide-gamut displays that exceed the color range of today's film prints and today's Digital Cinema projectors. A challenge arises if colors outside the gamut of one device are to be handled: some sort of gamut mapping (as explained in the *Color Gamut* section of this chapter) is necessary. Some colors are bound to be clipped or otherwise compromised.

I consider the eventual transfer from a wide-gamut master to today's film or Digital Cinema to be entirely analogous to today's situation of transferring a movie for video release. We have a wide-gamut master, and we seek to display it in a narrower gamut. It has not proved possible to have an algorithmic mapping of tone and color from today's film to video. A skilled colorist is required to make aesthetic judgments that are subject to approval by the cinematographer. I cannot imagine a completely algorithmic mapping from a future wide-gamut master to today's film or today's Digital Cinema gamut. Developments in understanding the color appearance properties of human vision are likely to enable some algorithmic assistance in both of these applications; however, the process must ultimately depend to some degree on craft and art.

My comments apply to the situation where a future wide-gamut representation is standardized. However, some people take the wide-gamut notion even further, suggesting that no standardization of device gamut is necessary. Some people think that future Digital Cinema devices should accept device-independent image data and subject the data to whatever gamut mapping is necessary for a particular display device.

Mapping between different native device color spaces is straightforward for colors that are shared within the gamuts of the spaces. Digital Cinema color processing would be very simple if colors outside the gamut of a particular device could simply be clipped to the closest realizable color. However, naïve clipping creates visible artifacts. To minimize artifacts associated with gamut compression, it is necessary to alter not only the colors at (and near) the gamut boundary but also colors within the color space.

I believe that cinematographers, directors, and producers will not tolerate color mapping in exhibition that alters colors in the interior of the expected color space. In my view, we must adopt an approach where creative staff can have full confidence that the movie as exhibited will be within a close tolerance of what they see at approval. I find it difficult to imagine how this goal can be achieved without having some sort of standardization of gamut in exhibition. There need not be a single standard: we could standardize a gamut that is representative of film gamut in the short term and standardize a wide gamut at some time in the future. But I cannot imagine the creative community ever accepting uncontrolled gamut mapping in the field, and I cannot imagine their approval of several different versions of a movie (one for each of several projector gamuts). We have two approvals today: one for film release and one for video release. I can easily imagine a third wide-gamut approval stage in the future for movies that are expected to benefit from wide-gamut release.

ACKNOWLEDGMENTS

The work reported in this chapter was partially supported by Warner Bros. and by c.o.r.e. Feature Animation. I extend my thanks to both companies.

4

The Mastering Process

Chris Carey
The Walt Disney Studios
Bob Lambert
The Walt Disney Company
Bill Kinder
Pixar Animation Studios
Glenn Kennel
Texas Instruments

Mastering is central to the Digital Cinema process, the nexus at which color, formatting, audio, subtitling, versioning, and metadata all converge. Mastering is a technically intensive but creatively nuanced art, the stage at which the source materials—film or digital files—are prepared for Digital Cinema delivery. This portion of the process relies substantially on input from the filmmakers to ensure that the digital version represents the original creative vision of the film. Ultimately, mastering determines whether the Digital Cinema material is equally or more appealing than conventional film and is responsible for the overall quality of the Digital Cinema experience.

This chapter sets out to define the terms of art in mastering and to describe the activities of the mastering process. It places mastering in the overall context of the Digital Cinema process, from the final post production of a film to the Digital Cinema delivery stage. *Digital Cinema mastering* includes a wide range of operations: acquiring or ingesting the source material; the creative manipulation of the digital data of the film images; the combination of audio, subtitle, caption, watermark, and other data; and the packaging of the final elements into a deliverable Digital Cinema file. In this chapter, we explore each of these stages in detail, providing a description of workflow, the technology involved, and the creative and technical decisions that drive each step toward the finished product.

In the general workflow of the digital process (see Figure 4.1), mastering is preceded by content creation—broadly, cinematography—and by post production. It is followed by data delivery to the theatre, storage, and ultimately digital display.

Capture, or *ingest*, is the first stage of Digital Cinema mastering. At this stage, source material is brought into the mastering process from original production content however it originated: from live action feature film elements, from conventional film animation, from computer-generated imagery, or from other digital source footage. The last stage of film post-production is also the first stage of the mastering process, a stage that yields the *Digital Source Master* (DSM) (see Figure 4.2).

Creative image manipulation (see Figure 4.3) is the second phase of the mastering process and perhaps the most crucial. Unlike conventional photo-chemical processes, digital manipulation of scenes offers a very wide range

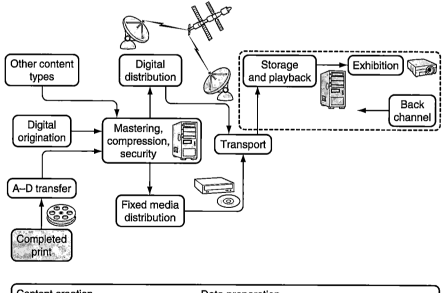

FIGURE   Digital Cinema system elements.

4.1

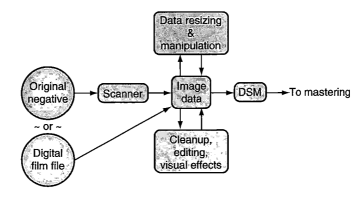

FIGURE   Capture and the DSM.

4.2

of options for the filmmaker, including the ability to make changes to the color, contrast, density, resolution, and positioning of the image, as well as dirt removal, retouching, and other enhancements and corrections. This stage also allows the creation of metadata for delivery alongside the image data to control color rendition at the point of projection.

Color correction or *grading* is one phase of creative image manipulation. It is the stage at which adjustments are made to the color and contrast of the source images, allowing the cinematographer to modify overall tint, color balance, brightness, contrast, and many other aesthetic aspects of the image.

Enhancements are also possible as another option in creative image manipulation. Common enhancements involve selective digital retouching of the image or replacing or altering visual elements.

Formatting and resizing is a key stage of Digital Cinema mastering. Source footage may need to be modified to fit a particular screen shape, such as reformatting wide-screen material to fit a conventional screen

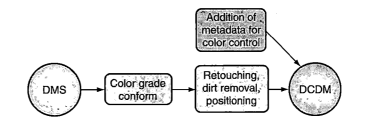

FIGURE   Creative image manipulation.

4.3

configuration or applying a digital *squeeze* (shrinking the image horizontally) for use with an anamorphic lens at playback.

Restoration, stabilization, and *cleanup* are optional stages of mastering, whenever touchups and enhancements are required to remove visual deficiencies, such as negative scratches or degradation due to age, or to reduce mechanical artifacts of the original photographic process, such as film camera gate weave.

Audio preparation brings the sound track into sync with the visual elements.

Related data placement involves adding non-picture and non-sound elements, including subtitles, captions, watermarks, and other metadata.

Subtitling and *captioning* involves creating on-screen text overlay at the point of projection or elsewhere in the theatre.

Watermarks are robust digital data, invisible to the moviegoer but sufficiently robust to survive manipulation and removal attempts by pirates. They can be used to provide forensic information in the event of theft. Along with other *metadata,* they may travel invisibly with the picture to aid in tracking content throughout the delivery path and to trigger certain events in the theatre, such as curtain openings. Image metadata may also be delivered to optimize the performance of specific types of projectors.

Packaging is the phase post-mastering where everything comes together as an integrated digital file. Once the DSM has been properly adjusted for color and other aesthetic considerations, it must be combined with the audio data files, text files, watermarks, and other metadata. This final form of the ready-to-ship digital file is known as the *Digital Cinema Distribution Master,* or DCDM.

THE PROCESS

In the overall workflow of preparing a Digital Cinema release, the mastering stage immediately follows the completion of post production of the feature film. It precedes the compression and encryption stages of content preparation. Once compressed, encrypted, and packaged, the Digital Cinema file is transmitted or transported to the theatre, where the digital product is unpacked, decrypted, decompressed, and then displayed.

At the stage of capture, the source material is brought into the mastering process from original production content, usually using scanning or data conversion. In the case of a live action feature, this typically involves scanning film elements or conversion of digitally originated footage to a format suitable for the next stages of mastering. The editor's role at this stage is to provide an *edit list* that enables frame accurate assembly.

Telecine or digital scanning technology for film to digital conversion continues to evolve. Common systems for scanning live action film are outlined further in the section Methods of Input, later in this chapter. In the case of animated features, production material usually is created digitally and at this stage of the process may simply need to be reformatted or resized. The end product of this portion of the post production process yields the *Digital Source Master,* or DSM. Depending on the particular facility conducting the work, the DSM may exist on high-capacity tape or on a Digital Cinema server similar to those used in theatres.

Creative image manipulation is the phase following image capture, and it involves the most creative portion of the entire Digital Cinema preparation process. Unlike conventional photochemical processes, which are limited to changing the density of the three primary colors, digital manipulation offers a very wide range of options for the filmmaker, including selected changes to the color, contrast, density, resolution, and positioning of the image as well as dirt removal, retouching, and other enhancements and corrections. These changes are typically made on a scene-by-scene or shot-by-shot basis, but they can be applied to individual frames or even selectively within a frame. Proper setup of the mastering facility screening room and projection system is a key component of the mastering process.

Color correction is one aspect of creative image manipulation. Color correction usually involves projecting the digital source master in a *digital mastering suite,* a specially designed and carefully calibrated screening room. Here, on-the-fly adjustments can be made to the image to create the final desired look of the production as it will ultimately appear in the digital theatre. Currently it is common for the director of photography to spend one to four weeks in the digital mastering suite on this particular stage of the process, iteratively reviewing and adjusting sections of the film. These adjustments allow many degrees of subtle changes to the tint, graininess, sharpness or softness, and other artistic elements, and they will have a major impact on the final work product. See the section, *The Digital Intermediate Process,* later in this chapter for further information on grading and correction.

Enhancements are also possible at this stage of the mastering process. Common enhancements involve adjusting the contrast of the image to compensate for over- or underexposure of the source image; creating a particular look, such as a sepia effect; or mimicking the performance of a particular film stock. Other enhancements may involve selective digital retouching of the image, such as boosting only certain shades of blue to increase the effect of the sky in a shot, lightening a shadow, or removing a visual element altogether. This stage of the process is particularly powerful in the digital realm: rather than only allowing adjustments to overall density or color balance as in the photochemical process, the filmmaker has an extraordinarily broad range of creative tools at his or her disposal to make changes in the subtlest ranges of visual performance (see Figure 4.4 in the Color Plate section).

Formatting and resizing may also be required in the Digital Cinema mastering process. Depending on the method of origination, the source footage may have been created in one of a number of aspect ratios and resolutions, since this DSM element may be used for purposes other than Digital Cinema, including conventional film release, DVD mastering, airline and broadcast masters, and other purposes. The formatting and resizing step takes all of these differences into account, and several different distribution masters are ultimately created to satisfy all the various distribution needs, with differing color gamuts, spatial resolutions, sampling frequency, and color component bit depth, among other metrics. In certain instances, such as when source footage was shot originally for a non-cinema use or for a different screen format (e.g., wide screen), it may be necessary to pan and scan or letterbox the material to fit the Digital Cinema aspect ratio.

Restoration, stabilization, and cleanup are all enhancement steps designed to remove from the image undesirable artifacts of the first stages of film production. Restoration may involve removal of negative scratches or dirt in the image, or artifacts of the initial film lab processing. Stabilization provides a digital means to reduce or eliminate the mechanical slippage that occurs whenever film moves through a film gate in a camera or when it is scanned without pin registration. While this subtle motion is often not noticeable in conventional photography and playback, it becomes increasingly important to achieve correct registration and continuity when live action photographic images taken by a mechanical camera are combined with digitally generated elements that have no mechanical variances. Other techniques are also possible at this stage to influence the visibility or invisibility of conventional film grain structures and filmic looks, depending on artistic and technical considerations.

Consistent color calibration of projectors is an essential step at both the mastering and display ends of the Digital Cinema process, since each stage of the pipeline must conform to a common set of performance characteristics to yield a similar result throughout the process.

Color encoding and *gamut mapping* are also necessary steps of the content preparation process. Encoding involves transformation of the picture data to a common format of colorimetric data. Gamut mapping refers to the process whereby metadata delivered with the image content is used to optimize the image to the performance characteristics of a projector or line of projectors.

Audio preparation is covered in additional detail in the section, *Audio Preparation: An Expanded Scope* later in this chapter. As far as its relation to the mastering process, this is the stage at which all elements of the audible portion of the final product must come into sync with the visual elements. Audio preparation involves attention to bit depth and sample rate of the digital audio material (all elements of the quality and accuracy of the sound), as well as channel count and channel mapping, or correct placement and routing of the audio files for multi-channel release.

Related data placement involves the generation and placement of a number of non-picture and non-sound elements, including subtitles, captions, watermarks, and other metadata—that is, data carried with the Digital Cinema files but never seen by the audience.

A distinctive feature of Digital Cinema is the ability of the release process to support multiple subtitling and captioning arrangements, such as might be used when more than one language subtitle is desired for a multilingual community. Subtitles, which transcribe the spoken dialogue, are usually generated in the mastering process and travel with the Digital Cinema file package as a separate set of data that drive a graphic overlay capability at the projector. Captions, which in addition to dialogue include descriptions of offscreen sounds and cues for attributing dialogue to particular characters, may be delivered in a data format similar to subtitles but are rendered on a separate display device in the theatre, such as a secondary projector or LED display for the hearing impaired.

Watermarks are another unique attribute of Digital Cinema mastering and delivery. At the mastering stage, it is possible to generate an embedded mark within the picture and/or audio unique to each version of the film, thereby allowing each shipped version to be traced back to its source or to its server. Watermarks can be combined with forensic *fingerprints* (marks generated on the fly at the projector or server) to allow an illicitly camcorded copy of any projected version to be traced back to a particular location and time of day.

Other metadata travels with the distributed product as well. This can include control track information designed to operate in-theatre equipment such as lighting, curtains, and special effects. Other metadata delivered with the picture may include *look-up tables* (LUTs) for colorimetry, key structures for security, and other data.

Following the image, audio, and metadata mastering stages, the data files will undergo *compression* followed by *encryption* and finally *packaging*, to make a transportable distribution package, called the *Digital Cinema Package* (DCP).

There may be future formats for Digital Cinema mastering, as well, as new projection systems are developed and display technologies such as digital 3-D projection are explored.

CAPTURE: CONTENT INGEST

Understanding Image Capture

Before we can get to the creative prize of digital mastering—namely, powerful creative picture manipulation—we must bring the imagery into the appropriate digital environment from its original state (see Figure 4.5). The mastering system must ingest this harvested raw material. Although the culinary metaphor has its limits, this is the prep stage: washing, chopping, and organizing.

Most often today, theatrically distributed movies originate on film, but standard or high-definition video is also sometimes used. And in the case of animation or visual effects films, digitally originated files are the source. This section will review current capture methods for each type of image origination. But first, there are some issues they all have in common.

Attributes

Size

The first, and usually most discussed, attribute is size: how much information is enough to capture the source material for ongoing manipulation? Many

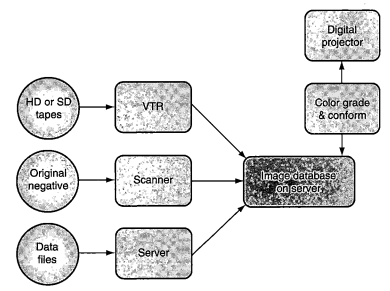

FIGURE

4.5

Digital ingest options.

take size to apply only to spatial resolution. But the image is made up of other important parts, the size of which must be chosen: aspect ratio, bit depth, and compression. From a quality standpoint, one might assert that the ultimate solution for each of these is to capture the maximum that can be mathematically described. Unfortunately, such complete descriptions often represent so much data that bandwidth and storage are strained beyond realistic limits. The practical solution lies in first determining the required end result and then settling on the budget and schedule necessary to achieve it.

Spatial Resolution

How many pixels will be permitted to describe the image? The simplest way to understand spatial resolution is as a fixed pixel dimension: width times height (e.g., 2048×1080, called 2K). The more pixels in the picture, the finer the detail that can be resolved by the eye. This becomes particularly relevant when the presentation is destined for large screens, particularly those from 10 to 80 feet in width. Discerning the difference among various spatial resolutions on a CRT display can require some very close viewing, mere centimeters from the glass. Even then the dot pitch of the monitor (i.e., the space between pixels) may make it hard to discern differences in resolution.

Spread those pixels across a 60 foot screen, however, and the difference is magnified without having to put your nose up against the screen. For comparison see Figure 4.6 in the Color Plate section.

Most of the high-definition television production and post production equipment in place today supports resolutions up to 1920 pixels horizontally by 1080 vertically (1080p). Current Digital Cinema projectors are capable of displaying up to 2048 pixels horizontally (2K). Recently, color correctors and digital disk recorders have been expanded to support 2048 pixels over a modified SMPTE 292M (serial digital) interface. The leap to presentation of 4096 pixels horizontally (4K) is a still larger barrier: not only is there no standardized method for recording and displaying such images, but even custom systems created to handle such data strain today's networks, disk speeds, and disk array sizes. Trade-offs of speed and flexibility in the creative production process will often be favored at the expense of maximum resolution.

Aspect Ratio

Aspect ratio is a way of expressing the image width compared to one or sometimes as a ratio of the lowest whole numbers. Analog broadcast television, for instance, is expressed as 1.33:1, or 4×3. There are several standard aspect ratios available to a film's director. Just as a painter must first select a canvas, the shape of the image represents an early creative choice in the conception of a visual style. For example, some argue that an epic action picture filled with vast armies may adapt best to a wide-screen frame such as 2.39:1, while an intimate interpersonal story may play best in 1.85:1. Yet some outstanding dramas and comedies are filmed in 2.39:1, and *The Seven Samurai*, which many consider among the best action films ever made, was filmed in 1.33:1.

Whatever the creative choice, maintaining the original aspect ratio is important through the life of a project, including image capture. Measures should be taken to maintain the proper dimension of the image without any optical or digital distortion. Leaders with circular patterns, edge markers, and center targets can be used to frame up images at each stage and check for proper aspect ratio and geometry. Such a *frame & focus leader* should be used on a project from the very beginning of production and carried through all the various stages of ingest and output (see Figure 4.7 in the Color Plate section). If the leader is carried forward through the production chain, those familiar with the geometric shapes and edge markings can use the leader to verify that what they are seeing is in fact the entire undistorted frame, regardless of the display medium.

Bit Depth

How many digits will be allowed to describe each color channel (red, green, and blue) for each pixel? The more bits used, the more processing power, disk space, network bandwidth, and time the project will consume. Practically speaking, 8 bits per channel is on the low end, describing standard video color. The highest end knows no limit: "floating point" means "may as many digits as needed fall after the decimal." However many digits it takes, that color channel is fully described. Woe to the color described by pi! Practical budgetary and technical limits place the typical high end between 10 and 16 bits. Each project supervisor must make choices appropriate to their workflow. Advocates exist for almost any bit depth being at the "limit of human perception," although recently tests sponsored by SMPTE DC28 have shown that 12 bits used with a gamma 1/2.6 power function (instead of linear) is sufficient for describing the range of human perception—even among *golden eyes,* or expert viewers.

The consequence of too few bits is banding, the failure of the math used to describe smooth ramps from color to color, resulting instead in gross steps that are visibly distracting. These issues are most challenging in subtle dark detail areas or subtle gradation, such as the complexion of a human face. The blue channel is particularly susceptible to visible banding. To scrutinize the worst in suspect images, select only the blue channel on a monitor, as seen in Figures 4.8a and 4.8b in the Color Plate section.

Project Specs

Putting all of these terms together in a practical workflow typical of current facility practices might yield an instruction like this: "scan 1.85:1 film at 2048×1080 12 bit log RGB DPX." Read on for an explanation of each of these terms.

While such recipes are the building blocks of lengthier specifications that eventually should describe a project plan, experience suggests that no matter how detailed and immaculate these spec documents get—and how much they appear to line up with creative, technical, and budgetary intentions—the first thing to be done, at the earliest possible moment long before production, is a practical test: go into the kitchen, test the recipe, and make a measured mess before beginning the full project.

The test should be set up to exercise as much of the actual production and post conditions as possible—not the run-of-the-mill situations but the worst ones. Be sadistic: create a torture test, designed to break the system. Only then will everyone get a clear idea of the limits of the pipeline. Only after results prove to match expectations successfully (or after expectations are successfully managed to match results) should the alphabet soup of techno-acronyms be chiseled into a formal plan for the mastering of a project.

Methods of Input

How one practically arrives at a specified ingested file for mastering will depend on how the material originated. Broadly, was it photochemically acquired by a film camera or was it made up of animation or digital effects rendered by a computer?

Camera (Film and Digital)

Film is still the most common origination medium for live action theatrical releases. Common commercial systems for transferring 35mm film to data are the Cintel C-Reality and Thomson Spirit Datacine, though systems exist for scanning other formats from Super8 through 65mm, with varying degrees of success. Systems typically yield SD or HD video, or digital file formats (e.g., DPX, TIFF, Cineon) at up to 4K resolution. Increasingly common, though more esoteric, are non-real time scanners, such as the Northlight, Imagica, Arri, and Kodak, which can yield 6K files at 14 bits. Apart from immensely detailed data files, the pin registered process can eliminate subtle weave and jitter that physical transports introduce while running at 24fps. But the additional cost of these benefits is incurred at the time of scanning in the ongoing burden of managing large amounts of data throughout the mastering process.

With highly optimized digital processing for real-time removal of dirt, scratches, and grain, these systems represent something akin to an over-achieving wet gate film lab process. It is possible, however, to overdose on these powerful treatments. The mission at the capture stage needs to be, as

Hippocrates said, "First do no harm." Overly aggressive grain reduction, for example, will yield a softened, de-focused look that blurs definition between subtle light to dark transitions.

Aside from treatment that qualifies as cleaning or repair, the aim in scanning is to get a pure, unmodified representation of the original material staged for creative manipulation. As a result, scans are typically done *flat*, with no image enhancement and therefore lack the contrast and saturation that some refer to as *snap* or *punch*. Those subjective attributes will come later. The purpose of the scan is to allow for maximum creative flexibility; no chef asks the produce supplier to spice the tomatoes on the vine. Many transfer systems can detect camera negative emulsion types via key code readers and based on the emulsion will present baseline color and contrast settings for capture.

Images shot using a digital camera can originate on anything from consumer MiniDV all the way up to a 4K, 14-bit Dalsa data recorder. As with scanning, the priority should be to capture the maximum dynamic range in the image—no clipping in the highlights, no crushing of detail in the blacks.

Sound

Typically sound accompanies camera-originated material on a separate double system format that requires synchronizing. Whether this format is hard drive, DAT, DVD, or CD, it usually makes financial sense to synchronize post transfer in editorial rather than during a costly scanning session. Whatever recording format is chosen, this is another area that bears testing through the production's entire pipeline to prove it works. When tests reveal sync issues, look for mathematical clues—e.g., a sync difference of 0.1% of program duration is usually pulldown related.

Data

Computer-animated films and visual effects-intensive films create images on the computer without a physical camera. The advantage of working with data is that the project is already in a digital state for creative manipulation with digital tools without the random, incidental artifacts of the photochemical process, including dirt, grain, flashing, or movement. But the downside is that data are relatively fragile: film frames can get dirty and scratched, but they cannot get corrupted or fall offline. Working with data requires robust hardware systems and rigorous file management to avoid these pitfalls. Compared to videotape formats, moving data is a non-real-time activity for many operations, in addition to being much less portable. A project cannot easily go to another facility across town to continue working there. And to some, those incidental artifacts symbolize film's "tactile," "material" quality. Of course, they are often simulated digitally with grain and other plug-ins for stylistic effect now.

The Discreet lustre is a leading data-centric mastering tool that can accept digital production imagery delivered over networked storage without ever hitting film or videotape.

While it might seem ideal for animators to work in the same file format as the mastering system, there are good reasons for the specialized artists to be working in specialized file formats. This fact introduces the problem of file conversions (from TIFF to DPX, for example), which are a cause of scheduling delays and a point of technical failure. When moving thousands of frames through file conversion stages and other automatically scripted operations, it is not uncommon for one of those frames to become corrupted for a number of reasons. Because it is difficult to check quality at every step in the process, such problems are often not detected until the project is mastered.

The Role of the Editor

It used to be that scanning, back when it was just called telecine, provided all the necessary media management data to the editor: roll numbers, feet and frame, key code, and so on. But with digital mastering there is now a round trip: the editor's cut lists and EDL data, whether delivered as text film logs, cmx, aaf, txt, or other scheme of arranging metadata, can be used to conform master-quality digital files into an approved continuity. This fast, flexible virtual negative assembly can be used not only for final output, but also for high quality creative review. And as color grading systems emerge with rudimentary editing functionality, so do editing systems with rudimentary color correction capability. New tools are causing old lines of labor division to blur. But for as long as computer systems are the least bit taxed by handling the highest quality images, there will likely remain an offline/online paradigm wherein the offline tool is leveraged for its ability to move through and manipulate massive amounts of lower quality content fastest, while the online tool will emphasize maximum quality at the expense of performance and broad feature sets. The two will be bridged by a maturing set of metadata systems that allow draft descriptions of timing, speed changes, color, image orientation, cropping, and so on, to be conveyed from the fast and cheap editing system to the slow and best mastering system.

CREATIVE IMAGE MANIPULATION

The creative part of the mastering process involves the color grading and reframing of scenes for display. While these practices and the supporting technologies are well established in traditional mastering for television and home video release, the additional requirements of Digital Cinema distribution are driving technological and process changes. A primary objective of the mastering process is capturing the creative intent of the cinematographer and director and translating it to the final display. This can be achieved only with rigorous attention to color calibration in both the mastering and exhibition environments. This section describes the color encoding for Digital Cinema distribution and the corresponding color decoding within the cinema projector, along with the use of metadata for gamut mapping.

Traditional Color Grading

The incipient Digital Cinema color grading process borrows both from traditional film color timing and from the traditional video mastering process for television or home video release (Figure 4.9). The latter starts with the telecine transfer of a timed *interpositive* (IP) film element. This photochemical IP is made by a film laboratory by printing the conformed negative using the color timing information from the answer print. Telecines commonly used in traditional video mastering include the Thomson Spirit[1] and Cintel C-Reality.[2] The color grading process is controlled by a color corrector, which provides an ergonomic interface for the *colorist* to adjust and store the color correction information on a scene-by-scene basis. Popular color correctors include the DaVinci 2K[3] and the Pandora MegaDEF.[4]

[1] www.thomsongrassvalley.com/products/film/spirit/stick_desc.html
[2] www.cintel.co.uk/
[3] www.davsys.com/2k.htm
[4] pogle.pandora-int.com/Pixi.html

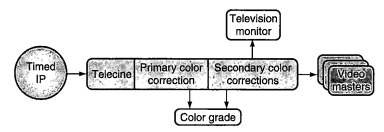

FIGURE   Traditional mastering process.

4.9

The color corrector controls the internal settings of the telecine for *primary and secondary color correction*, as well as additional color processing and windowing operations within a downstream color corrector, in cases where an outboard corrector is used. Primary color correction includes telecine calibration as well as gain (white level), gamma (midscale), and lift (black level) controls that are adjusted by the colorist on a scene-by-scene basis. Typically, a knob is used to adjust overall levels and a trackball to balance the three color channels (red, green, and blue). Secondary color correction allows the colorist to isolate colors by hue and rotate the hue or to window areas of the frame for local color grading.

Color correction decisions are made by displaying the video output on a calibrated studio (CRT) monitor set to D65 color temperature and a peak white of 35 foot Lamberts (ftL). The monitor is placed in front of a neutral gray wall or curtain and, lit to approximately 3 ftL (10%). The lighting in the mastering suite is subdued and the black level of the monitor is set with a PLUGE signal.[5]

Additional Requirements for Digital Cinema Color Grading

Digital cinema mastering also involves color grading (Figure 4.10), but with additional requirements. First, the CRT monitor is replaced by a Digital Cinema projector and this requires a bigger room with lower ambient light. Typical mastering screens are 10 feet high by 24 feet wide. The colorist's console is placed a minimum of 20 feet back from the screen (2 screen heights) and

---

[5] whatis.techtarget.com/definition/0,,sid9_gci796789,00.html

DIGITAL CINEMA MASTERING AND DISTRIBUTION PROCESS

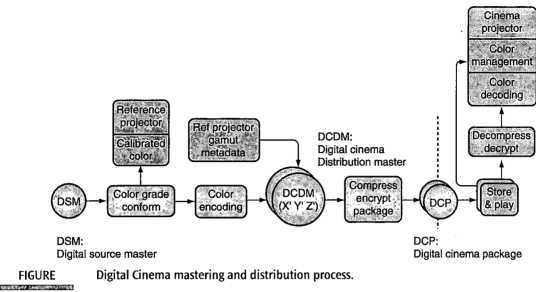

DSM:
Digital source master

DCP:
Digital cinema package

FIGURE   Digital Cinema mastering and distribution process.

4.10

the projector is placed in a booth with a throw of 36 feet or more. A ceiling height of at least 12 feet (ideally 15 feet) is required. With a peak white luminance of 14 ftL and providing for a minimum sequential contrast ratio of 2000:1, the ambient light falling on the screen must be limited to less than 0.01 ftL. This requires the elimination of all stray light and the use of matte black surfaces on walls, floors, and chairs to minimize reflection.

The DCDM has several characteristics that go beyond those of television masters. To conform with the published DCI specification,[6] the required bit depth is 12 bits, rather than 10, and the projector is calibrated for a display gamma of 2.6, rather than 2.5. The color encoding is 4:4:4 $X'Y'Z'$ rather than 4:2:2 $Y'P_b'P_r'$. And the image resolution for Digital Cinema mastering is either 4096×2160 lines (4K) or 2048×1080 lines (2K), compared to 1920×1080 lines for HDTV. To color correct and display a 2K Digital Cinema master, the interfaces between the telecine, color corrector, and projector must all be dual-link SMPTE 372M, running in 12-bit 4:4:4 mode.

---

[6] www.dcimovies.com

Process Implications

Digital cinema requirements will drive changes in the mastering process. Theatrical release deadlines will not allow the sequential steps of film answer printing and color timing, followed by the telecine transfer of a timed IP and subsequent retransfer for home video markets. Time pressures and cost efficiencies are driving a consolidated digital mastering process, commonly called *Digital Intermediate* or DI.[7] This process was pioneered by Cinesite for the mastering of *Pleasantville* (1998) and *O Brother, Where Art Thou?* (1999) and has been implemented on a broader scale by EFILM, Technicolor Digital Intermediate, and Warner Bros. in the Los Angeles market.

Recently, several software color correctors have been introduced that support the color grading of 2K or 4K digital files for DI. These include the Discreet lustre,[8] Baselight from Filmlight,[9] Nucoda Film Master,[10] and Quantel QColor.[11]

The Digital Intermediate (DI) Process

In the DI process (Figure 4.11), select takes of the original negative are scanned at 2K or 4K resolution and loaded onto a server. If working at 4K resolution, it is necessary to generate 2K or 1K image proxies to provide interactive color grading. With the scanned pictures stored as files in a database, the next step is to conform the picture to an *Edit Decision List* (EDL) provided by the film editor. This eliminates the need to cut and splice the original negative. The digital intermediate process also allows digital effects shots to be imported into the database and traditional optical effects (fades and dissolves) to be directly rendered as part of the conforming process.

Once the color grading is complete (and a scene-by-scene color list has been compiled), the color corrections can be rendered to the 4K master as a background process. The color-corrected digital picture master can then be married with the audio and subtitle tracks and compressed, encrypted, and packaged for Digital Cinema release. It can also be delivered to a laser film recorder and output to a film *internegative* (IN) for traditional film release

---

[7] *Digital Film Mastering*, ASC Manual, 8th Edition (Hollywood: The ASC Press, 2001)
[8] www.discreet.com/lustre/docs/lustre_techspecs.pdf
[9] www.filmlight.ltd.uk/baselight.html
[10] www.nucoda.com/
[11] www.quantel.com/domisphere/infopool.nsf/html/CA7D8524EF4380C380256D11004E4B5A

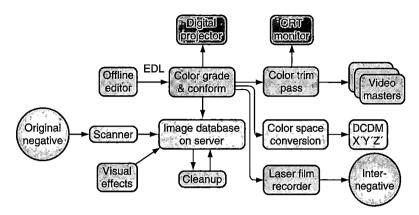

FIGURE   Digital intermediate process.

4.11

printing.[12] This same master can also serve as the starting point for the home video and television releases, whether SDTV or HDTV. It is only necessary to reframe the picture for 1.33:1 (pan/scan) or 1.78:1 aspect ratio television display and to make a color trim pass to compensate for the home viewing conditions—a smaller, brighter display in a brighter setting.

With the pictures stored in files rather than on film, it is possible to share these images with other networked workstations. This means that cleanup (dirt removal) operations can be performed in parallel with the creative color grading. Other operations that can be performed in parallel include pan/scan for 1.33:1 display and stabilization to correct for camera shake and enhancement to correct for focus problems in selected scenes.

Matching Film

Before the Digital Cinema color grading begins, an important creative decision must be made. Is the creative intent to make the digital release look like a traditional film print, or is it to produce the best digital picture? If the intent is to match the look of a traditional film print, or if the distributors want the film and Digital Cinema release to look as close to each other as possible, then the best approach is to use a *three-dimensional display look-up-table* (3-D LUT) in the color correction process that emulates the characteristics of the color print

---

[12] www.discreet.com/docs/whitepapers/digital_intermediates.pdf

stock (for example, Kodak Vision 5383). These display LUTs are available from Kodak,[13] Arri,[14] and Imagica,[15] or they can be built in a calibration process that measures the film output of a series of color test patches. With the 3-D print film LUT enabled, the process of grading to match film is greatly simplified; this LUT includes the print film stock's highlight and shadow characteristics and mixes colors to match film.

If a 3-D LUT is used in the color grading, it is necessary to render this LUT into the data when the DCDM is created. This means that the color rendering process *bakes in* all of the creative color corrections as well as the characteristics of the print film LUT. The DCDM can then be faithfully displayed on any cinema projector that is calibrated to match the reference projector used in mastering (see the next section).

Color Calibration of the Reference Projector

It is critically important that the *reference projector* used in mastering be carefully calibrated to the performance parameters outlined in the draft SMPTE recommended practice.[16] Likewise, the Digital Cinema projectors used in exhibition must be calibrated. Both calibrations are necessary to ensure that the creative intent and the color characteristics of the DCDM are faithfully reproduced in the downstream cinema exhibition. Figure 4.12 outlines the key performance parameters of the reference projector.

One of the key requirements of Digital Cinema distribution is that a single DCDM must play on all projectors and look the same, eliminating the need for multiple inventories of distribution masters. This can be achieved only if all projectors (regardless of the display technology or manufacturer) are calibrated to match the SMPTE recommended practice and have gamut mapping capability (see the section Gamut Mapping). Beyond this basic calibration, proprietary color processing is not permitted. Of course, proprietary color processing to create a special look can be used in the mastering process, as long as this processing is rendered into the DCDM.

The draft SMPTE standard for the DCDM Image Structure[17] also specifies the color metadata that must be packaged with the DCDM picture

---

[13] www.kodak.com/US/en/motion/index.jhtml
[14] www.arri.com/entry/products.htm
[15] www.imagica.com/Galette/English/
[16] Draft SMPTE RP, Reference Projector and Environment for Digital Cinema Mastering.
[17] Draft SMPTE Standard, DCDM-Image Structure.

Parameter	Target
Luminance, center 100% white	48 cd/m² (14 fL)
Luminance, corners and sides	75% of center
White point chromaticity, center	x=.314, y=.351
Color uniformity of white field, corners	±.002 x, y of center
Red primary (Xenon)	x=0.680, y=0.320
Green primary (Xenon)	x=0.265, y=0.690
Blue primary (Xenon)	x=0.150, y=0.060
Sequential contrast (room + projector)	2000:1
Intra-frame contrast (room + projector)	150:1
Gray scale tracking	± .002 x, y of white point

FIGURE

4.12

Reference projector performance targets.

essence. These metadata include the color primaries, peak white luminance, and sequential contrast ratio of the reference projector. With this information it is possible to faithfully reproduce the color on a calibrated cinema projector, compensating for its intrinsic color gamut or contrast.

Color Encoding and Decoding

The DCDM color is encoded as $X'Y'Z'$ colorimetric data, as specified in the draft SMPTE standard.[18] This means that a color transformation is necessary from the source $R'G'B'$ data (the prime symbol denotes gamma correction). This color transformation involves a LUT that linearizes the data for a gamma 2.6 display, followed by a linear matrix in display space and an inverse LUT. This color transformation can be applied in the color corrector or it can be rendered with batch software such as Apple's Shake.[19] Figure 4.13 shows the color encoding process.

Inside the projector, the operation is reversed. The projector applies a gamma 2.6 LUT to the $X'Y'Z'$ data to linearize it for display. A linear display

[18] Ibid.
[19] www.apple.com/shake/

• R'G'B' color space of reference projector is converted to device-independent X'Y'Z' color space of DCDM with a linear space matrix

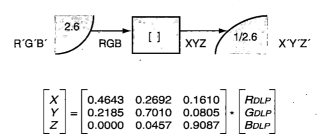

$$\begin{bmatrix} X \\ Y \\ Z \end{bmatrix} = \begin{bmatrix} 0.4643 & 0.2692 & 0.1610 \\ 0.2185 & 0.7010 & 0.0805 \\ 0.0000 & 0.0457 & 0.9087 \end{bmatrix} * \begin{bmatrix} R_{DLP} \\ G_{DLP} \\ B_{DLP} \end{bmatrix}$$

FIGURE
4.13
Color encoding.

space matrix is applied to convert from *XYZ* to the native *RGB* primaries of the cinema projector. If the color primaries of the cinema projector match those of the reference projector, then the decoding color matrix is simply an inverse of the encoding color matrix. Figure 4.14 shows the color decoding process.

Gamut Mapping

The draft SMPTE standard for the DCDM is designed to be extensible to wider gamut projectors in the future. The *X'Y'Z'* color encoding encompasses the full color spectrum. Displaying today's masters on future wider gamut projectors is straightforward. However, once wider gamut (perhaps laser-

• X'Y'Z' color space of DCDM is converted to projector (device specific) RGB color space with a linear matrix

$$\begin{bmatrix} R_{DLP} \\ G_{DLP} \\ B_{DLP} \end{bmatrix} = \begin{bmatrix} 2.6146 & -0.9796 & -0.3765 \\ -0.8198 & 1.7420 & -0.0091 \\ 0.0412 & -0.0876 & 1.1009 \end{bmatrix} * \begin{bmatrix} X \\ Y \\ Z \end{bmatrix}$$

FIGURE
4.14
Color decoding.

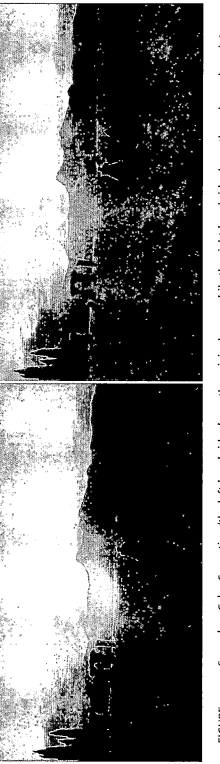

FIGURE 4.4 Secondary Color Correction (the left-hand side shows the original scan, while the right-hand side shows the enhanced scan). Images from *Van Helsing* courtesy of Universal Studios Licensing LLLP.

A frame from *A Bug's Life*, courtesy Disney/Pixar.

At 720×486, 2MB.

At 1280×1024, 5.2MB.

At 1920×803, 10.2MB.

At 2048×857, 11.8MB.

A comparison of SD, 128×1024, HD, and 2K images. *A Bug's Life* image courtesy of Walt Disney Pictures/Pixar Animation Studios.

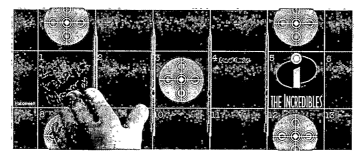

FIGURE

4.7

Frame & focus leader. *The Incredibles* image courtesy of Walt Disney Pictures/Pixar Animation Studios.

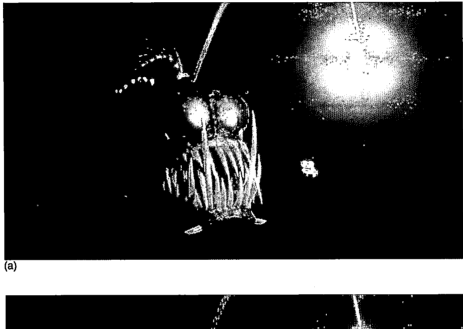

(a)

(b)

FIGURE

4.8

A demonstration of banding in an 8-bit MPEG compressed image (a) made more visible through blue-channel-only monitoring (b). *Finding Nemo* image courtesy of Walt Disney Pictures/Pixar Animation Studios.

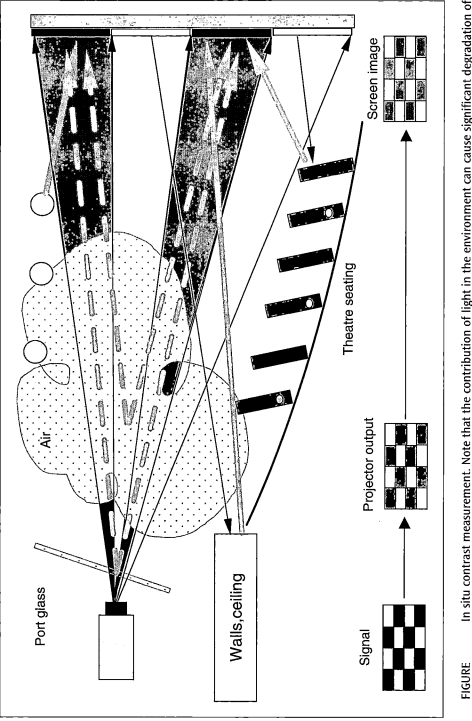

Port glass

Air

Walls, ceiling

Theatre seating

Signal

Projector output

Screen image

FIGURE In situ contrast measurement. Note that the contribution of light in the environment can cause significant degradation of
9.7 the black level of the image in the simultaneous (ANSI) contrast of an image.

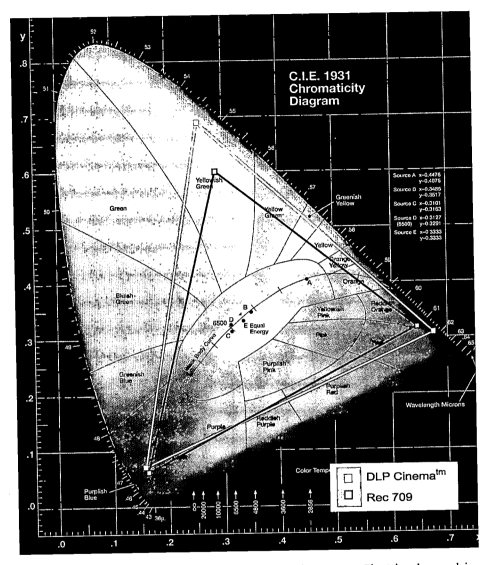

CIE diagram showing the color gamut visible to the human eye. The triangles overlying the diagram represent the color display capabilities in current HDTV (Rec. 709) and Digital Cinema (DLP Cinema™). CIE chart courtesy of photoresearch Inc. © Photoresearch Inc. All rights reserved.

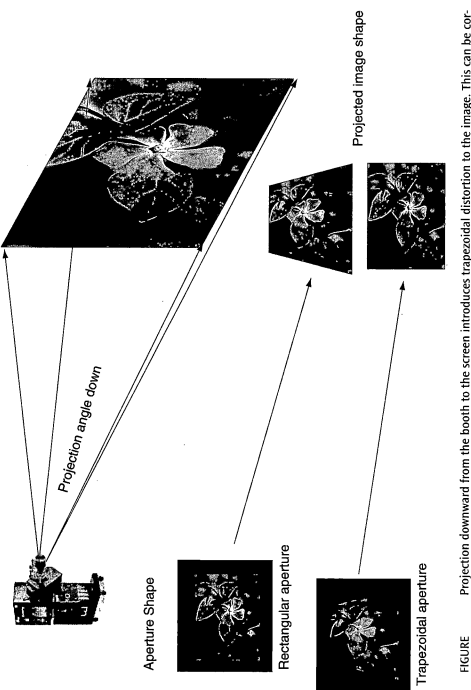

Projection angle down

Projected image shape

Aperture Shape

Rectangular aperture

Trapezoidal aperture

FIGURE
9.12

Projection downward from the booth to the screen introduces trapezoidal distortion to the image. This can be corrected by using a trapezoidal mask in the aperture of the projector. Digital projectors apply this mask electronically.

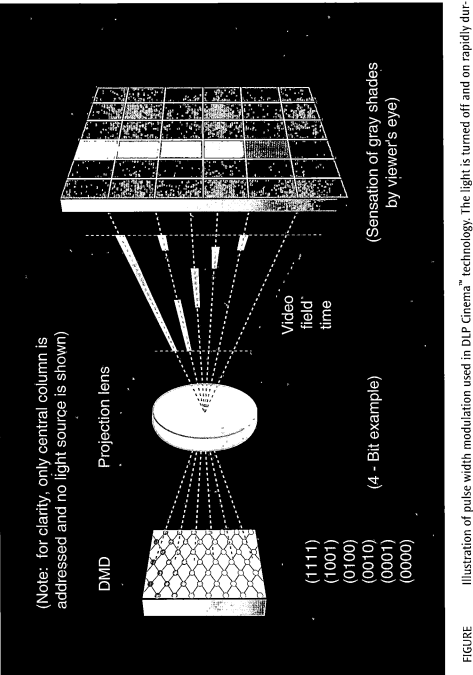

(Note: for clarity, only central column is addressed and no light source is shown)

DMD   Projection lens

(1111)
(1001)
(0100)
(0010)   (4 - Bit example)
(0001)
(0000)

Video
field
time

(Sensation of gray shades
by viewer's eye)

FIGURE
9.14

Illustration of pulse width modulation used in DLP Cinema™ technology. The light is turned off and on rapidly during an image frame time. The retina will integrate this to create the sensation of gray scale. The intensity of the gray depends on the on time during the frame.

based) projectors are available for mastering, the issue of backward compatibility with the installed base of Xenon projectors becomes important. These wider gamut masters will contain colors that exceed the display gamut of the legacy Xenon projectors.

Therefore, SMPTE recommends that all Digital Cinema projectors include the capability to map the gamut of the master into the native color gamut of the cinema projector.[20] SMPTE is drafting a Recommended Practice to describe the preferred technique for gamut mapping. This process will use the metadata that describe the gamut of the reference projector: the color primaries, peak white luminance, and sequential contrast ratio.

Formatting and Resizing

The two common theatrical projection formats are Academy 1.85 and wide-screen, with projection aspect ratios of 1.85:1 and 2.39:1, respectively. Wide-screen can be originated either in anamorphic 2.40 (often called CinemaScope) or Super 35. Since the camera aperture and thus the image recorded on the negative film is larger, the mastering process involves cropping and resizing the display data from the original full aperture scans. Typically, this extraction is centered vertically, but it can be pushed up or down to frame the action better. The nominal extractions are illustrated in Figure 4.15, using scanned image dimensions as the input and a 2K Digital Cinema master as the output.

With the CinemaScope (sometimes called Scope) format, the camera uses an anamorphic lens that squeezes the picture horizontally by a factor of 2.0. The inverse lens is used on the film projector. For a 2.39:1 aspect ratio display, this means that a 1.195:1 aspect ratio image is extracted from the original negative, utilizing close to the full height of the camera aperture. This imparts a higher vertical resolution to the CinemaScope display.

The high-quality results obtainable from the digital intermediate process have given new life to Super 35 production, in which a full aperture (original Academy camera aperture) is used to capture images in the camera with spherical (flat) lenses, and the film is released as a wide-screen anamorphic print. With a digital intermediate, it is a simple process to extract the 2.39 image and squeeze it for output to a Scope internegative. This digital

---

[20] Draft SMPTE DCDM-Image Structure.

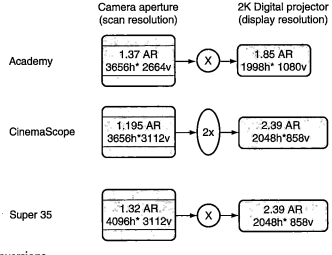

Camera aperture (scan resolution) 2K Digital projector (display resolution)

Academy 1.37 AR 3656h* 2664v X 1.85 AR 1998h* 1080v

CinemaScope 1.195 AR 3656h*3112v 2x 2.39 AR 2048h*858v

Super 35 1.32 AR 4096h* 3112v X 2.39 AR 2048h* 858v

FIGURE Format conversions.

4.15

squeeze produces images that are much sharper than when using an optical printer with an anamorphic lens. Films such as *O Brother, Where Art Thou?* and *Seabiscuit* used this approach.

Although wide-screen (letterboxed) releases for home video are becoming more popular, the primary home video version is cropped for a 1.33:1 video display. Capturing all of the important action requires a manual process known as *pan and scan,* in which the colorist re-frames the picture for 1.33:1 by extracting a panning window from the original wide-screen format. This is particularly important with pictures framed for 2.39:1 display.

Projects that were born as composited or rendered 3-D modeling environments have a flexibility that camera-originated or flattened bitmapped digital projects do not because they can be recomposed for new aspect ratios.

Other Operations

The digital mastering process provides opportunities to do more than color correction and formatting. Offline software image-processing tools can be used to subtly *sharpen* (enhance) a shot that is out of focus or to *stabilize* (remove unsteadiness from) a shot in which the camera is unsteady or bumped. Care must be taken not to take this processing too far, which could result in visible artifacts.

Another common step is *cleanup* or *dirt removal,* the process of identifying and removing the shadow images of unwanted dirt particles from the picture. A *cleanup pass* on the color-corrected video has been a routine part of home video mastering for nearly a decade, with pioneering software packages from MTI.[21] The Discreet lustre color corrector provides collaborative tools so that the cleanup operation can be performed by an assistant working in parallel with the colorist.[22]

Digital grain reduction is frequently used in the mastering of archival films for home video release. Reducing the grain with an adaptive temporal median filter improves the picture while making it easier to compress for television or DVD, by removing the random high-frequency information that stresses the compressor. Again, care must be taken not to go too far, which could remove textures and make the images look artificial. An example of a commonly used grain reducer is the DVNR from Digital Vision.[23]

Digital restoration techniques have been widely used to restore archived films for home video release. Software tools are available that automatically correct for dye fade (which results in reduced color contrast), sharpen pictures, realign misregistered color records, and correct for unsteadiness and flicker. REVIVAL is a comprehensive restoration software package available from DaVinci.[24]

AUDIO PREPARATION: AN EXPANDED SCOPE

Audio preparation for the Digital Cinema mastering process begins as a relatively straightforward process of assembling the appropriate sound track(s) to be associated with the image. However, consider that for a worldwide release there may be 30 or more different language tracks for a feature film, and the process takes on a significantly expanded scope. Many of these are identical in total length to the original version, but some will be of different lengths because of edits that are needed for local censorship reasons.

If the language version is being dubbed, then the dubbing service provider will perform any sound editorial changes needed to accommodate

---

[21] www.mtifilm.com/
[22] www.discreet.com/lustre
[23] www.digitalvision.se/products_mediamastering.htm
[24] www.davsys.com/rs2.htm

censorship review. In the case that the original sound track language version is being used but there are editorial changes needed to conform to censorship, the original version masters are brought back to a sound editorial service for conforming and for preparation of elements needed to complete the final version. Each of these localized composite sound tracks must be monitored and ultimately married to the appropriate picture, which may also have localized elements, to create a final language version composition.

File Types and Standards

Technical preparation of the audio elements for use in Digital Cinema is limited in scope. The audio tracks are used exactly as mastered from the theatrical mixing stage. The current practice is to use uncompressed, *pulse code modulation* (PCM) linear digital audio files in broadcast WAV file format. These are used without any compression or data packing. This is the standard digital audio file format used in most post production sound facilities today, although there is some diversity of sampling resolutions (common bits depths are 16, 20, 24 bits/sample) and sampling frequencies (44.1, 48, 96 Khz, and numerous variations on these to provide speed matches to video sources). There is rarely anything more than a simple file type conversion needed to prepare these tracks for Digital Cinema use. Audio track assignment of up to 7.1 channels currently follows the de facto industry standard of L/R, C/Sub, Ls/Rs, Le/Re conforming to AES data stream pairs. Current practice has been to pass through Dolby EX encoding as LST/RST to be decoded conventionally by the Dolby processor. Future track assignments will be carried as metadata within the packaged composition.

Downstream Uses

In other downstream distribution channels these tracks are often evaluated and may undergo some form of dynamic range constraint in consideration of a restricted overall dynamic range capacity of a particular distribution medium. For example, the VHS cassette or television broadcast audio systems are not capable of peak audio levels in excess of 20 dB above a calibration of nominal 0 dB. This can be accomplished with a fairly simple audio compression/leveling system, and these exist as outboard audio processors from a large number of manufacturers.

This unassisted method of reducing dynamic range can have unwanted side effects, however; one example is reducing dialogue intelligibility by lowering the overall level to allow room for the peak level areas. As a result, there has been an increasing trend in the motion picture industry to create a unique *home video/television mix*. This puts the creative control for addressing this problem into the hands of the creative team that produced the sound track in the first place. These other distribution channels may then employ compression and/or conversion from one digital audio file format to another, but the Digital Cinema audio systems that are in place now and will be in the future have no such performance restrictions.

Audio Watermarking

The next consideration in audio preparation is that of *audio watermarking*. This is the process of embedding an inaudible signal into the audio stream that will allow for downstream devices to perform detection and respond to those signals. Although today there is no standard practice for the use of an audio watermark technology in Digital Cinema, it deserves comment here, as there are numerous implementations of audio watermarks in other distribution mediums, and it certainly is a relevant topic for the future of Digital Cinema. Watermarking can be used for a number of applications; the most commonly discussed is that of copy control, or forensic analysis in the case of theft, and unauthorized redistribution of the material, but this can also be used to trigger other devices in the theatre itself. These watermark detection devices may be used to enhance the sensory experience (e.g., environmental changes such as smell, temperature, vibration, and moisture), or they may be used to trigger auditorium systems such as lighting and curtains. Once this audio watermarking has been completed, we are ready for the final step in the mastering process.

Layback and Synchronization

We have come to the creation of the final composite master. Currently the majority of Digital Cinema masters is delivered to the compression/encryption/packaging phase using a high-definition videotape format, which requires a *layback* of the audio track to the video master for each version. The advantage to this method is that a single physical element represents the definitive finished product, and audio sync can be derived from this master for future purposes.

But there are clear disadvantages to using a videotape format. For one, there is no ideal videotape format available from a picture quality point of view. Several of the currently used formats (HD-CAM, D-5, D-6) are all quite capable of handling audio losslessly, but each compromises picture quality because of data compression, limited color channel resolution, or both. In addition, there are no spatial resolutions above 1920×1080 in any current video standard; thus true 2K image files cannot be carried this way, to say nothing of 4K. Finally, the videotape mastering method is an expensive and time consuming process because the video and audio must be laid down in real time. Therefore the trend continues to move away from a composite videotape master for each of the distribution master versions to work in an entirely file-based model, starting from a master image essence file, and then combining audio and other related files to produce the DSM.

RELATED DATA CREATION

Current Uses of Related Data

In the current 35mm film distribution model, *related data* is information carried physically in or with the film print. This includes the label or packing or assembly list printed and enclosed in the film container with the print, which gives the theatre operator clear identification of the title, number of reels, length, sound format, aspect ratio, and any other instructions regarding the film.

For international language releases, related data include subtitles, which may be fixed to release prints directly by laser etching or a hot wax stamp method. For larger print quantities an overlay negative or integrated negative may be created for duplication. Ratings cards or translated main insert and end titles are similarly assembled into the print or duplicating negative at the film lab to create a specific language version of the film. In some instances more than one language version of a film is used in the same market, indeed even in the same theatre. For example, for a family-oriented film in Japan, the theatre operator will have two versions. A fully dubbed Japanese language track will play in the morning and afternoon shows to accommodate children who have had little or no exposure to English yet. In the evening, the preference is to play the English original version soundtrack, with Japanese subtitles. This allows adults to hear the original movie star performances and refer to the subtitles only when necessary. In Belgium, the population is split among French and Flemish speaking. Theatres run prints in both languages on different screens within the same complex (see Figure 4.16).

Related Data in Digital Cinema

In the case of Digital Cinema, all the related data can be created electronically, assembled virtually at the time of packaging through the use of metadata and then unpacked in the theatre prior to display. Currently the use of related data in Digital Cinema distribution is limited to uses similar to 35mm print distribution described above. In future Digital Cinema distribution, the range and diversity of the related data will be far greater than in the film distribution model and promises to bring significant advantages in efficiency and flexibility. For example, this will create opportunities to reach emerging markets with a print customized to that market at a small incremental cost, thus offering better movie going experiences in a broader and more diverse range of new theatrical markets.

Audio-Visual Data

Audio-visual data include subtitles, captions, sound tracks for the visually impaired, watermarks, censor or ratings cards, distributor logos, and translated main, insert, and end titles. The need to create these elements already exists so we simply add digital specifications to the deliverables list during the creation of these elements for incorporation into the Digital Cinema mastering and packaging process. This material will be formatted as audio/video assets, image data files, and other data file types.

Other Data

Other data are the elements that are either invisible to the moviegoer or are entirely unused in the actual rendering and projection of the content but

Element	Treatment	Definition of Treatment	Where used
Soundtracks	Original English	The original mix of the film	Used in an average of 23 territories; 6 territories utilize it as is with no subtitling; balance with local language subtitles either physically etched on the prints or printed in at the lab via overlay printing
	Dubbed	Localized mix incorporated foreign language dubbed dialogue	Average 28-32 versions
Main Titles	Original English	The original Main title as seen in the US	6 territories
	Translated custom Main titles	Main title in a localized language re-created to match the font, animation, efx etc. of the original English title	9-11 versions
	Local language subtitle or 'byline'	The original Main title as seen in the US with the local language subtitle added underneath via physical etching of the print or printed in at the laboratory	19-21 versions
Inserts/Narrative Titles	Original English	Narrative text on screen used as seen in the US; no changes or localizations made	6 territories
	Translated custom insert titles	Narrative text on screen with story point value when possible is localized and re-created to match the font, animation, efx etc. of the original English title	9-11 versions
	Local language subtitle or 'byline'	The original a local language subtitle is placed on screen translating the narrative title/insert	19-21 versions
	Neutral Inserts	Customizing of a narrative title/insert that is not language specific thereby can be used on all dubbed versions	created once but used by all dubbed versions
End Credits	Original English	Original English end credit as seen in the US; no changes or localizations made	6 territories
	Int'l End credits & crawl - English	Customization of the end credits and crawl in English to allow addition of localized dubbing talent and technical credits within the body of the existing credits	all dubbed versions
	Localized Int'l End credits & crawl - English	Completely translated version of the int'l end credits and crawl	2 versions
Subtitles	Local language translation of dialogue	Localized dialogue subtitles etched onto prints or printed in at the laboratory via overlay	17; some territories utilize dual language subtitles (i.e. French & German on screen at the same time)

Distribution Specific Variants	MPAA rating card	Removed for int'l prints	all versions, all prints
	Studio logo	Int'l distribution logo	all versions, all prints
	Censor or import. cards added to prints	Physically spliced onto prints or printed in at the lab usually at the head of the prints	China, India, Malaysia, UK; Thailand censor put a light scratch at the start of the film barely visible to audience.
	Intermission	Card added in the middle of show to allow for intermission	Italy only

FIGURE 4.16   International print localization overview.

that nevertheless carry important information about the content. This would include information such as the title, number of "reels," running length, rating information, trailer attachment information, subtitle language(s), and color metadata (described in detail in *Creative Image Manipulation* in this chapter). The file format used for this information will be MXF.

Metadata

All of the data described above must be formatted and transmitted in a way that is meaningful to the playout server. At this time, standardization of the file types, definition of terms, and protocols for communicating the wide range of information that can be conveyed is under development both within SMPTE and Digital Cinema Initiatives.

Mastering the Rest of the Master

The number and complexity of the mastering elements needed for a feature film to satisfy all of its downstream distribution channels is at an all-time high. With both PAL and NTSC video standards in wide use around the world today for standard definition television, and high definition needed for a smaller yet growing number of distribution channels, distributors find themselves with the unenviable challenge of trying to create a single video master to accommodate all possible combinations of uses.

Formatting and Standards Conversion

The Digital Cinema master is just one of the multitudes of masters that ultimately must be created to satisfy all downstream distribution needs of a motion picture. In fact, there can be as many as a dozen or more downstream masters required for each title, including full frame, 16×9, 4×3 pan-and-scan, and 4×3 letterbox—all in both PAL and NTSC video, as well as high-definition 1080i and 720p masters. The number of individual masters grows even further if the original presentation was in the anamorphic (2.39:1) format. Figure 4.17 depicts a typical flow of element creation from either a film or digital original element.

114

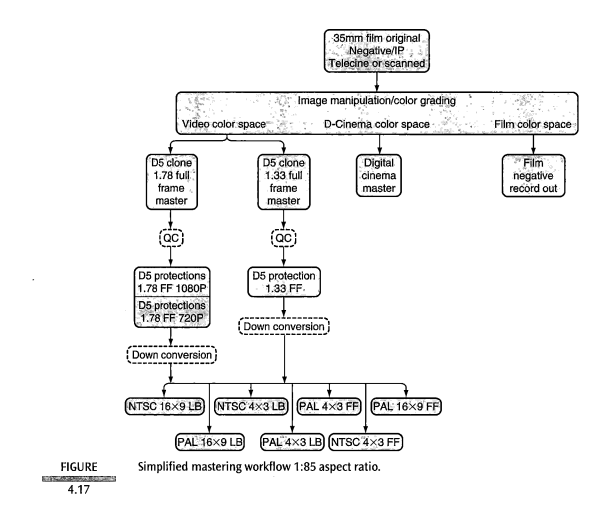

FIGURE 4.17   Simplified mastering workflow 1:85 aspect ratio.

Repurposing the Work

The essential creative and technical elements of the Digital Cinema mastering process are indeed repurposed for all of these video distribution elements. Color correction for each of the display media—i.e., film, Digital Cinema, and direct view monitoring—remains a subjective process. Typically the first correction is done for the film color space, whether by traditional Hazeltine photochemical timing process, or as the first digital color correction as part of a digital intermediate workflow. Then Digital Cinema and downstream video color corrections are done as a secondary adjustment, or *trim pass*.

This topic needs further review, as there is currently a widely held belief in the creative community that a substantial amount of human intervention is required to accurately translate creative intent from one display gamut to another. At the same time, much work is being done to develop software tools that will mathematically produce color space conversions in a single step correction process. If the resulting conversions prove equal in quality and accuracy to work done with creative supervision, the full potential of a single motion picture master will have been achieved.

Other steps in the mastering process, such as dirt and scratch removal, frame registration, and other repairs, are fully repurposed for all downstream masters. In some cases the dirt and scratch removal work done in the mastering process is actually more necessary for the video and television distribution masters than for film and Digital Cinema distribution. This is because in the nonlinear environments of DVD and video on demand, the consumer (or distributor) has the ability to stop and freeze one frame to detect a piece of dirt or scratch, whereas at a movie theatre, in real-time playback, one- or two-frame flaws will likely go unnoticed. In the end, a distinct advantage of a digital intermediate process is that even the final film and Digital Cinema distribution elements can benefit from these advanced "dirt fix" techniques that are employed during the image manipulation process.

Quality Control

As these downstream masters are created, they receive extensive quality control review with an eye towards the distribution channel that will be receiving them. There is a broad diversity of quality control standards throughout the world. Different distribution sectors and even regions of the world have different criteria for "acceptable quality" in their delivery requirements, resulting in a complex, iterative process to ensure the master is acceptable to all distribution channels worldwide.

Inventory and Archival

Once all of these myriad distribution masters are created, there remains the final responsibility to inventory and archive these elements. Prior to the digitization of the post-production process, the archival elements comprised the cut camera negative and separation elements created from that cut negative for protection. (These *separation elements* are often called *YCMs* because the image on the negative is separated into its three color components of yellow, cyan, and magenta, which can later be retrieved to produce a new negative whose positive images will contain the inverse colors of blue, red, and green, respectively.) This was a manageable challenge for motion picture archivists. First, the lifespan of the storage medium (35mm film) is well known to be several decades at minimum, and the technology to retrieve the information (i.e., lenses, projectors, and telecine machines) is widely available and not at risk of obsolescence.

But consider what changes in an all-digital world. The original camera negative is replaced by high-resolution 4K data scans or, soon, digital camera direct data output where there is no camera negative at all. The extensive digital image manipulation that occurs before recording out the 35mm distribution negative or producing the DCDM means that the true original archival final element is the digital source master. All this makes the film industry's archiving process more and more dependent on the information technology (IT) industry for data storage technologies.

However, in the IT paradigm we find continuous introduction of new storage products at a dizzying pace, and the prior storage technology is left obsolete. This is basically at odds with the film industry's practice of treating archives as deep storage, where elements are typically left undisturbed for decades, in proper conditions, until the movie is reissued. This problem has already surfaced in the first phase of the digital transformation of the entertainment industry, and much attention must be placed on this in the coming years.

THE FUTURE OF MASTERING

We can expect that there will be continuing advances in the creative and technical tools that are available to further improve the performance of every phase of mastering, from image capture to manipulation and output/conversion systems. There will also, we suspect, be a significant change in the workflow of mastering and its place in the overall filmmaking process. One factor is a continuing pressure on the film business to offer our product worldwide on the same date (*day and date*), combined with a shortening of the downstream distribution windows (i.e., Video/DVD, Pay TV, etc.). There have even been suggestions to offer a film into all channels of distribution at the same time and simply modulate the price of each channel of distribution over time. Imagine being able to purchase a new blockbuster movie for viewing at home on the same day it opens in theatres but at a comparably higher price than if you purchased it 4 months after it opened. Although there are many reasons that this extreme example of a distribution model may never completely materialize, we can rest assured that the trend to more worldwide day and date releases, and shrinking windows, will continue to bring pressure to integrate the mastering process more completely into the production and post production of a film. Further support for this trend to integrate will come from the emergence of digital cinematography into the mainstream. This will create a necessity to bring the digital image management tools, systems, and expertise forward all the way to the production trailer.

Future of Image Capture

The future of image capture as it currently exists is a bleak one: extinction! OK, not exactly, but eventually for new film production we will not need to scan film at all because all images will be captured digitally, so the capture of a photochemical element will be relegated to restoration of archival film elements and other non-theatrical production work. Fear not, scanner manufacturers, this is a long way off and lots of scanned images from now. In the meantime, we expect scanning resolutions will not need to develop much further than today's 4–6K resolutions, and color channel resolutions are also at or beyond human perception, but the speed at which these images can be scanned is very much in need of dramatic improvement.

Image Manipulation

This area is a fertile ground for continuing improvements in the techniques and tools that can be applied to the manipulation process. Many of the improvements in this area will come from software tools that allow faster, more precise, and more effective results in essentially every area of activity covered here.

The logical extension of these developments is that image mastering could occur on the set. The portability and speed of the technology could reach a threshold that will permit the director of photography to deliver his or her creative intention directly from the camera. The need for an offline editing stage could vanish, with editors and directors only ever reviewing "master quality" imagery.

Doubtless, this technology will have an effect on style—just as the capability to pack oil paint in tubes helped give rise to *plein air* impressionism in the 19th century. We will soon come to see films made in the 21st century as products of these technical developments, just as we now see hand-held, zoom-lensed films shot on location with fast film stocks that are the product of the 1960s.

Audio Preparation

As with color grading, the trend to create two somewhat different sound tracks that maximize the performance and environment they are intended for will continue to become the norm. Particularly as we start to take advantage of the extended channel count, speaker placement, and performance capabilities afforded by the Digital Cinema systems, we will find there may be a necessity to follow this dual inventory path. Other advances may well come in the form of using the metadata to add other sensory inputs to the theatregoer. These effects will likely change the way a sound track is mixed. This could be seen as possibly a negative side effect of greater flexibility—namely, greater complexity!

Related Data

This area is just in its infancy; the first step in its evolution is simply having a distribution and exhibition system that can accommodate these related data. One can expect a great deal of growth and refinement in how and for what the related data will get used, expanding beyond subtitles, playlists, and rights expressions to uses that help expand and improve the moviegoing experience.

The Rest of the Masters

This is an area, as mentioned in the opening paragraph, where many workflow changes will likely occur because of substantial changes in the underpinning technology: the transition from a videocentric to a datacentric model within the mastering process, the eventual obsolescence of standard definition video, and the ever-emerging HD videotape formats that promise to provide lossless HD video in a cost-effective package for future video distribution servicing.

Archiving will attract special consideration here from content owners seeking to protect their assets from formats that grow obsolete on 18-month cycles. Against the yardstick of film, a digital format would need to withstand the elements and the march of technology for a century before being competitive in this regard—or at least be convertible to this year's model safely and economically on an ongoing basis.

This revolving data door may be more likely than a single, monolithic standard. After all, archiving is not about putting things away but getting them back, and such a format shuffle would constantly prove that data are being retrieved. As storage costs spiral downward over the next century, we may all wind up with entire studio catalogs, uncompressed, residing on our personal media players, awaiting a small, biometrically verified transaction to decrypt them for our viewing pleasure.

Finally, we hope that the future of Digital Cinema is one of broad and rapid adoption, giving all theatregoers a markedly superior experience and keeping them coming back for more.

5 Compression for Digital Cinema

Peter Symes
Thomson Broadcast & Media Solutions

Compression is one of the enabling technologies for Digital Cinema in that it makes storage and distribution of the cinema-ready product practical and economically feasible. Used appropriately, compression has little—ideally nothing—to do with the quality of the final cinematic experience; it is just one of the technologies used in taking the image to the projector.

Given this, compression has probably received far more than its fair share of attention in Digital Cinema discussions and in the standardization processes. It is an emotional subject in the Digital Cinema community. Some purists believe that compression is, by its very nature, something that should never be part of the path from lens to screen. Others are fierce proponents of one technology or opponents of another.

Assuming we accept the need for compression in the Digital Cinema distribution process, any of the principal compression technologies may—if used correctly—provide a practical degree of compression without visibly degrading the image. Any technology, if used wrongly, or if used to provide excessive levels of compression, will degrade the images.

The politics surrounding compression are complex. Some part of this is seen at the end of this chapter where intellectual property and licensing are discussed. But before that, we examine the technologies and see how they may be used as enablers for Digital Cinema.

WHAT IS COMPRESSION?

Compression is the general term for a set of tools and techniques that can reduce the quantity of data necessary to represent some digital entity. When a digital entity is reduced in size it can be stored more easily and more cheaply, and it can be transmitted using less bandwidth and/or less time. Time, bandwidth, and storage capacity all cost money, so sometimes the sole objective of compression is economic. More often, compression is used to make the impractical practical: to store something in a reasonable amount of storage medium, to transmit it in a reasonable time, or to transmit in real time a stream that otherwise would need an impractically large bandwidth.

Compression works by removing redundant information, and this falls into two categories. There is information that is redundant because its loss cannot be perceived; this information can just be discarded. There is also information that is redundant because the "real" information has been coded in an inefficient way. It is possible to re-code using fewer bits, and then recreate the original, or a sufficiently good approximation, at the point of use.

The most well-known compression standards for images have been developed within the *Joint Technical Committee* (JTC) of the *International Organization for Standardization* (ISO) and the *International Electrotechnical Commission* (IEC). Two working groups within the JTC are responsible for a great deal of compression technology. The *Joint Photographic Experts Group* (JPEG) has developed standards for the compression of static images, and the *Moving Pictures Experts Group* (MPEG) is well known for its standards for compressing video. *MPEG-2* is the most widely deployed compression system, being the basis for DVDs and for all current digital television systems.

Digital Cinema is not video, but both Digital Cinema and video are moving image sequences, and the same techniques are applicable to both, even though the parameters may be very different.

WHY IS COMPRESSION NEEDED FOR DIGITAL CINEMA?

Compression in Digital Cinema is all about practicality. The quantity of data needed to represent high-quality imagery in its native uncompressed form is staggering.

The *Digital Cinema Initiatives* (DCI) specification calls for a container with 4096 pixels horizontally. A movie with an aspect ratio of 1.85:1 is 3996×2160 pixels, for a total of 8,631,360 pixels per frame. Each pixel is represented in the *Digital Cinema Distribution Master* (DCDM) by three 12-bit values; this works out to 310,728,960 bits, or nearly 40 megabytes, per frame. A 2-hour movie is 172,800 frames (at 24 fps) for a total of nearly 7 terabytes. This is a phenomenal amount of data; the largest commonly available portable medium is the 2-layer DVD that can store 9.4 gigabytes, so the 2-hour movie would need over 700 DVDs in its uncompressed form. Transmission of a single movie over a satellite transponder, even if we assume a totally error-free circuit, would take more than 2 weeks.

Such storage or transmission is physically possible but wildly impractical. With today's storage and transmission technology, Digital Cinema cannot become a practical form of distribution, or a business, without a way to reduce substantially the quantity of data used to deliver the movie to the theatre. This is the role of compression.

Lossless Compression

Some compression techniques are completely reversible; it is guaranteed that the "bits out" after decompression will be identical to the "bits in" before compression. In one respect this is obviously the ideal form of compression in that (assuming error-free transmission) there can be no possibility of degradation. This is *lossless compression,* and it does have practical applications. Well-known computer programs such as PK-Zip and Stuffit are lossless compression systems. They can take a computer file, make it more compact for storage or transmission, and then restore a perfect copy of the original.

Unfortunately, lossless systems generally do not provide sufficient compression for large-scale imagery applications such as Digital Cinema distribution. Typically, lossless systems can compress image data by factors in the range of two or three to one; a useful degree of compression, certainly, but not enough to make Digital Cinema practical. Recently there have been claims that new techniques can provide much higher compression ratios but—at the time of writing—no independent tests have verified these claims.

So the majority of this chapter will be devoted to the characteristics and design of lossy compression systems; systems that are likely to meet the practical needs of Digital Cinema distribution.

However, lossless compression does still play an important role. These techniques may be used with almost any source of data, including the output data of a lossy compression system. So practical compression systems usually consist of a lossy front end followed by a lossless section (known as the *entropy coder*) to reduce the bit rate even further.

Lossy Compression

For the foreseeable future, Digital Cinema will require the use of compression systems that are not lossless: systems that discard or distort some of the information in the original image data, or *lossy compression*. The intent of such systems is to provide the maximum amount of compression of the image data consistent with an acceptably low level of distortion of the images, *as perceived by a human viewer* viewing the images *under the intended conditions*.

These are vitally important points. The *human visual system* (HVS) consists of the eyes, the optic nerves, and the sections of the brain that interpret all the information and create the perception of the image that we see. It is an incredibly complex and versatile design, but it does have limitations. The HVS is not capable of perceiving all of the information in a scene or in an image under all conditions. A lossy compression system exploits these limitations. The first step is to omit or distort information that cannot be perceived by the HVS. If this does not result in sufficient compression for the application, the next step is to omit or distort information that results in a substantial data reduction in exchange for a small perceptual effect.

By definition, the output of a lossy compression system is different from its input. The differences, of course, can be measured. The greater question is whether they can be perceived by a viewer and, if so, to what degree and under what conditions?

A lossy compression system can distort the image in a number of visible ways. The most obvious is that fine detail in the image may be lost. Also, shaded areas may appear less smooth and, with severe distortion, may exhibit visible quantization steps, characterized by *contouring* or *banding*. The compression system may introduce *artifacts*—elements in the image that were not present in the original. One notable example from some compression systems is *blocking*—visibility of a rectangular structure used by the compression system to divide the image for processing.

The HVS is very sensitive to errors of this type; we can perceive incredibly small errors if they are correlated along straight lines. Another common artifact is known as *mosquito noise*. This is perceived as "busy-ness" introduced by the compression system in areas of fine detail and along sharp edges.

Many of these errors are visible in moving image sequences but are much easier to identify definitively in still images, particularly if a split-screen system permits direct comparison of the processed image with the original (pre-compression) image.

However, it is important not to focus exclusively on errors in static images. Digital Cinema has to provide excellent quality in moving images. Errors in the individual static images will cause problems, but so will inappropriate changes between sequential images. The HVS is very sensitive to change in the peripheral vision area. If a viewer is looking at the center of the screen, a very small change at the edge or corner of the screen can attract the viewer's attention. In 2004 tests of one compression system it was found that grain visibility changed slightly from frame to frame. This was quite sufficient to catch the attention of a viewer and to make this implementation unsuitable for Digital Cinema.

We could—and some in the industry believe that we should—require that compression used in Digital Cinema be visually undetectable, even to expert viewers who are allowed to approach the screen, freeze the images, and compare the compressed images directly with the original. This is a very stringent requirement that would result in much less compression (much more data to store or transmit) than a more relaxed requirement.

Or we could define a requirement that the "average" viewer in, say, a central seat in a "typical" theatre not be annoyed by disturbances created by the compression system. This would be much easier to achieve and would permit a higher level of compression (much less data to store or transmit). Under these conditions, it would be obvious close to the screen that information was missing from the images and/or that there were visible artifacts introduced by the compression system. People in the front seats would, presumably, be annoyed by the visible effects of the compression system.

The compression level could be reduced so that the "no annoyance" test was met in the front seats, but even this might leave a more subtle problem. Even if there are no obvious losses or annoying artifacts in the pictures, can we be sure that the viewing experience has not been compromised at all? If the experience is less satisfactory, customers might not return to digital presentations—even if they could not identify any specific reason for the experience being less satisfactory.

Clearly this is not an acceptable risk in the proposed re-invention of a multi-billion-dollar industry. The developers of Digital Cinema will ensure that the compression system chosen is capable of being used in a way that is essentially transparent. Compression must not represent a barrier to the deployment of new technology for movie distribution or be the cause of any dissatisfaction in cinema audiences.

This is not difficult to achieve. As mentioned in the introduction, any good compression system can achieve this quality of performance if used correctly. Unfortunately the converse is also true. No matter which system is selected, if it is used incorrectly, or if commercial constraints dictate excessive compression ratios, the result will be degraded images and an inferior experience for the theatre viewer.

The Concept of Visually Lossless

As discussed in the preceding section, it can be very difficult to judge whether or not a given distortion, viewed under particular conditions, is relevant to the quality of the viewing experience. Some of the changes introduced by a lossy compression system do not affect this experience. For example, the original image may contain fine detail that is invisible to a normal viewer, even seated in the front row of a theatre. Slight losses in these areas—provided no other artifacts are introduced—probably do not impact the viewing experience.

In an attempt to set a standard requirement, workers in the Digital Cinema field have determined that the compression used should be *visually lossless*. Various groups have struggled with the definition, and there are a number of slight variations in wording. However, the intent is clear to most, and this wording conveys the concept as well as any:

Visually lossless is understood to mean that the reconstructed moving pictures after decompression shall not be distinguishable from the original by a human observer when exposed to typical viewing conditions in a theatre set-up. This applies to different kinds of material such as live action and computer generated. These conditions include assessment by experienced viewers and projection on a large screen in a typical theatrical environment.

SAMPLING OF IMAGES

Compression systems operate on digital data, generally obtained by sampling images. In the case of an electronic camera, sampling occurs at the image sensor in the camera; for images captured on film, sampling is performed in the film scanning process.

The *sampling* process measures the light received from the scene or transmitted through the film at each sampling point or—more precisely—the total light received over a small area surrounding the sampling point, as shown in Figure 5.1. The measurement (still an analog value at this stage) is then *quantized* so that it may be represented by a digital word.

Quantization applies a code word that represents either the light intensity or the film density. The number of bits used in quantization determines the number of possible code words and, therefore, how accurately the measured value can be represented. Figure 5.2 shows a 3-bit quantizer where any analog value is represented by the nearest of eight possible values, each represented by a 3-bit code. This is, of course, a very crude approximation, but it serves to illustrate the principle.

Generally the coding is arranged to be nonlinear with respect to light because a small step in the quantity of light close to black (in a dark area of a scene) is much more significant than an equal step close to white (in a light area of a scene). *Density coding*, or *logarithmic coding* of light, or *power-law* (gamma-corrected) *coding* of light, all approximate to perceptual uniformity—in other words, all the quantization steps represent roughly equal increments to the HVS. The DCI specification calls for power-law coding

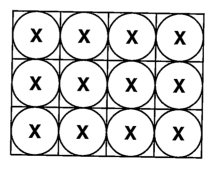

FIGURE
5.1

A representation of the sampling process. The squares indicate pixels, where one pixel is the area of the image represented by a single sample value. The sample points are shown as Xs. The circles show an example of the area from which light might be collected for a single sample.

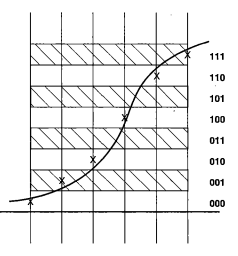

111
110
101
100
011
010
001
000

FIGURE

5.2

A simple 3-bit quantizer. The curved line represents an analog signal, and the vertical lines the sample points. Each sample value (X) falls into one of the eight bands, and is allocated the corresponding binary value. Some sample values are accurately represented; others are approximated. The deviation between actual values and quantized values is known as *quantization noise*.

with a gamma value of 2.6, and 12 bits per color per sample (4096 possible values for each of X, Y, and Z).

Sampling is an extremely important part of the overall process. In one sense this is obvious: it is the sampling that generates the digital data that forms the basis of Digital Cinema. However, this step is critical in another respect. If the sampling is performed improperly, it can introduce errors that cannot be removed later. Of particular relevance to this chapter, errors introduced by improper sampling may prevent a compression system from performing as designed.

To understand sampling, and to understand compression, we need to think about image frequencies and sampling frequencies. Normally *frequency* suggests measurement with respect to time, but frequencies can be measured in space as well, and spatial frequency is an important concept for sampling and compression.

Spatial frequency is the rate of change of lightness within an image as we move within the image. It is most obvious when we think of the gratings within a resolution test chart. As we move within the image, the lightness changes from black to white and back to black. In some areas the changes are spread out (low spatial frequency); in others they are very close together (high spatial frequency) as shown in Figure 5.3.

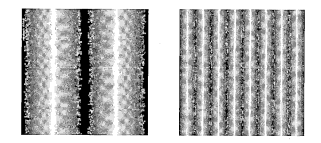

FIGURE   Low spatial frequencies (left) and high spatial frequencies (right).

5.3

Spatial frequency can be measured in a number of ways, such as cycles per millimeter, or line pairs per picture height. Similarly, spatial sampling frequency can be expressed as samples per millimeter, or samples per picture height. Spatial frequency can be measured in any direction, but it is generally adequate to consider just the horizontal and vertical directions.

Sampling theory is very complex, but the most important rule is easy to understand. It is known as the *Nyquist theorem*. Nyquist tells us that sampling is valid only if the highest frequency sampled is less than half the sampling frequency. In terms of samples of an image, this means that the highest spatial frequency in the image must correspond to more than two samples. This makes sense: there must be at least one sample for "up" or "light" and one for "down" or "dark." Less obvious is what happens if we do not enforce this rule. Frequencies above the Nyquist limit are translated by the sampling process into low-frequency sampling artifacts.

Figure 5.4 shows an artificial example that illustrates the mechanism of artifact creation. The "x" marks represent sampling points. The solid line shows a frequency above the Nyquist frequency for this sampling—in other words, the spatial frequency represented by the solid line is more than half the spatial frequency of the sampling. The dotted line represents a much lower frequency, but the values that would be measured by the sampling system are identical! The result is that if the high frequency is present in the image when it is sampled, the samples will represent the lower frequency and this frequency will be present in the displayed image even though it was not part of the original scene.

Unfortunately, once the sampling has been performed there is no way to tell whether the low frequency is "real" (i.e., part of the scene) or an artifact created by sampling at a rate too low for the image content. It gets worse: at

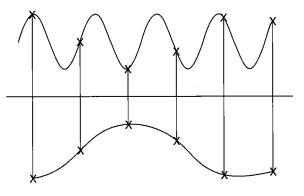

FIGURE

5.4

Violation of Nyquist (see text). The upper signal is above the Nyquist frequency, so the samples "X" will be interpreted as if they are the (identical value) samples of the signal shown below, and this lower-frequency signal will appear on the display.

the spatial frequencies of interest for imagery, the HVS is much more sensitive to the lower artifact frequencies than to the high-frequency image content, so the artifacts are very visible.

This phenomenon is responsible for filmed wagon wheels appearing to go backwards, moiré patterns, and other common misrepresentations of reality.

COMPRESSION SYSTEMS FOR MOTION PICTURES

Motion picture systems such as film and television rely on a phenomenon of the human visual system related to persistence of vision. It is found that if a sufficiently rapid sequence of images of a scene is presented to the HVS, it is interpreted as an acceptable representation of the scene, even if it includes moving images.

In the case of moving picture film, or its equivalents, we photograph the scene repeatedly. Each exposure is recorded on a separate film frame generally at 24 fps, and usually the print is shown at 24 fps, with each frame being displayed twice for a flash rate of 48 fps.

So one way of compressing a motion picture sequence is simply to compress each frame as a static image. Each individual frame is then decoded for projection. Figure 5.5 shows the concept. Such a compression scheme is described as *intra-frame* because all of the information is derived from

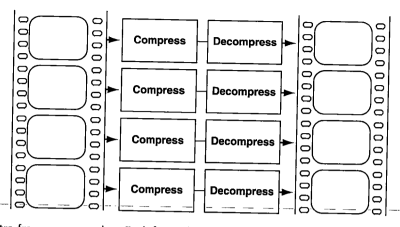

FIGURE

5.5

Intra-frame compression. Each frame is treated as a separate entity, and compressed without any reference to other frames.

within the single frame being processed at the time. This is a viable approach and, at the time of writing, a compression system of this type is being considered as a standard for Digital Cinema.

However, it is easy to see that intra-frame techniques do not exploit all of the redundancy in a motion picture sequence. If we hold a strip of motion picture film up to the light, we see a sequence of very similar images, as shown in Figure 5.6. Moving objects appear at slightly different places in each frame, and if the camera is panning, the background is slightly displaced frame to frame. Nevertheless, there is typically a great deal of commonality from frame to frame. In other words there is redundancy; it should be not be necessary to send information repeatedly that represents the same image content.

If we can find a way of exploiting this redundancy, it should be possible to increase the compression efficiency significantly. Such techniques are called *temporal compression* because use is made of redundancy over time, or *inter-frame* because coding of one frame may use information from one or more other frames.

Note that the use of inter-frame encoding can provide more compression, but this does not in itself imply lower quality. Inter-frame compression can provide the same quality at a lower bit rate than intra-frame—or it can provide higher quality at the same bit rate.

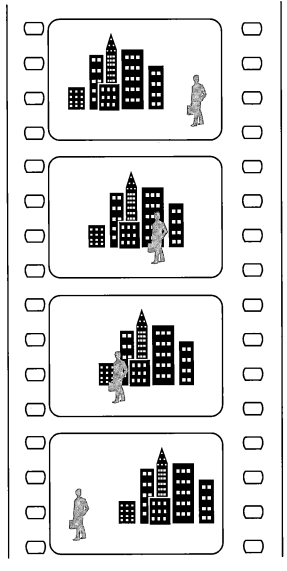

FIGURE

5.6

Even though the foreground object is moving, and the camera is panning, there is a great deal of image content common to the four frames.

Spatial Compression

Spatial compression is intra-frame encoding. These techniques take a single image, or part of an image, and compress without using information from any other image. Spatial compression in Digital Cinema is very similar to compression of a single still photograph, except that the process is performed for each frame of the movie.

FUNDAMENTAL CONCEPTS

Real image data is, to some extent, correlated. This means that there are dependencies among lightness values in parts of the picture. An image created by a lens capturing a real scene cannot have lightness values that are completely random. This means that, to a certain degree, some values can be predicted from other values, at least in terms of their probability. It follows that, given sufficient understanding of the nature of these dependencies, the data can be coded in a more efficient manner.

Communication theory uses the concept of *entropy*. A sampled monochrome image, quantized at 8 bits, uses 8 bits per pixel when coded in a simple manner. However, if we design a perfect coding system specifically for that data set, then when we examine the whole image it might be possible to use only 40% of the bits, for an average of 3.2 bits per pixel. The entropy of the image is said to be 3.2 bits per pixel.

It is possible to build coding systems that—quite losslessly—represent images at very close to their entropy value, but this generally represents compression of around 2:1—not enough for our needs.

The entropy of the data representing an image can be calculated, and this value—according to current communications theory—represents the theoretical limit for a lossless encoder. To obtain greater compression we need to turn to lossy techniques. However, the techniques just described can be applied to the output of a lossy compression system as well.

TRANSFORMS

A *transform* is a set of mathematical equations that can be used to represent a set of data in a different way. For example, image data may be transformed from one color space to another: *RGB* to *XYZ* to *YUV*.

Some transforms are reversible; the transformed data may be passed through an *inverse transform,* and, given sufficient precision in the calculations, the original data are recovered. Some transforms are inherently non-reversible. For example, *RGB* data of a full-color image may be transformed into data representing a monochrome image, but there is no way to recreate the color image from the monochrome data. Generally, transforms used in compression are fully reversible.

Lossy compression systems need to determine what data are unnecessary or can be more crudely represented without significant harm to the image as perceived by the HVS. A system cannot just discard samples, or reduce the precision of some parts of the image because the viewer can choose to look at any part of an image. In this respect the HVS has no significant limitations.

However, if we look at images a different way, we can find some HVS limitations to exploit. The HVS has a *contrast sensitivity* response that varies with spatial frequency. We need to consider both the spatial frequencies in the image and the viewing distance, but these can be combined by calculating frequencies as cycles per degree at the observer position.

The HVS is extremely sensitive in the range of 1 to 5 cycles per degree; under ideal conditions it can detect lightness variations of around 0.1% in this frequency range. Outside this range the sensitivity decreases substantially. At high spatial frequencies in particular, there must be a much greater variation before the change can be perceived. At about 20 cycles per degree the sensitivity is almost zero. This suggests that higher spatial frequencies could be encoded using a lesser number of bits.

Figure 5.7 shows a contrast sensitivity chart. It shows a range of spatial frequencies on one axis and a range of contrast values on the other. When viewed from an appropriate distance it should be possible to see the full contrast range at some frequencies and observe that other frequencies are visible only at high contrast.

Unfortunately, the image data that come from sampling just tell us the lightness (or color) value at each point. Individual samples provide no information about spatial frequencies in the image.

The transforms used in present-day compression systems convert pixel data sets into data sets that represent the spatial frequencies present in the image or part of the image.

Two families of transforms are in common use, known as the *discrete cosine transform* (DCT) and the *wavelet transform*. These transforms are quite different in the mathematics and the way they are applied, but they both do the same job: convert location (pixel) data into frequency data.

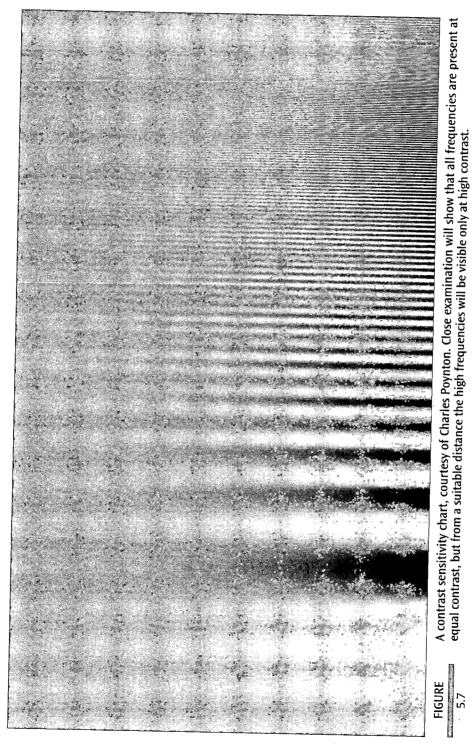

FIGURE
5.7
A contrast sensitivity chart, courtesy of Charles Poynton. Close examination will show that all frequencies are present at equal contrast, but from a suitable distance the high frequencies will be visible only at high contrast.

DCT transforms

The DCT is a derivative of the *Fourier transform*, optimized for use on blocks of sampled data. However, it is not necessary to understand Fourier transforms to gain an appreciation of how DCT works.

Most DCT systems operate on blocks of data representing a square section of an image, eight pixels horizontally by eight pixels vertically, but we can look at the operation by considering just one row of eight pixels. Prior to the transform, each of the eight values represents the lightness or color of one pixel. The transform has to convert these values to values representing the various spatial frequencies in this part of the image. There are only a few possible frequencies because of the Nyquist limitation; with only eight samples there must be fewer than four complete cycles of image information.

DCT works by defining a set of *basis functions* representing the possible frequencies. The basis functions for the 8×1 DCT are shown in Figure 5.8. Each is itself a set of eight sample values, and each represents one possible frequency that may be present in the image samples.

The basis functions are chosen so that some combination of (positive or negative) multiples of the basis functions can match any set of eight sample values. The set of multipliers becomes the transformed values, or *DCT coefficients*. The process of calculating these coefficients is quite laborious; each basis function is multiplied, pixel by pixel, by the original set of values, and the result is integrated.

One analogy for this process is a paintbox with patterns rather than colors. By choosing the correct mix of the eight basis function patterns, it is possible to "paint" any set of eight pixel values. The transform coefficients are the "quantities" of each pattern that were used. Given sufficient precision this shows that the transform is reversible; by definition, multiplying the transform coefficients by the known basis functions will generate the original set of sample values.

In image compression a 2-dimensional DCT is used on blocks of (usually) 8×8 pixels. In this case there are 64 two-dimensional basis functions, each representing some combination of horizontal frequency and vertical frequency. The 64 two-dimensional basis functions are shown in Figure 5.9. The principle is the same; some combination of different multiples of the 64 patterns can generate any possible set of 8×8 pixel values, and the set of multipliers is the set of transformed coefficients. In this case, each 8×8 pixel block generates an 8×8 block of DCT coefficients.

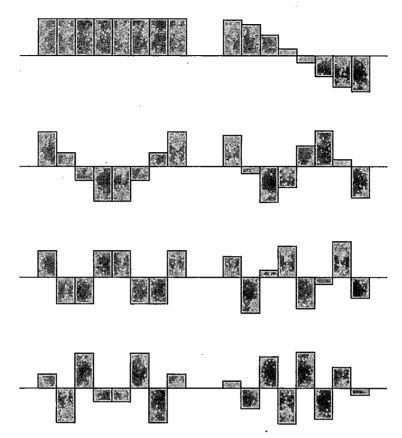

FIGURE 5.8

The set of 1-dimensional DCT basis functions representing the different spatial frequencies that may be present in a row of eight samples. The combination of these with their vertical equivalents generates the 64 2-dimensional basis functions shown in Figure 5.9.

It should be noted that this process does not reduce the amount of data—in fact, to maintain enough precision to make the transform reversible the transform coefficients need more bits than the original pixel values. The importance of the transform is that the image content is now expressed in terms of its frequency content, and we can make decisions based on the known characteristics of the HVS. However, before examining this process we will look at the chief competitor to DCT, the wavelet transform.

Wavelet Transforms

The wavelet transform is quite different from DCT and is used in a different way to analyze the image, but there are also strong similarities.

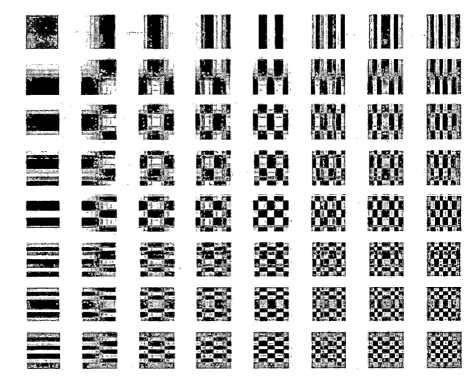

FIGURE   The 64 2-dimensional DCT basis functions.

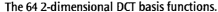

5.9

DCT is used to analyze small discreet blocks of an image; it has a set of basis functions, all the same size as the image block. When a DCT is performed, all of the frequency-based information for a small area of the image is extracted at one time. The resulting transform coefficients are also in blocks; the same size and the same number as the pixel blocks of the original image.

The wavelet transform needs only a single basis function (although it is usually implemented as separate horizontal and vertical functions). The wavelet basis function is more complex, but the process of point-by-point multiplication followed by integration is similar to that used with the DCT basis functions. However, instead of being applied to a block of pixels, it is moved, pixel by pixel (mathematically, *convolved*), over the entire image. Figure 5.10 shows a typical basis function, usually known just as a *wavelet*.

The wavelet convolution process measures the contribution of a single frequency band to the image, and the wavelet can then be scaled to extract another range of frequency information. One "pass" of the wavelet extracts a part of the frequency information from all, or a large part, of the image.

Actually, the implementation is even more clever than this. The first convolution measures (creates coefficients for) the highest frequency band. Once this is known, those frequencies can be extracted (filtered out) from the image. When the highest frequencies have been eliminated, the number of samples in the image can be reduced, because the Nyquist limit has been lowered. In practice, the number of pixels in each dimension is halved (reducing the number of pixels to one-quarter). The identical wavelet can then be used again, but because of the smaller image it will extract a lower range of frequencies. This process can be repeated until the image is reduced to just a few pixels that can be coded by any convenient process. This iterative process creates successively smaller sets of coefficients for lower and lower frequencies.

Wavelet transforms are more complex than DCT, but there are two distinct advantages. Because the wavelet operates on the complete image, there are no blocks. At low bit rates (high compression ratios) the block structure of DCT-based systems can become visible as a very objectionable artifact. Wavelet-based systems also produce artifacts at low bit rates, but these tend to have a "smeared" appearance and are not so immediately objectionable. This is not a very significant factor for Digital Cinema because other requirements make it unlikely that such low bit rates would be used.

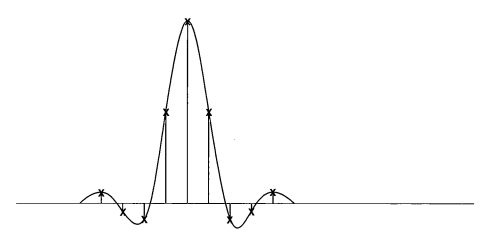

FIGURE

5.10

A typical wavelet. The wavelet is generally visualized as the curved line, but the implementation is really the series of sample values shown.

The other advantage of wavelet-based systems is potentially very important to Digital Cinema. By its very nature, the compressed bit stream produced by a wavelet system contains decodable representations of smaller versions of the image. A decoder can start with the very low frequencies (small image) and decode successively higher frequency bands (larger images) until it has decoded the desired image size, *and then it need go no further*. If a 4K image is compressed by a wavelet-based system, it is possible for a decoder attached to a 2K projector to decode just the 2K image and ignore all the remaining data in the bit stream.

Quantization

Either of the transforms discussed above can convert image data into a form in which the image is described in terms of its spatial frequency content. In itself, this has not achieved any compression—in fact, both of these transforms generate coefficients that require more bits than the original pixel values! However, the intent of the transform is to put the information into a form in which the limitations of the HVS can be exploited.

The next step is quantization. Of course, the original data are already quantized; the precision was one of the fundamental parameters of the digital image. If the bit depth of the lightness values is reduced, contouring will be visible and the image will be drastically impaired. With the transformed data, however, we have more flexibility. Because of the contrast sensitivity response of the HVS, we can reduce the bit depth of some of the transform coefficients quite considerably without significant change to the perceived image.

The contrast sensitivity response of the HVS falls rapidly with increasing spatial frequency. High spatial frequency detail that has low contrast is just not perceived and need not be transmitted. Less obvious, but verifiable, is the fact that the coefficients representing the higher spatial frequencies can be coarsely quantized without significant visible effect. At these higher frequencies the HVS needs only an approximation of the original amplitude to provide a visual experience indistinguishable from the original.

So, in a compression system the transform coefficients are reduced in precision according to some formula. Obviously this reduces the quantity of data that must be transmitted, but there is a far more significant effect. With real images many of the transform coefficients are very small. When the precision is decreased, the small coefficients are truncated or rounded to zero.

The result of these operations is a set of transform coefficients, some represented by a relatively small number of bits and many equal to zero. The reverse transform will yield a set of pixel values that will form the reconstructed, or decompressed, image. Providing the quantization is not excessive, this image, when viewed at the intended distance, can be indistinguishable from the original.

The qualification is very important. We have made use of the limitations of the HVS and, in particular, its contrast sensitivity response. This function relates sensitivity to spatial frequency measured in cycles per degree—a value dependent on both image content and viewing distance. If the reconstructed image is viewed at a substantially different distance, the assumptions made in the quantization process will be invalid.

Lossless Coding

The final step in a compression system is to code the remaining information in the most efficient manner possible. This is typically a two-stage process. The first stage uses knowledge of the image structure and the transform to arrange and pre-code the data in a form suitable for the second stage, the *entropy encoder*.

Various techniques are used in the first stage. In DCT systems, the block of transform coefficients is scanned in an order calculated to maximize runs of zeros in the scanned sequence. *Run length coding* (a special code that indicates several repetitions of the same value) is very efficient. In another example, wavelet systems use tree structures to predict zero values. All systems use predictive techniques to remove further redundancy from the data.

Finally the data is processed by the entropy coder. In its simplest form, the entropy encoder uses short codes to represent values that occur very frequently and longer codes to represent the less common values. This is known as *variable length coding* (VLC). VLC systems depend on knowledge of the statistics of the data to be coded.

Modern compression systems use enhanced versions of VLC such as *context-adaptive variable length coding* (CAVLC) or more sophisticated entropy encoders such as arithmetic coding, and *context adaptive binary arithmetic coding* (CABAC). These technologies can adjust to varying statistics of the data and are a specialist subject in their own right.

Summary

The elements of a generic spatial encoder are shown in Figure 5.11. Note that this diagram applies to both DCT and wavelet systems. The transforms are different and, as a result, so are the prediction and ordering steps. However, the fundamentals are the same: transform into the frequency domain, quantize, and losslessly encode the quantized data.

TEMPORAL COMPRESSION

Spatial encoders are intended to remove redundancy from a single image. As discussed above, usually there will be image content that is common to many frames, and this obviously represents redundancy.

It is possible to design 3-dimensional transforms: DCT, wavelet, or others. Unfortunately, transforms usually work well only when the data to be

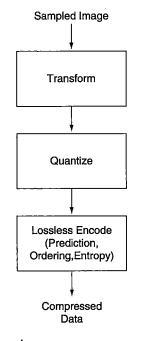

FIGURE   The elements of a spatial encoder.

5.11

transformed conform to the Nyquist limit. We can ensure this for spatial data, but frame rates in cinema (and video) are too low for all but the slowest motion. In simple terms, there are not enough temporal samples to accurately "track" a moving object. Three-dimensional DCT systems have been tried without great success. Work continues on 3-dimensional wavelet transforms, but no viable system has been demonstrated at the time of writing.

However, the redundancy still exists, and practical temporal compression seeks to extract it by using picture fragments that have previously been encoded as part of another frame.

In a scene where the camera does not move, we could code one frame, decode it at the theatre, display the frame, and also store it for further use. Then, for subsequent frames, instead of coding the background areas, we could just instruct the decoder to use the background areas from the previously stored frame.

This simplistic approach does not help with objects in the scene that move, and it fails completely if the camera pans because the background is no longer in the same position on the frame. To increase the coding efficiency significantly and reliably, we need a method of reusing parts of a previously coded image, even if they appear in different parts of the frame. This is the role of motion estimation.

Motion Estimation

Motion estimation in compression systems is the process of searching for an area in a previously encoded image (the *reference picture*) that matches the area being coded in the current picture. For example, the current image may contain a red car. The process of motion estimation is to take a fragment of the image of the red car and to see if an identical, or almost identical, fragment exists in an image that has already been coded, sent to, and stored at the decoder. If we find such a fragment we can instruct the decoder to retrieve the information from the stored image and use it in the current image.

This technique is most easily applied to DCT systems because the coding is performed in blocks. In the MPEG-2 system, for example, the DCT blocks are 8×8 pixels; motion estimation uses *macroblocks* that are 16×16, or four DCT blocks. Motion estimation has been used with wavelet-based systems, but it is more difficult to obtain substantial gains in efficiency.

Motion-Compensated Prediction

Motion-compensated prediction is the process of using motion estimation to predict the content of parts of the current image. The motion estimator attempts to find, in a reference picture, image fragments that correspond to image fragments in the picture currently being encoded. If such fragments are found, this means that part of the current picture may be encoded by a simple pointer to the fragment in the reference picture. The pointer must be a vector, because the fragment may not be in the same position in the reference image. This vector is called a *motion vector* and represents both a horizontal and a vertical displacement. The motion vector tells the decoder where to go in the stored reference picture, relative to the position in the current picture, to get the predicted fragment. The result is that we can assemble a prediction of the current picture (probably incomplete) from fragments extracted from one or more reference pictures.

Two further steps are necessary. All parts of the current picture for which no equivalent was found in the reference picture(s) need to be encoded by the spatial coding techniques discussed above. We must also transmit a motion vector for each fragment used in the prediction. If every prediction was a perfect match this would be all that was needed. In reality, however, the fragments often do not match perfectly, and it may be necessary to send correction data called *residuals* to achieve the required accuracy. Residuals are formed by subtracting the predicted fragment from the current image data and encoding the differences using spatial techniques. A good encoder will always check that the sum of coded motion vectors plus coded residuals is less than the data required to spatially encode the same picture fragment.

I-Pictures, P-Pictures, and B-Pictures

I-pictures are "free-standing" pictures where only intra-frame techniques are used for coding. All coded data are derived from the current picture without reference to any other picture. *P-* and *B-pictures* both use motion-compensated inter-frame prediction to achieve (generally) higher coding efficiency.

Motion-compensated prediction can be performed only if the reference picture already exists at the decoder because the decoder will be told to extract a fragment from it to use in the current picture. This means that the reference picture must have been encoded and transmitted to the decoder before the encode process is started for the current picture.

P-pictures (*predicted pictures*) use the obvious approach. The P-picture uses a reference picture earlier in the sequence. However, if we are prepared to reorder the pictures for transmission, all reference pictures do not have to be "earlier" in the picture sequence. For example, in the picture sequence shown in Figure 5.12 we can choose to encode and transmit frames 1 and 5, and put frames 2, 3, and 4 aside until this has been done. We can the use picture fragments from both frames 1 and 5 while coding frames 2, 3, and 4. This reordering increases memory requirements at both encoder and decoder. It also increases delay in real-time systems, but this should not be significant in Digital Cinema.

B-pictures in MPEG-2 are coded using two reference pictures, one before and one after the current picture. The latest MPEG-4 *codec* (an abbreviation for coder-decoder) permits the use of multiple reference pictures, before or after the current picture.

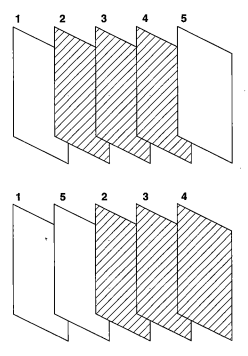

FIGURE
5.12

The display order of a sequence of frames is shown in the upper diagram. However, for bi-directional prediction the two reference frames must be sent to the decoder before the dependent frames, so the transmission order is as shown in the lower diagram.

Summary

Temporal compression is sometimes criticized in the context of Digital Cinema because it is often used in the video world to help provide very high levels of compression—with consequent artifacting. However, temporal compression can provide significant improvements in coding gain without loss of quality.

At the time of writing, the designers of Digital Cinema have provisionally selected a wavelet-based system for Digital Cinema. It is probable, therefore, that (at least) the first large-scale implementations of Digital Cinema will not use temporal compression.

COMPRESSION SYSTEMS AND STANDARDS

This section provides a very brief overview of standardized compression systems that may be relevant to Digital Cinema. Early experimental deployments have used a number of techniques, mostly proprietary. Examples include a variable block-sized DCT-based system from QUALCOMM and a wavelet-based system from QuVis. This latter system demonstrated in early 2004 playout of a 2K presentation from a 4K compressed file.

MPEG, ITU, and JVT

The MPEG-2 system, widely used in television, is limited to 8-bit precision, and most commercially available components can provide only 4:2:0 coding. However, the syntax of MPEG is very robust and extensible, and some early experimental Digital Cinema systems were based on proprietary extensions of MPEG-2.

MPEG-4 Part 2, the original video codec of MPEG-4, is more complex and offers more coding choices than MPEG-2 but not much greater coding efficiency. For this and other reasons it has gained little market acceptance.

For its latest offering MPEG teamed up with the experts group of the International Telecommunications Union (ITU) and formed the *Joint Video Team* (JVT). This team produced a new codec that, in some applications at least, offers about twice the coding efficiency of MPEG-2. The codec is variously known as *H.264* (the ITU designation), *MPEG-4 Part 10*, or the MPEG *Advanced Video Codec* (AVC).

AVC as originally standardized in 2003 is 8-bit only, 4:2:0 only, so it is quite unsuitable for Digital Cinema. However, at the time of writing, JVT is completing work on the *fidelity range extensions* to AVC, offering various profiles up to 4:4:4 at 12-bit resolution. These extensions should make AVC technically capable of meeting the needs of Digital Cinema. Unfortunately, the proposed licensing terms may be seen as an inhibiting factor.

JPEG2000

The original JPEG was a DCT-based system designed for static images. This standard was subsequently extended in a number of proprietary systems to provide coding for motion images.

JPEG2000 also started life as compression for static images, using wavelet technology, but this time the committee also standardized the extensions necessary for motion imaging. Motion JPEG2000 does not use temporal compression; each frame is wavelet-compressed individually. JPEG2000 provides the capability of compressing a 4K file and extracting only the 2K image if that is all that is required.

In 2004 DCI selected JPEG2000 as the technology of choice for digital cinema. It appears to offer all the technical attributes desired, and—for now—is believed to be royalty-free. However, DCI has chosen constant-quality encoding, and to use MXF packaging, so the tools in the Motion JPEG2000 extensions will not be used. The initial tests with JPEG2000 used 10-bit RGB files, and these were encoded at rates of 75 and 125 Mbps for 2K resolution, and 100 and 200 Mbps for 4K resolution. Tests with 12-bit $X'Y'Z'$ files will be conducted later in 2004, along with tests to determine the peak bitrates for both 2K and 4K.

INTELLECTUAL PROPERTY AND LICENSING

Compression systems are incredibly complex and rely on a great deal of research and development from the companies that participate in and contribute to creating the standards. These companies need to see a return on their investment, and they expect to achieve this by licensing the patents they are awarded for their technologies. Unfortunately, licensees' and licensors' ideas of "reasonable" royalties do not always coincide!

The situation is complicated by the fact that many companies hold patents that are essential to any given compression standard. It would be impractical for every potential user to have to negotiate a license with each patent holder, so the patent holders of MPEG-2 formed a consortium to offer licenses and share out the royalties to the patent holders. Not everyone liked the MPEG-2 license, but it was acceptable to a large number of potential users, and this was one of the factors leading to the enormous success of MPEG-2.

A similar arrangement was made for MPEG-4 Part 2, but there was an inordinate delay in publishing licensing terms, and the terms when published were almost universally rejected because of their pricing structure. Revised terms were published a few months later but still failed to generate any enthusiasm. A number of factors contributed to the marketplace failure of MPEG-4 Part 2, and the failure to agree in a timely manner on acceptable licensing terms was certainly one of them.

This history has made potential users very nervous about the licensing terms for MPEG AVC. At the time of writing, two organizations are trying to form consortia of patent holders and are publishing very different proposed licensing terms. There has been movement to satisfy the complaints of some potential users, but the situation is far from clear. For the field of Digital Cinema this may be academic. The history of MPEG-4 licensing has left many in Hollywood opposed to adopting any MPEG standard. In contrast, JPEG200 is thought (again, at the time of writing) to be royalty-free, but it is impossible to be certain.

CONCLUSIONS

Compression is a vital part of Digital Cinema. For the foreseeable future, electronic delivery of high-quality movies will be quite impractical without it. However, any one of a number of compression systems is capable of meeting the technical requirements if used correctly. Equally, any compression system will produce unacceptable results if used improperly.

The choice of compression system for the first Digital Cinema standards will be based on a combination of factors. The ability of wavelet-based systems to provide multi-resolution playout from a single file is attractive. Other factors will include compression efficiency and licensing terms. Finally, any candidate compression system must be tested and verified using the chosen color components and bit depth, currently expected to be $X'Y'Z'$ at 12 bits.

Security and Packaging

Security

Robert Schumann
Cinea, Inc.

Security within the Digital Cinema infrastructure is of paramount importance. The average cost of making and marketing a movie by the MPAA member companies in 2003 was $102.9 million.[1] The value of the content is both this sunk development cost plus any profits derived from future revenues. In addition, even though thousands of copies will be made for the cinema release, each individual digital copy carries the entire value with it. Thus, for all practical purposes, security in the context of Digital Cinema is the equivalent of protecting considerably more than $100 million during shipment from the studio, while stored in the theatre, and during playout.

SECURITY PRIMER

Protection of electronic goods is similar to protection of any other valuable property. Many of the same techniques and tools, although updated in their electronic form, are employed. This should not be surprising given that the problem of stopping and finding thieves has been around for as

---

[1]www.mpaa.org

long as civilization, and we have a lot of experience in understanding what works.

The techniques employed fall into one of two categories: stopping thieves from getting unauthorized access to the data and finding and prosecuting thieves if and when they do succeed at getting access. Before determining how to protect against threats, however, it is critical to perform an analysis of the potential threats, the likelihood of their occurrence, and the impact if they occur. Finally it is helpful to understand that all security systems will eventually fail: thus, a critical component of any design is to understand how and when renewal of the security system will occur.

Stopping the Thieves

Theft of digital content can occur in many ways, primarily differentiated by the nature of the access that the potential thief has. A perfect protection system could be developed by locking the digital content into a Kryptonite safe and destroying the key. Of course this approach, while providing perfect security from thieves, also prevents usage of the content. An alternative is to leave everything completely unprotected, no locks on the doors, and no passwords. Doing this solves the usage problem but obviously makes an extremely easy target for thieves. The goal, therefore, is to build systems such that legitimate use of the content is enabled while providing reasonable security.

The basic building block of content protection is the partitioning of environment into two areas where the content needs to be available for use and areas where it is just being stored or moved around. The area where the data are accessible for use is referred to as a *protected enclave.* A protected enclave is, by definition, deemed to be a secure location, and the security of the overall system is determined, in part, by the security at the boundary of the enclaves in which the content is available for use.

Content Encryption

When digital data are outside of a secure enclave they are protected using technology that is known as *encryption.* Encryption is the act of obfuscating the original data (*cleartext* or *plaintext*) such that one cannot convert the encrypted data (*ciphertext*) back into plaintext without the knowledge of a secret (the *key*). These encryption schemes are known as *ciphers*. Over the millennia there have been thousands of different encryption systems developed to protect personal, business, military and government secrets. Almost every encryption system has been broken as well. Historical examples of ciphers and protection systems include the Cipher of Mary Queen of Scots, Navajo Code, and the Enigma Machine developed by Arthur Scherbius. For an informative overview of the history of encryption, *The Code Book* by Simon Singh is recommended.[2]

Modern digital ciphers are almost always based on mathematical and/or logical manipulations of digital data and can be broken into two classes: *symmetric* and *asymmetric*, based on whether the sender and receiver use the same (symmetric) or different keys (asymmetric). Symmetric ciphers require that both the sender and receiver have access to exactly the same secret keys. Symmetric ciphers typically use smaller key sizes and as a result can be much more efficient and operate much faster using significantly smaller computational resources than asymmetric ciphers. The two most commonly used modern symmetric ciphers are *Digital Encryption Standard* (DES), and *Advanced Encryption Standard* (AES), with AES being the newer of the two systems.

DES was adopted as a Federal Information Processing Standard (FIPS) specification in 1976. It is the 56-bit version of the Lucifer cipher developed by Horst Fiestel of IBM. DES processes 64-bit blocks of data. Brute force attacks on the 56-bit version are now feasible with off-the-shelf hardware; thus, most modern systems use a variant (FIPS 46-3) called 3-DES (or *triple DES*) that performs three 56-bit passes that provide an effective 168-bit key length.

AES was adopted by the U.S. government in May 2002 as FIPS 197 after a multi-year analysis and selection process. AES is based on the Rijndael cipher developed by Joan Daemon and Vincent Rijmen of Belgium. AES processes 128-bit blocks of data and FIPS 197 specifies 128-, 196-, and 256-bit key lengths as standard.

Asymmetric ciphers are based on certain mathematical properties such that a pair of matched keys is created. However, these keys are not identical and knowing one of the pair does not enable one to determine the other matched key. Items encrypted with one key can be decrypted with the other,

---

[2]Simon Singh, *The Code Book: The Science of Secrecy from Ancient Egypt to Quantum Cryptography,* (Anchor; August 29, 2000)

matched, key. However, these ciphers have the characteristic that the key used to encrypt data cannot be used to decrypt the data. The keys used in these asymmetric ciphers are commonly known as public/private key pairs, as one side will keep secret the *private key* while publishing the *public key*. This is often used for email systems where an individual can send the public key to everyone he or she corresponds with. The correspondents can then use the public key to encrypt their message. The message, however, can only be decrypted using the private key, thus, even other people with knowledge of the public key cannot read the message. Messages can therefore be safely sent to an individual with the knowledge that only that individual can read them. Note that when the private key is used to encrypt a message, anyone with the public key can *decrypt* the message, but the receivers can be assured that only the holder of the private key could have *sent* the message. In this way asymmetric ciphers can be used not only to protect the confidentiality of the data but to provide authentication of where the data came from.

Modern asymmetric ciphers tend to be very computationally intensive, as they require long keys and the ciphers themselves are quite mathematically complex. Thus these ciphers are typically used for small data sets (often including the delivery of symmetric keys). The most commonly used asymmetric cipher is the *RSA* cipher developed by Ronald *R*ivest, Adi *S*hamir, and Leonard *A*dleman in 1977. It is based on the use of large prime number pairs as the basis for determining a matched key pair. The strength of the cipher is based on the computational difficulty in factoring prime numbers. In practice, this requires 1024- or 2048-bit keys to ensure that brute force factoring cannot be applied.

Key Management

Having the strongest protection materials in the world does no good if the keys to unlock the data are not equally protected. For example, having a kryptonite door on your house does you no good if you leave the key under the mat. Thus the mechanisms for creating, storing, transporting, and using the keys are critical features of any security system. In protecting digital content, symmetric ciphers are almost always used. Since these ciphers require both the sender and the receiver to share a common key, the problem becomes how to securely teach the receiver the necessary symmetric key. It is common to use an asymmetric cipher, such as RSA, to encrypt the symmetric key. The receiver can publish its public key, which the sender then uses to encrypt the symmetric key. This solves the issue of transporting the content keys between the secure enclaves in which they are created and used.

Certificates

The use of asymmetric ciphers solves the issue of protecting sensitive keying information during transport. However, it does nothing to help the sender of the sensitive information understand whether or not the public key provided by the receiver actually came from the legitimate receiver or whether the delivery has been intercepted by an adversary (bad guy) who has injected himself or herself into the transport path. In small closed systems, this problem is solved by having a trusted entity deliver, in a trusted fashion, the public keys.

In large environments, such as email, this problem has been addressed by using the idea of a digital certificate. A digital certificate is the digital equivalent of the old wax seal. In practice, all members of the group have knowledge of one or more trusted *roots*. They are taught, in a secure way, the public key of the root. Service providers operate the root and provide a service whereby they digitally "sign" certificates for each member in the group. The sending device can now present its certificate, along with the data (such as the public key). The receiver can validate the certificate (as it has the root's public key) and thus validate the sender's transmission.

In practice these certificates can be and are chained, so the root need not know about every leaf in the tree. However, a receiver can always follow the chain until it finds a certificate whose signer it can verify. At worst, this would require following the chain all the way to the root. A common certificate format used today is the *ITU-T X.509* certificate format standard.

Digital Rights Management

In the area of content security there are two components that must be addressed. The first is cryptographic security (encryption, key management, and certificates) described above. The second component is the set of business rules that control when and how the content may be decrypted (in the case of Digital Cinema, displayed). The process of defining the rules and the systems that interpret the rules is often referred to as *Digital Rights Management* (DRM).

Logging/Auditing

The last major component of a content security system is a mechanism to log events that occur. These events include those associated with content, such as encryption and decryption, as well as with potential security breaches, such as those generated by tamper detection circuitry. From the perspective of protecting the infrastructure, the logs are extremely useful. They can be reviewed and analyzed to detect unusual activity, such as repeated access attempts. In addition the log data can be used in some environments for business purposes, e.g., billing and transaction auditing.[3]

THE VALUE OF SECURITY IN THE SUPPLY CHAIN

Why do we even care about security in Digital Cinema? More important, how much effort should be put into the security systems and operations for this business? In order to effectively answer that question, it is helpful to understand the motion picture industry from an economic perspective. Remember that content piracy is all about economics. First, if distributors gave away their content for free, there would be no piracy. Second, piracy cannot take back the revenue that has already been earned by a distributor. Thus, all anti-piracy efforts are related to protecting the *future* revenue stream generated by a piece of content.

A distributor's revenue streams are affected when individuals who would normally pay the studios to see a movie through a legitimate distribution chain (e.g., in a theatre) are able to acquire and watch the movie through other means that return no revenue to the distributor. This includes individuals who buy "bootleg" DVDs or CDs on the streets around the world as well as those who download movies over the Internet.

Review of Movie Windowing System

The potential economic loss to a studio from illegitimate distribution is directly related to when the illegitimate copies are made available and the

---

[3]There are many valuable resources for further reading into digital security. One is the RSA securities Cryptography FAQ, which can be found at www.rsasecurity.com/rsalabs/faq/index.html.

quality of those copies. The movie business distributes its content in a very controlled series of releases into different distribution channels. This release strategy is commonly referred to as the *window system* and individual channels have their own release window. The normal release chain is:

◆ Theatrical exhibition—Where it is available for public viewing in movie theatres.

◆ In-flight/Early window—Where it is made available for public viewing in more confined or secondary markets such as hotels, airlines, and cruise ships.

◆ Home Entertainment (sometimes still called Home Video)—Where it is first available on DVD or VHS for viewing within customers' homes as rental movies from rental stores and as "sell-thru" product at video and general merchandisers.

◆ Pay-Per-View—Where it is first available on cable and satellite pay-per-view channels.

◆ Premium Cable—Where it is first available on HBO, Showtime, Cinemax, Starz, etc.

◆ Over-the-air TV—Where it is finally available to watch for free on the broadcast TV networks.

Figure 6.1 shows these release windows graphically, overlayed with the percentage of the overall revenues received from each of the windows. From a security perspective, the more important issue is the remaining value of each movie during each of the windows, as shown in Figure 6.2.

This is the amount of money that is at risk at the start of any given window and represents the value that the security mechanisms in that window are protecting. Before the theatrical release the entire future value of the movie is at risk, whereas after the home video window more than 70% of the total revenues have already been wrung out of a movie, thus the risk from pirate copies (as well as the value of the security system) is significantly lower.

What this means is that for a movie such as *Finding Nemo*, which has brought in over $850 million in worldwide theatrical box office receipts, each copy of that movie in a theatre represented $850 million dollars on opening day and its widespread release to pirates could potentially jeopardize that entire amount. Of course overall piracy does not, today, cause that magnitude of loss, although even a 1% loss in this example would mean

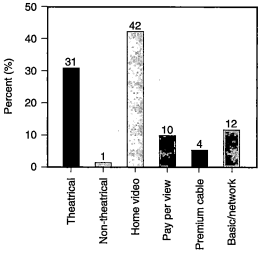

FIGURE
6.1

Release windows shown graphically.

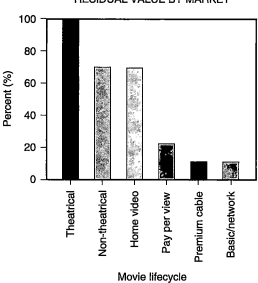

FIGURE
6.2

Release windows with remaining value.

that an additional $8.5 million of revenue was lost to distributors and exhibitors alike. Note that only one copy of a movie is necessary to start the piracy chain.

Potential Losses from Piracy

The economic value (and associated loss to the studio) of a pirate copy is generally related to two factors: the price difference between a pirate copy and a legitimate copy and the quality difference (including convenience) between a pirate copy and a legitimate copy. The two most commonly discussed pirate scenarios exhibit two different extremes.

Professional Pirates

DVD and VCD copies sold by professional pirates are often of inferior quality. Nevertheless they usually command a significant price, and in fact pirate "brands" known for higher quality pictures are able to command a price premium. Why? These professional pirate copies compete in a market in which there are usually no legitimate copies available (either on DVD or in the theatres), and as such even the worst quality copies find some market. In some cases the availability, and quality, of these pirate copies is so great that no legitimate market for the movies is even viable. In countries such as China investment in modern theatre complexes is strangled due to the competition from pirated copies, which are almost always available before a movie is available in what few legitimate theatres exist.[4] This problem is exacerbated by the industry policy of delaying foreign releases for months after U.S. release. Recently studios have experimented with global day and date releases for some major motion pictures, including *Harry Potter and the Prisoner of Azkaban* and *The Matrix Reloaded*. While helping to combat piracy this approach carries significant additional cost and production burdens.[5] It is estimated that this professional piracy results in revenue losses to MPAA member companies (the seven major studios) of more than $3 billion per year.[6]

---

[4]Marcal Joanilho, "China: Don't Drive Us Away, Say Cinema Operators," *The Standard Newspaper*, 29 March 2004, Hong Kong.
[5]Sharon Waxman, "Rings" Shows Trend Towards Global Premieres, *New York Times*, Dec 22, 2003.
[6]Valenti's Views. *Harvard Political Review*, www.hpronline.org/news/2003/01/25/Interviews/Valentis. Views-347207.shtml

Electronic Downloads

Electronic copies distributed via the Internet, including on file-sharing networks, are another increasingly common pirate mechanism. Here the consumer price is $0, and the product competes favorably with legitimate studio content in availability, quality, and convenience of acquisition and viewing. Further, the perceived risk of being caught for the content consumer is nil.

In all cases, the higher the quality of the pirated copy, the greater the loss to the studio as the value to the consumer of the legitimate copy shrinks. This effect can be seen in studies of pirate content on the Web.[7] Initial copies on the Web are often of lower quality (e.g., made by hand-held camcorders). As better-quality copies become available they quickly replace the lower-quality copies. Studies of content downloading in the United States show that low-quality copies available during theatrical release have a limited distribution. When higher-quality copies are available (often at the time of DVD release), there is a much bigger spike in downloads.

So far we have focused on piracy and economic loss to distributors by copies being distributed outside of normal, legitimate channels. Like all retail channels, however, there is also loss at the point of sale. These losses result from unauthorized, or unreported, showings at otherwise authorized facilities. For example, a theatre reports that it has two showings of a movie per day while actually performing three showings per day, with the receipts from the third showing going unreported (usually directly into employees' pockets). While this is not a primary focus of Digital Cinema security systems, it is a significant secondary issue to distributors as well as the major exhibitor chains.

REVIEW OF EARLY FIELDED SYSTEMS

We will now briefly discuss security within the current film-based theatrical environment as well as the security architectures of the first generation of the Digital Cinema rollout.

---

[7]Simon Byers, Lorrie Cranor, Eric Cronin, Dave Kormann, and Patrick McDaniel. "Analysis of Security Vulnerabilities in the Movie Production and Distribution Process," *Proceedings of the 2003 ACM Workshop on Digital Rights Management*, October 27, 2003, Washington, DC.

Film

Until relatively recently, the security provided by the traditional film-based distribution system was quite good. It was secure not because it was difficult to acquire a film copy but because it was difficult to cause much economic loss from the copy. Twenty years ago, the only effective tool for theft was to steal a print that could be played at another screen, resulting in a small absolute loss to the studio. This was true because the telecine equipment necessary to convert the film print into a video form usable by the pirates was extremely expensive. In addition, there was no means for the pirate to distribute to a consumer (the VCR was just coming to market).

Over the past 20 years, however, several technology developments have made film-based distribution much more susceptible to theft. The first VCRs (now DVD players) provided a convenient distribution mechanism for pirate copies. With the advent of personal video cameras, pirates were able to film a movie directly from the screen on which it was shown. Initially the quality was poor, and the cameras were quite large. Nevertheless this has become a favorite method of pirates, and today there are very high-quality pirate copies made using digital camcorders, often set on tripods in private midnight showings with the audio cable plugged directly into the theatre sound systems. These copies can be of surprisingly high quality. In addition, very small hand-held camcorders can now be snuck into theatres by regular patrons, sometimes with the recording portion located outside the theatre, receiving a wireless feed. The MPAA estimates that a significant majority of all professional pirate copies originate from camcorders.[8]

Digital Cinema

While there were early demonstrations of digital projection in cinemas in the late 1980s and early 1990s, including the Pacific Bell "Cinema of the Future" demonstrations in 1993 and Hughes Digital Cinema in 1993–1995, the remainder of this chapter will focus on the recent Digital Cinema era. This era has been enabled by the emergence of the Texas Instruments DLP Cinema™ projectors and their use in showings of *Star Wars: Episode 1* on June 18, 1999.

---

[8]Rick Merritt, "Compression schemes take screen test for Digital Cinema," *EE Times*, March 31, 2004

Early Trials (Physical Security)

Preparations for the showing of *Star Wars: Episode 1* were overseen by Dave Schnuelle, who was working for LucasFilm/THX at the time. These first showings were focused on simply getting the system to work and incorporated no electronic security. Content was delivered on uncompressed hard disc arrays and played using SGI computers with unprotected SDI connections directly to the projector. Security was accomplished through physical means. The content was hand carried and installed by a studio representative who remained in the projection booth throughout the showing to ensure there were no playback issues. This same representative made sure the discs did not disappear and were locked up while not being used. This arrangement was very expensive and not very operationally friendly.

The RAID arrays were rapidly replaced with QuVIS Qubit servers that were intended for use by normal theatre personnel and allowed for the delivery of compressed copies. The Qubit machines had no cryptographic security provisions, although the content was compressed in QuVIS' proprietary scheme that provided some measure of obfuscation. Due to operation and security issues, the content continued to be delivered and installed by studio installation personnel, although once content was installed the players were left alone. Security here was completely dependent on the small number of playback locations, their high visibility, and the use of hand-carried content delivery.

THE NEXT GENERATION

While the physical security employed in the early trials was effective and appropriate for the very small number of locations involved, everyone involved knew that it was completely insufficient for any commercial rollout. Both of the first two vendors who rolled out networks of projectors in 2001 recognized this fact. As a result, these networks had significantly improved security infrastructures. The two architectures, however, were radically different and posed different challenges and opportunities to their developers.

Technicolor/QUALCOMM

Technicolor Digital Cinema (TDC) was formed as a joint venture between QUALCOMM, which provided the technology, and Technicolor, which provided the operational expertise and relationships with distributors and exhibitors. TDC began rolling out their network in 2001 and by 2003 had installed approximately 40 screens. In the late 1990s, QUALCOMM recognized the coming opportunities in Digital Cinema and began a large-scale development program to create a complete Digital Cinema content distribution and playback system. This system was based on QUALCOMM'S proprietary Adaptive Block Size DCT compression scheme, which is a block adaptive version of MPEG-2.

From the beginning of their development efforts, the QUALCOMM team recognized the critical value of content security for this market, and their designs included appropriate security capabilities from the ground up. The QUALCOMM engineers had the advantage that they were building a proprietary infrastructure that did not need to interact with other entities from a security perspective.

While not much is publicly known of the design, several items are available. The system designers clearly viewed both transport and the theatre as insecure environments. They went to great lengths to protect the content in the theatre, both during storage and playback. The system was based on 3-DES for the content encryption cipher, and content was delivered and stored in an encrypted form. In fact, content remained encrypted until it was within the same silicon chip that performed the content decompression. The system provided for conditional access windows with the ability to control playback of content by projector and time. The system did not include link encryption, championing instead the idea of placing decoders within the projectors themselves.

The security network was managed from a central network management facility and keys were delivered "out-of-band" over network connections. Audit and logging data were returned to the centralized control facility. These communications were occasional and a theatre could operate without continuous outside network connections. It is presumed that QUALCOMM used standard tools such as RSA and Diffie-Helman for authentication and communications sessions setups. QUALCOMM performed all authentication and certification of the equipment.

Boeing

Boeing Digital Cinema, similarly to TDC, put together and fielded screen installations in conjunction with a closed content delivery network. This network also was rolled out in 2001 and similarly reached almost 40 screens. From a security architectural perspective there were two core differences. Where TDC avoided the link encryption issue by targeting decoders inside projectors, the Boeing network was designed for external cinema network playback devices and as such needed link encryption. Second, and most important, the Boeing network was designed to support heterogeneous playback servers. In fact, Boeing fielded servers from both EVS and Avica within their network, and both Avica and EVS created a custom version of their servers to support the Boeing proprietary security architecture. Boeing developed a proprietary content delivery architecture including theatre management servers and a satellite receiver network.

The Boeing network used AES to encrypt the content. This encryption was applied in mastering and removed only at the point at which the content was ready to be decompressed for display. Unlike the QUALCOMM system, the Boeing servers performed this decryption in software on the playback servers. Content keys were released to the decryption software from a Boeing custom component that was based on the *TecSec CKM*™ technology. Boeing used the CKM system to provide key management and playback window access controls. In addition, the Boeing system featured link encryption using TI's CineLink technology between the playback server and the projector. Last, for content traveling over the satellite network, Boeing added an additional encryption and receiver control hurdle, such that only those locations scheduled to receive the content would even store it to begin with.

Like TDC, the Boeing Digital Cinema Network was centrally managed. Unlike TDC, Boeing maintained ongoing network connections with each theatre via the Boeing satellite network. This was used for content distribution, secure key delivery (using CKM), and network operations and monitoring. Standard secure IP network practices were followed with *virtual private networks* (VPNs) used extensively.

Cinea

In 2002, in conjunction with EVS in Europe, Cinea fielded a system that allowed the separation of content delivery from the content security functions. The Cinea Cosmos security architecture, while still a proprietary implementation, had many of the elements of the current DCI/SMPTE architecture. It provided separation between the individual security functions, such as real-time content decryption, link encryption/decryption, and the larger security management component. The security management component provided the DRM capabilities, secure log management, real-time clocks, back-end key management communications, and playback device authentication.

The Cosmos system supported protection of content during delivery using both 3-DES and AES. Content keys were delivered to the network using occasional telephone or IP connections to the Cinea back end. This back-end communication used standard techniques (RSA and Diffie Hellman) to mutually authenticate the end-points and to set up a secure session for transmission of keys, DRM info, and log data. At the time of playback, the Cosmos Security Manager would release the content keys to a hardware-based decryption module integrated into the decompression subsystem. The Cosmos system supported several unique features including the ability to localize in-theatre content at receipt through re-encryption. This re-encryption was required if the content was delivered in 3-DES as the real-time decryption modules supported only AES.

The Next Generation: DCI/SMPTE-Based Systems

In looking at the evolution of the Digital Cinema infrastructure since 1999, one of the clear trends has been toward the design of modular, interoperable systems. This direction is supported by both the content owners and the theatre owners in the belief that it will help build a marketplace for competitive products and services. The challenge in such an environment is to design a security architecture that provides the critical aspects necessary for an effective "end to end" security infrastructure while facilitating the use of plug and play components.

DESIGN PHILOSOPHY

The SMPTE DC28 Digital Cinema committees, and more recently the studio-funded Digital Cinema Initiatives (DCI), have been grappling with effective mechanisms to enable strong security while providing for equipment and provider interoperability. From these discussions an architecture has emerged that, while not ideal from a security point of view, nevertheless provides a reasonable compromise between absolute security, interchangeability of components, renewal of security, and business model flexibility.

Before delving into the technical details, it may be helpful to discuss briefly the critical business issues and requirements on which the architecture is based. Note that some of these business issues continue to be very contentious, and it has been the goal of the SMPTE committees to define technical designs such that the final business agreements between distributors and exhibitors on these issues can be dealt with as operational patterns.

Business Issues

No Dark Screens

Both exhibitors and distributors agree that the goal of the Digital Cinema systems is to play content and that there should be no *dark screens* (occurrences when the movie stops playing and the screen goes dark). Behind this statement, however, quickly come caveats: movie opening dates are set by contract and the movie cannot play before those dates, except of course for test screenings, which must happen before those dates to make sure everything is ready for the opening. There are contractual end dates after which the movie should not show. Movies should play only at theatres to which they are contracted; however, they should be able to play on any screen in that theatre.

The crux of the security issue is a concern on the part of exhibitors that the existence of sophisticated digital conditional access controls could allow distributors to become the de facto operators and schedulers of their theatres. As an example, the access rights controls defined in the DCI spec provide for the basic dark screen situations, i.e., correct location and date/time window. But the DCI spec also defines several other circumstances that distribution might consider as dark screen issues for security and business reasons (e.g., inoperative fingerprinting unit, inoperative logging system, invalid "certified" devices, and illegal access to a secured container). Although the Digital Cinema security systems may have many potential features, the use of those features will depend on negotiations between distributors and exhibitors and, more specifically, the business relationship between both parties.

Control, Ownership, and Sharing of Audit and Playback Information

The most contentious issue was, and continues to be, what should happen to the logging information that is generated by the systems. Everyone agrees that there is tremendous value in the logs and that these data should be collected. However, when, where, and under what conditions this data should be provided to various parties remains unclear. As a result, the current architectures strive to define the data collection mechanisms within a theatre (to enable interoperability) while remaining silent on how the data collected within a theatre are then further distributed.

System Maintenance and Other Operational Issues

The question of support for general operational issues, including system maintenance, is not contentious but is often overlooked. The system design must support mechanisms for the installation, transfer, and replacement of content playback equipment without causing unacceptable dark screen conditions. For example, if a content playback device fails on Friday night, the system must support a way for the technician to plug in a new player without waiting until Monday morning to get security authorizations. This, of course, must be balanced against preventing content thieves from just plugging their capture equipment into the chain.

Single Inventory

All parties agree that a requirement of the system is to provide for a single inventory that can be played on all screens. Given this constraint, the security system must support a common format for decryption of the content at playback.

Interoperability of Equipment

All parties further agree that interoperability of equipment within a theatre is highly desirable. There is also agreement that limitations on specific implementation architectures should be avoided where possible. For example, some theatres might have a single projector and a single stand-alone content player. Other theatres might have a centralized *storage area network* (SAN) on which all of the movies are stored and during playout streamed from the SAN to an embedded media block within a projector. Still other theatres might have a central SAN with independent content players, perhaps from different manufacturers, at each screen.

Technical Issues and Threats

With business requirements and their implications in mind, what are the threats that the security system is intended to protect against?

Content Delivery

Protection of the content during delivery to the theatre is a basic requirement of the system. The content should be deliverable using a variety of means, including physical media, such as DVDs or hard disc drives, and electronic delivery via satellite or terrestrial broadband connection. The assumption here is that the bits are fairly readily available to a pirate who manages to get access to them during transit. This requirement is easily met with a strong encryption algorithm.

Key/DRM Delivery

Delivery of the necessary content key(s) and any associated DRM information to the theatres must also be protected. Here the protection envelope's job is to prevent discovery of the content key(s) and to ensure that the DRM information has not been manipulated and that it is from an approved source. Obviously the key needs to stay secure, but why worry about the access rights information? To protect against redistribution by unauthorized distributors of the encrypted content, it is critical that the DRM information be authenticated by the security system that receives the keys. For example, if the keys are securely protected but the DRM information is editable, then a pirate could make a copy of the encrypted movie and deliver it, along with a newly created set of access rights containing a new time window or even a newly authorized theatre, to a client.

Content Storage at the Theatre

Unlike film prints, which are very difficult to copy, digital prints are very easy to copy. They are stored on standard computer drives that can be easily duplicated without any trace of that duplication having occurred. In addition, theatres eventually will all be networked internally, with potential external network connections as well. These network connections serve as further conduits through which content can be copied, again potentially without trace.

Because of the ease with which electronic copies can be made, the content should be stored fully encrypted until the last possible moment, i.e., content playback.

Content Playback

During content playback it is necessary to first decrypt the content in order to decompress it. During playback, the content can be collected on the link to the projector or between the decryption and decompression subsystems. The goal is to make a secure enclave within which the content can be safely decrypted, decompressed and, if necessary, re-encrypted for delivery to the projector.

Systems Architecture

Now that we have examined the requirements and goals of the DCI/SMPTE security architecture, let us review the details of the architecture itself. The DCI architecture makes a clear distinction between events that occur *outside* a theatre and those that occur *inside*.

Extra-Theatre

To a large degree, the external systems are designed to deliver content, keys, and access rights to a theatre complex using one-way delivery mechanisms. The design target is to allow the creation of a single delivery master that can be copied as many times as necessary. The theatre-specific components, specifically keys and access rights, are delivered separately in a *key delivery message* (KDM).

Content Master

In order to enable a single Digital Cinema package, DCI has recommended a single standard for the packaged encrypted content. Content is segmented

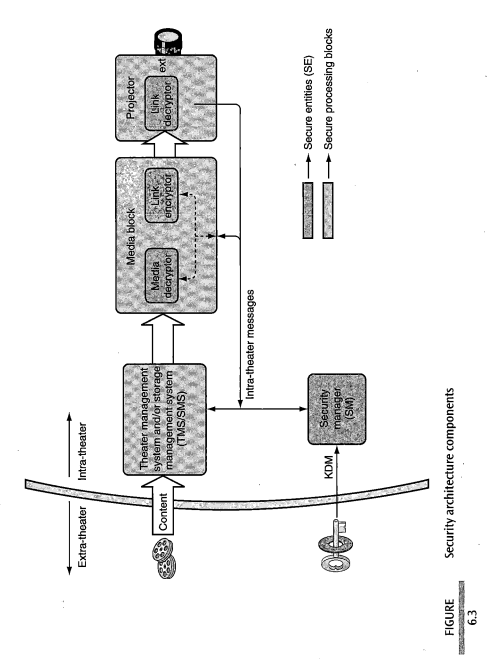

FIGURE

6.3

Security architecture components

into *reels*. Individual reels are composed of a collection of *track files*, each of which is a *Material Exchange Format* (MXF) file containing a single essence stream. Reels are then put together into a *composition list* that describes which reels should be played in which order.

Reels are individually encrypted with 128-bit AES keys in *cipher block chaining* (CBC) mode. The entire track file is not encrypted; the MXF headers remain in the clear and only the *essence* (*content data*) itself is encrypted. Draft SMPTE spec describes the track file structure. Figure 6.3 shows the DCI MXF structure including the security headers. The headers permit only a section of the essence to be encrypted by defining an offset into the essence before encryption begins. The key used to encrypt the track file is identified by a ContentKeyId. Each track file can have its own key (and thus ContentKeyID), or the same key could be used for all track files in a reel or across an entire composition. The CompositionID is the primary index into the KDM described in the following section.

To support replacement of small pieces of a movie in the field without requiring re-delivery of the entire movie, reels can be as short as 1 second, and new compositions can be created referencing the new reel and the old reels. Under normal conditions a composition is intended to be similar to the reels used in current film-based print releases. Thus a typical 2-hour movie would contain six segments (emulating 20-minute film reels), where each segment would include a separate track (MXF file) for each essence element in that segment. Typical essence elements are video, audio, subtitles, and metadata. Thus a typical reel would have four tracks and the full movie composition, with six reels, would have 24 total track files.

To support checking of the integrity of a distribution set, the composition, and individual track files contain HMAC-SHA-1 check fields, which provide a mechanism for validating the integrity of the elements of the composition as well as the individual track files.

Content Keys and Access Rights

Access rights and the necessary keys to play a composition are delivered via one or more KDMs. Individual KDMs correlate to a specific composition and may contain one or more content keys (used to encrypt track files). In addition multiple KDMs can exist for any given ContentID, either to carry all of the necessary content keys or to provide for multiple playback windows. Content playback is allowed if any of the KDMs for a ContentID is permissible. Each KDM has a unique KDM-ID that can be used to revoke a KDM should that become necessary. Just as the DCI specification does not specify how content is transported to the theatre, it does not specify how KDMs are delivered to the theatre. This is left to appropriate market forces.

Because the distributor/exhibitor relationship is based on trust, the KDM provides an extremely rudimentary set of access controls as compared to many other modern DRM environments. Most modern DRM mechanisms provide for complex digital rights expression languages with rich sets of primitives that enable fine controls over date and time of playback, number of playbacks, and other parameters. The DCI and SMPTE groups explored these mechanisms as well, and the direction from the main business stakeholders (both distributors and exhibitors) was that this type of complex DRM was not appropriate for theatrical exhibition. As a result, the base KDM provides only fixed fields for a start and stop date (time window) during which the content may be viewed. To ensure the authenticity of these fields, they are signed in conjunction with the content key block.

Last, each KDM contains a certificate (or chain of certificates) that provides authentication that this KDM is issued by the legitimate content owner. These certificates provide the signature basis for binding the content keys, usage dates, and content key IDs, ensuring that they cannot be moved from one KDM to another.

Intra-Theatre

Once the content and KDMs have been delivered to a theatre, the second half of the DCI security specification comes into play. This deals with content security during storage and playback within the theatre. Figure 6.3 shows the components of the DCI intra-theatre security architecture. These components represent logical functions that exist within the theatre playback environment and are part of, or interact with, the security subsystem. Later in this section we will discuss practical examples of how these logical elements can be realized within physical devices in a theatre complex.

From a security perspective, the DCI intra-theatre architecture differentiates between those components that are directly involved in, and responsible for, the handling of content and keys (*security entities* or *SEs*) and those components that have no direct responsibility for security. SEs are the secure enclaves within a theatre and as such process cleartext keys, content, or both. The identification of specific SEs is helpful, as it makes clear which subsystems need to take security into account and which do not. For example, theatre management systems and content storage systems have no direct security responsibility and are not viewed as SEs.

Among the security entities within a theatre, the *security manager* (SM) plays a special role. The SM is the focal point for content security and is responsible for enforcing security policy within the theatre. The SM is responsible for authenticating the playback chain and releasing the content keys in preparation for the playback of the content. Before releasing keys, it checks the playback rules for the content and enforces those rules through selective release of the keys to the *media decryptor* (MD), contained within the media block. The SM also acts as the focus point for theatre management systems to interact with the security components. By concentrating all these functions within one component, the architecture is able to simplify significantly the requirements of the other SEs in the content display chain. In particular, only the SM must perform authentication, have strong random number systems, have a secure clock and understand the relationship of compositions to reels and tracks. Lastly, by placing most of the more complex security "application" logic within the SM, the architecture simplifies the logic within lower level "shared" or embedded components (SEs). This increases the likelihood that they will continue to be secure and that replacement will need to occur only at the SM level.

By compartmentalizing the security control logic into the SM, the architecture also enables multiple SMs within a theatre complex. This provides significant flexibility, both from a technical and business perspective, and helps to isolate the most likely component to change as a result of compromise or business paradigm changes. The use of a separate SM also ensures that theatre owners could install a single SM (and receive a single KDM for the theatre) independent of which equipment is used for playback and projection. The use of separate SMs further allows exhibitors to purchase the degree of security sophistication appropriate for their environment.

Multiple SMs may be used to provide operational redundancy for each other. Support for multiple SMs is also critical to enable field updates and renewals of the security subsystems should they be hacked, which they eventually will. In addition, support for multiple SMs can be used to provide partitioning between content owners should that be desirable.

Theatre Management to SM Interaction

The security subsystems operate within the context of the larger playback environment and as such are controlled and directed by the theatre management and screen management systems.

As described earlier, the *Theater Management System* (TMS) is the master of the SM—that is, it initiates all communications with the SM and instigates all interaction of the SM with other components within the theatre complex. The TMS and SM set up a *Transport Layer Security* (TLS) session, with the TMS providing an X.509 certificate to the SM such that it can authenticate that it is taking direction from a known system. The use of TLS prevents someone from plugging in any PC and beginning to direct the SM.

The TMS initiates communications with the SM and informs the SM of the separate SE components within a theatre. It does this by providing the SM with a list of each SE, its type, and its IP address. This information is then used by the SM to initiate its communications with the SEs. In other words, the SM "learns" the theatre configuration from the TMS.

For determining what content is playable, the SM supports TMS queries about particular content IDs and their availability, relying on the existence of KDMs for the content and the associated playback windows. When playback is initiated, the TMS uses this link to request that the SM authenticate and initialize the playback chain. Last, the interface supports the ability of the TMS to pass content through the SM for optional ingest processing. This optional ingest processing could be used to localize content within the complex or to insert a forensic watermark at content load. This stage is optional but exists for future flexibility.

Secure Entities

Within the DCI architecture, *Secure Entities* (SEs) are viewed as boundaries within which the content and keys for decryption can be safely in the clear. Individual SEs communicate with the SM to receive the appropriate security information necessary to play back content. In addition the SEs must store all appropriate content access information and other security issues (such as attempted hacks) in a secure log. This logging information is then passed up to the SM. Each SE has its own X.509 certificate that is used for authentication. Examples of SEs in the DCI architecture are media decryptor, link encryptor, and link decryptors.

In some cases a device may have multiple SE stages that require secure processing between them. These combination devices are known as *secure processing blocks* (SPBs) and represent secure enclaves that contain a set of related security entities. Examples of SPBs are media blocks, which decrypt, decode, and then link-encrypt; and baseband watermarking modules that might link-decrypt, watermark, and link-encrypt. To simplify communications and provide for security boundaries at the SPB, the SPBs have their own certificates and act as proxies for the SEs within them.

The SM communicates with the individual SEs (or their SPB shells) via TLS sessions over IP. The X.509 certificates from the SEs are used by the SM to authenticate the endpoint and ensure it is authorized to receive the content. Security entities do not need to authenticate the SM as the only purpose would be for the SE to decide that the SM should not have gotten the key (i.e., cannot be trusted). This is already accomplished by the content owner providing (or not providing) the KDM to the SM.

Once the session is initialized the SE/SPB passes waiting log data up to the SM for collection. Note that in the case of multiple SMs, an SE/SPB will pass log data only to an SM for which that particular SM provided the content keys. This ensures that SMs cannot see log information for content they have not directly authorized.

Content handling keys are also passed from the SM to the SEs as appropriate. For SPBs that by definition decrypt content on input and encrypt content on output, the SM can further define a linkage between the keys used at input and the keys used at output. This is critical to ensure that a rogue SM cannot be used to key the downstream link with a key known to the attacker, thus enabling access to the content. The SPB is responsible for ensuring that this linkage takes place. In order to minimize the impact of communications or SM equipment failure in the theatre, the specification allows for key releases to include a period of validity. It is anticipated this will be between 24 and 48 hours. In this way, once the playback chain is set up by an SM, the equipment in the chain will be able to play a show without requiring additional SM communications.

Unaddressed Issues

The DCI architecture assumes that watermarking is applied by a studio, prior to the image and/or audio entering the DCDM phase. Therefore, the DCI spec does not cover watermarking. For security reasons, the fingerprinting system (clearly part of the theatre system) will not be functionally defined in the DCI spec. However, DCI has indicated that they intend to define the interface between the theatre system and fingerprinting system. In addition, the specification does not yet provide any guidelines related to the mechanisms to be used to provide secure boundaries around SEs and SPBs. It is anticipated that these issues will be addressed prior to the release of the final specifications.

Implementation Examples

Like most well-designed systems, the DCI architecture provides a flexible framework within which a variety of specific implementations can be accomplished. The actual fielded implementations will depend in large part on business issues that remain unresolved at this point. As these business issues are necessarily determined by individual discussions and arrangements between distributors and exhibitors, they are not yet known.

However, to clarify how the DCI architecture would be implemented in practice, we will briefly look at some sample physical implementations and associated business assumptions. It is anticipated that some combination of these implementations will be fielded.

Basic Single Theatre System with Embedded SM and Self-Managed Security

In this model the exhibitor has two pieces of equipment: a projector and a server. These two pieces of equipment contain all of the components necessary to operate the theatre. Figure 6.4 shows this implementation.

Note that in this example implementation, an SM module is implemented within the server, and this SM is owned and operated by the exhibitor. In this model, keys and access information (KDMs) are delivered to the exhibitor, perhaps via email. The exhibitor stores and maintains the access logs from the SM. The exhibitor is responsible for also loading all authentication information into the SM and reviewing logging information for security violations. This model presumes that the exhibitor is approved by the distributors to manage his or her own security operations.

Basic Single Theatre System with Embedded SM and Third-Party Security Operations

This model is similar to the prior model except that a third party has been contracted (by the exhibitor and/or distributor) to provide security opera-

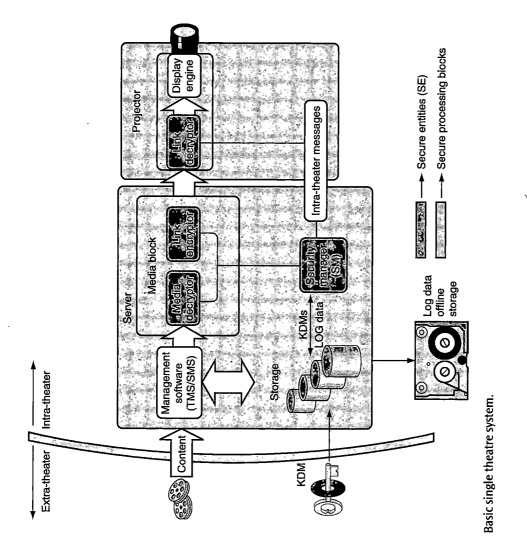

FIGURE 6.4

Basic single theatre system.

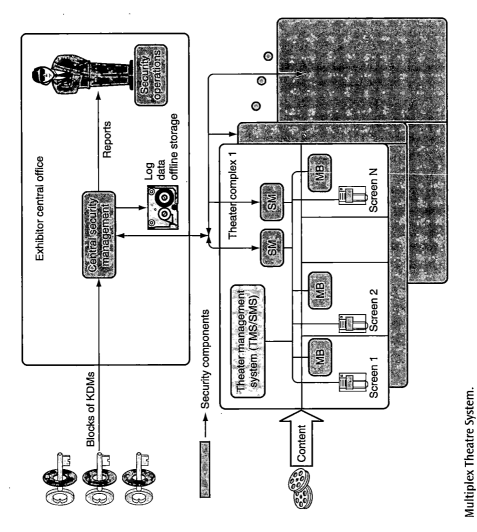

FIGURE
6.5

Multiplex Theatre System.

tions support. This third-party security service communicates keys, access rules, and authentication information to the SM in the theatre. It receives from the theatre the SM logs for security analysis and storage. Essentially this is an outsourcing of the security operations. This is a likely scenario for smaller chains and single location exhibitors. Note that this model may also include the provisioning of an SM, at each theatre, by the third party.

Multiplex Theatre System with Self-Managed Security

This model is shown in Figure 6.5. The basic assumption here is that the exhibition *circuit* (or chain) that owns the theatre complex has decided to purchase and operate a distributor-approved SM solution.

In this example, each complex has two redundant SMs that communicate with the remainder of the equipment in the complex. These SMs are part of a larger circuitwide security management system that operates from the circuit's central operations center. In practice, the central operations facility receives KDMs for each of the individual theatres from distributors. These KDMs are then distributed within the circuit's internal network to the individual SMs by the central security management system. The central security management system also collects, stores, and provides reporting based on the logging information passed up from the in-theatre SMs. This information is reviewed by the circuit's internal loss-prevention and operations staff and is shared with the distributors as agreed on.

Multiplex Theatre System with Third-Party Security

This model is shown in Figure 6.6. The basic assumption here is that the circuit has decided not to provide its own Digital Cinema security operations. As a result, they will need to contract with (or let the distributor contract with) a third-party security provider. As in the individual screen example described before, the in-theatre SM may be provided by the third-party security service. There may be one or more of the SMs, depending on the business arrangement. In this scenario the third-party security service receives all of the KDMs for each theatre and is responsible for delivering the KDMs to each theatre, providing acquisition, analysis, and monitoring of the logging information and ensuring that playback equipment within the theatre is authorized (and not revoked).

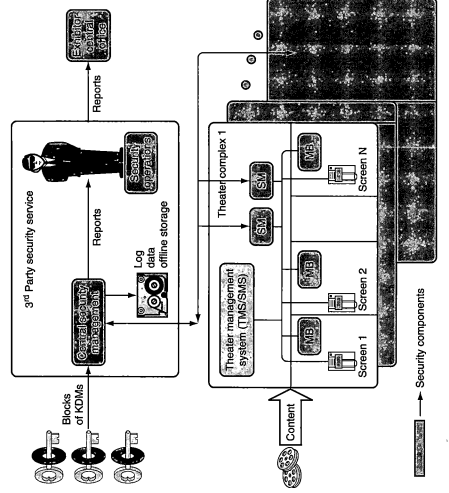

FIGURE
6.6

Multiplex Theatre System with Third-Party Security.

Summary

The protection of digital movies within the theatre involves the implementation of cooperating security components among distributors, exhibitors, and equipment manufacturers. Because of the tremendous residual value in digital theatrical prints, the security subsystems must be robust, well designed, and able to withstand concerted attacks by professional thieves. This need for protection must be balanced with the needs of the users to have implementations which work in the real world.

Packaging

Chris Carey
Studio New Technology
The Walt Disney Studios

Collecting and organizing all the elements that together comprise the *distribution package* is a substantial task with many possibilities for error. Thorough inventory control and quality assurance are critical issues at this stage of the game. The purpose of the packaging process is to organize all the elements that comprise the distribution master, along with the related data that will provide information relevant to the unpacking, decryption, and ultimate playout of the material, and then to wrap these elements into a standardized file format or structure such that theatre systems can unwrap this distribution package in a predictable and standardized fashion.

The packaging process occurs after compression and encryption, and it yields a *Digital Cinema Package* (DCP) that is ready for transport to the exhibition venue. As of this writing, the packaging of the *Digital Cinema Distribution Master* (DCDM) is typically limited in scope to combining all the necessary elements required to make one theatrical presentation in a single theatre. The definition of a DCP, however, allows for more than one presentation in more than one theatre. The upper limit of what may be included in a single DCP is constrained only by the maximum amount of materials one would practically want to transport as a single package. For example, several versions of a presentation (e.g., different languages) intended for several different screens of a single multiplex theatre facility may be combined into a single DCP.

Formats

As mentioned above, one of the principal purposes of the packaging process is to organize all of the materials needed for a theatrical presentation into a standardized format. This is not currently the case; there is a separate format or type of package required for each of the Digital Cinema servers in the use today. QVis, Avica, EVS, GDC, and Technicolor each have different ways of organizing the essence and metadata (in fact, there are several image compression types as well), such that there must be separate packages produced for a single film release to accommodate this lack of standardized packaging. There is currently an industry effort to increase interoperability between the various manufacturers, known as the *Interop Group*. This effort is beginning to align the file types used; for example, they have agreed on the image data as MPEG-2, audio as PCM linear, metadata as MXF files, and subtitles as PNG files. Standardization of these file types and the resulting interoperability of Digital Cinema systems are of course fully addressed in the DCI Digital Cinema specification.

Scope of Materials

The materials that can be included in the distribution package comprise all of the essence data, the related data, and usage data. These data are organized in a hierarchical structure beginning with the highest level information, e.g., package name or title of the film, and ending with the most elementary data-like track file.

Final Step

Once all of the materials have been compiled, verified, and formatted, all that remains is to place the distribution package into a container for transportation. The size of the distribution package for a single film on a single screen will be in the range of 50 GB to 100 GB. This size is not constrained in any way by the packaging process but is simply a result of what is included. Today a variety of storage media are being used, including Exabyte Mammoth II tapes, DLT tapes, DVD-R disc, and removable hard disc drives. Having placed the distribution master onto one of these media, we are ready for transportation!

7

Audio For Digital Cinema

David W. Gray
Dolby Laboratories, Inc.

The potential of a new digital delivery system for feature film into theatres offers tremendous opportunities to improve, expand, standardize, and future proof all the various system components—specifically audio—for this discussion. For audio, pundits and designers have the unique situation of a relatively clean sheet of paper. Certainly legacy audio formats can neither be forgotten nor can they be considered much of a burden. This clean sheet is both blessing and curse in that the capability to do anything must always be weighted against the desire to do something. The chapter will point to a number of dichotomies that currently exist with the state of audio in the process of defining Digital Cinema. This chapter will explore the opportunity and the road on which audio has traveled for the past 3 years as well as look into what the future may hold for audio in Digital Cinema.

The following is excerpted from the SMPTE DC28.6 Audio Report.

> The transition from analog to digital sound in all forms was well under way at the end of the twentieth century. Recording, editing, mastering, and distribution of audio entertainment all have been changed wholly or in part by the changeover to digital methods and delivery media.
>
> The development of digital audio for the cinema has reached a state of "adolescent maturity" in the year 2000. A significant percentage of the sound played in first run movie theatres emanates from one of three brands of digital delivery systems developed in the prior decade. Over 85% of feature releases carry both analog and digital sound tracks of some kind. Images are still projected from 35mm film, however, and all cinema digital sound systems to date are either synchronized to or reproduced from signals that are stored photographically on the film prints. Film-less

(digital) cinema releases are now occurring. At the time of this writing over 30 theatres have been equipped with digital projectors and have presented movies played from digital tape or hard-disk HDTV players.

    Improvements in cinema sound are still possible, and the transition from analog cinema using 35mm film projection to the all-digital cinema made possible by the advent of high quality digital cinema projectors and digital media for distribution is the appropriate time to make the move to a higher level of audio performance in theatres.

While nearly 4 years old, this excerpt from the SMPTE Audio Report is still timely and completely pertinent.

THE HISTORICAL VIEW AND OPPORTUNITY

Audio for film has had tremendous improvements and innovations from the inception of sound for film in the late 1920s. Although numerous systems came and went, the industry had settled by the late 1940s on an optical sound format utilizing a dual bi-lateral variable area optical track of 78 mils on the right side of 35mm film (see Figure 7.1).

    This format had a two-channel or stereo capability that was not exploited until the mid-1970s. In the 1950s and 1960s both four-track and 6-track magnetic became popular sound formats as well. These formats offered multichannel audio for either 35mm (Figure 7.2) or 70mm release formats as shown in Figures 7.2 and 7.3.

    The mid-1970s brought significant change in film audio. Dolby Laboratories, Inc. developed its Dolby Stereo system for optical sound tracks, thereby allowing quality improvement in frequency response, dynamic range and channel count compared to traditional optical-based sound tracks. Dolby utilized a noise reduction system, improving the dynamic range approximately 10 dB and, more importantly, allowing lower noise so that noise control need not be done via traditional high-frequency roll-off. The system also incorporated a matrix system whereby four channels of audio are encoded to two channels of the optical sound track. On playback in a Dolby-equipped theater, the two channels of the optical sound track are decoded back into the original four channels, while in a non-equipped theater the track is considered mono-compatible and plays back in conventional mono. Although it is a proprietary system, by the 1990s Dolby Stereo had become the de facto optical sound track format, and many of the components of the Dolby system were formally standardized.

    Dolby also improved the 70mm six-track magnetic by applying noise reduction, utilizing channels 2 and 4 as low-frequency enhancement chan-

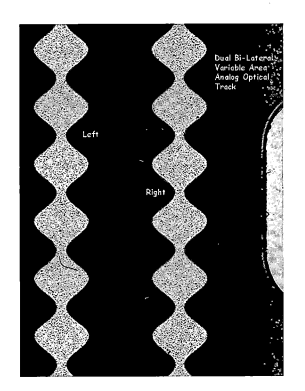

Dual Bi-Lateral
Variable Area
Analog Optical
Track

Left

Right

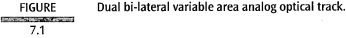

FIGURE 7.1

Dual bi-lateral variable area analog optical track.

nels and a method for stereo surrounds. While clearly the premier format, 70mm prints were expensive and thus the format was only used on larger studio releases. A typical large-budget studio release in the late 1980s would rarely have more than 200 70mm prints and some 1500 plus 35mm optical sound track prints.

As the cost of 70mm continued to increase, the pressure from the industry was to find a way to get the sound quality of the premier 70mm audio format at the cost of a traditional 35mm optical sound track release. In the late 1980s a SMPTE ad hoc committee was formed to look into the optimum channel count and speaker location for the future. That committee's work culminated in a report that described what we know today as the 5.1 channel format (left, center, right, left surround, right surround, and sub woofer—the .1 channel). As the nineties dawned, a number of companies were looking into ways to provide digital audio via 35mm release prints (see Figure 7.4). By the mid-1990s, three separate digital audio systems had come to market to

35mm magnetic.

70mm magnetic.

meet the desire for a lower-cost six-channel system for 35mm film. Two of the companies, Dolby and Sony, released systems in which the six channels of audio are physically located on the 35mm film. A third company, Digital Theatre Systems (DTS), devised a system where the six channels are housed on a separate CD-ROM with a control track located on the film.

The debate will undoubtedly continue for eternity on how this situation came to pass, but all will agree that what was termed The Sound Wars raged for a few years as some studios endorsed one system and not others. By the late 1990s most studios where releasing in two and in some cases all three formats.

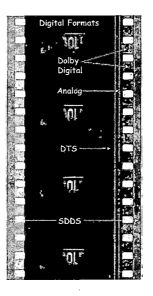

FIGURE   Digital formats.

7.4

THE CURRENT STATUS OF CINEMA AUDIO

Currently most films produced utilize at least one of the digital 5.1-channel film sound track formats. Most recently published numbers (Dolby Laboratories, Inc. and SMPTE A12.68) show that the Dolby Digital format of Dolby Laboratories, Inc. is installed in approximately 42,500 theatres. DTS's format is installed in approximately 22,000 theatres, and while no longer available for purchase, Sony's SDDS format is in approximately 8000 theatres. No statistics exist for how many of these theatres have multiple format capability, making it impossible to have an accurate number of digitally equipped theatres in the world. However, the number is certainly greater than 55,000.

POTENTIAL NEW FEATURES

One of the most often cited reasons for standardizing audio in a new Digital Cinema system is to avoid repeating the Sound Wars syndrome of

Potential Features	Advantages	Issues
Additional Channels	Ability to convey the sound space in a more realistic manner.	Money and implementation challenges balanced against usefulness.
Discrete Audio Channels	No matrix encoding.	More bandwidth required
PCM or Data Reduced Audio	PCM is an open standard and high quality.	More bandwidth and storage required
Smart Audio—Controllable Dynamic Range	Closer presentation to the director's intent.	More time in dubbing.
Smart Audio—Automated down-mixing or up-mixing	Ability to send one master that adapts to the theatre's configuration.	It will always be a compromise and require more time in dubbing.
Smart Audio—Metadata Control, Information, Dynamic and Static Capabilities	Better presentations.	None.
Audio Digital Rights Management—Encryption	Security from piracy	On going operation and key management is necessary
Audio Digital Rights Management—Access Control	Content provider always knows what is going on and has control there over.	Big Brother is watching-creating business rules
Watermarking—Location and Time	A deterrent to piracy.	None
Constant Clock Rate	Audio would no longer be forced to follow picture.	Audio would no longer be forced to follow picture. Potential for changes in equipment infrastructure.

Standard Interfaces—Connectors and Type	Easy interchange and mixing equipment from various manufacturers.	None
Multiple languages	Would allow simpler day and date worldwide presentations and accommodation of multiple language venues.	Additional Bandwidth and storage required
Multiple versions (ratings)	Theatres could have PG in matinees etc. and R at night for example.	Creative issues for directors and more time required in editing and dubbing.
Time, thus money, savings in post-production: No optical negatives No printing	Time, Money and Management.	None.

FIGURE 7.5   Potential features of digital cinema audio format.

the 1990s. A single format has many advantages and is the most desired outcome of an audio specification for Digital Cinema. The question then becomes what should this audio format include and not include? Potential features are presented in Figure 7.5 without ranking order of desirability.

THE DEBATE—HOW AND WHY

The goal in any proposal or format is to balance the needs and desires of the various stakeholders in the process. Digital Cinema has in essence three major stakeholder groups and untold numbers of sub-stakeholders. The content providers (studio distributors), the content presenters (exhibition), and equipment manufacturers form the three major groups. In just about any area of Digital Cinema these three groups have divergent needs and desires, thus creating opposition of some form at every turn. Although at times the process feels like it will never come to fruition, history has shown us that standards and agreements can be achieved.

From an audio perspective (audio has fewer subjective issues) one would expect more agreement than disagreement and generally this is the case. A single format is a desire of both distributors and exhibitors, as both feel this will be the most economical and efficient. Manufacturers may or may not agree, because many believe the marketplace is too small for many vendors and the only way to recoup their R&D is to have some protection via proprietary systems. For example, the current total units sold in roughly ten years by all three digital audio systems combined are approximately 70,000 units. That is not a very big market, leading some manufacturers to prefer a proprietary approach and/or consumer spinoffs to recoup R&D costs. Although the most visible issue, a single format is not the only feature in audio with or without consensus. All the other possibilities for audio have varying degrees of acceptance (the devil is in the details) in the three major groups and are presented in Figure 7.6.

In general, distributors will support features that give them more flexibility and grander presentations, exhibitors will support features that will help them sell more tickets at the box office, and manufacturers want something to differentiate themselves from the crowd.

Feature Possibilities	Studios/Distributors	Exhibitors	Manufacturers
Additional channels	Generally yes	Maybe	Generally yes
Discrete audio channels	Yes	Yes	Yes
PCM audio or data reduced audio capable	PCM unless bandwidth is limited	PCM or a single digital coding format	Generally not concerned
Smart audio	Yes	Maybe	Maybe
Audio digital rights management	Yes	Maybe	Will provide if desired
Watermarking	Yes	Generally yes	Will provide if desired
Constant clock rate	Generally yes	Generally not concerned	Many want constant sample rate as well
Standard interfaces — connectors and type	Yes	Yes	Yes
Visually impaired and hearing-impaired capabilities	Yes	Yes	Yes
Multiple languages	Yes	Maybe	Generally not concerned
Multiple versions (ratings)	Maybe—potential issues with artists and post production time	Maybe	Generally not concerned
Time, thus money, savings in post production	Yes	Maybe	Generally not concerned

FIGURE

7.6

Acceptance of potential features of Digital Cinema audio format.

THE STANDARDS

In any new format, professional or consumer, one of two methods of deployment and implementation occurs. The first can be called the *market standard* method. A market standard method is one in which a company or companies succeed in getting critical mass in the marketplace, usually with a proprietary system or design. If critical mass is reached, the industry organizations and standards bodies such as SMPTE embark on annotating these methods into "after-the-fact" standards. An excellent example is the original Dolby Stereo system, from which the frequency response, system levels, low-frequency utilization, and other parameters of the format all became common de facto industry standards and finally SMPTE/ANSI standards, SMPTE Recommended Practices, and SMPTE Engineering Guidelines.

While this process to obtain a standard is possible in Digital Cinema, it is highly unlikely to occur given both distributors' and exhibitors' desire for one format that is standardized before deployment. The second method, called the *standards process* through the standards bodies, is a multifaceted beast interwoven with technologies, politics, and business models. This process at its worst produces absolutely nothing and at its best a complete standard that allows no deviations on how and what will be implemented. The DVD standard and the high-definition television (ATSC) standard are excellent examples of successful standards efforts. It should be noted that neither of these came to fruition through standards bodies but rather industry committees put together to accomplish the task.

At this time Digital Cinema has the following entities involved in the creation of standards:

1. Society of Motion Picture and Television Engineers (SMPTE) www.smpte.org
   a. DC 28 Digital Cinema Technology Committee
      i. DC 28.10 Mastering Committee
      ii. DC 28.20 Distribution Committee
      iii. DC 28.30 Exhibition Committee
2. European Digital Cinema Forum (EDCF) www.digitalcinema-europe.com
3. National Alliance of Theatre Owners (NATO) www.natoonline.org
4. International Theatre Equipment Association (ITEA) www.itea.com
5. Digital Cinema Providers Group (DCPG) www.dcpg.com
6. Digital Cinema Initiative (DCI) www.dcimovies.com

*The following sections contain extracts from SMPTE draft documents. These extracts have been approved for publication in this context by the Chair of the SMPTE DC28 Technology Committee and by the SMPTE Engineering Vice President to illustrate the level of detail and the progress that has been made in the draft documents. It must be emphasized that these are only draft documents—they are **not** approved Standards or Recommended Practices. There may be substantial revisions before approval, so these extracts should not be relied upon for any purpose.*

The standards effort is extremely difficult, as large differences exist within the major groups. The seven major studios' demands are not necessarily the same as the small independent distributor, just as the big theatre chain does not necessarily have the same issues as the small independent single screen. Add in the differences in philosophy and desires of the manufacturers and you have the protracted process we are currently enduring.

Even with broad-based agreement, the detailed objections can be difficult to overcome. Currently, for example, the original audio committee DC 28.6 and the current audio ad hoc group under DC 28.10 came up with a very basic but needed document called Digital Cinema Audio Characteristics. This document attempts to standardize the digital audio via the number of channels to 16 and, the reference level of these channels to −20 dBFs and defining the bit depth to 24 bits and sample rate 48,000 samples per second. The key features as taken from the draft document are as follows:

Bit depth
The bit depth shall be 24 bits per sample. Material having other bit depths shall be justified to the most significant bit.

Sample rate
Irrespective of the associated image frame rate or rates, the audio sample rate shall be forty-eight thousand samples per second per channel, commonly expressed as 48.000 kHz.
The 48.000 kHz sample rate can be expressed in relation to image frame rate in several ways. Examples are shown in Annex B. All frame rates imply an audio sample count per image frame that is a simple integer ratio.

NOTE: A called out sample rate is actually an average over time. Instantaneous deviations of the sample rate from its average (jitter) affects the quality of the audio output in digital-to-analog conversions and so must be considered in implementation designs. This standard does not specify audio sample rate jitter.

Channel count
The delivered digital audio file system and the playout equipment shall support a channel count of sixteen full-bandwidth channels, not all of which need be used for a given title. Two of these channels are reserved for HI (hearing impaired) and VI (visually impaired, or descriptive narration) channels. Other channels are named and allocated according to a separate SMPTE specification.

Reference level, digital
Digital inputs and outputs shall have a nominal reference level of −20 dBFS.

Reference level, analog
For compatibility with existing cinema audio equipment in conventional exhibition environments, analog outputs delivered by the playout equipment shall have a reference level of −10 dBV, either as a single-ended signal, or as a floating, symmetrical ("balanced") signal that does not change level difference between its two output terminals if either is connected to ground to create an unbalanced signal. A trim of this level of +/−6 dB is recommended.

For professional environments, the delivered analog signal shall have a reference level of +4 dBu, supplied as a floating, symmetrical ("balanced") signal.

These are completely basic issues that any manufacturer needs to know before it can build anything and any content provider needs to know before a master can be made. The debate has continued for nearly 2 years in SMPTE and a year in DCI. The major stumbling block is the sample rate, with passionate proponents of a 96-kHz sample rate and equally strong proponents of a 48-kHz sample rate. One camp puts forward that Digital Cinema must have a 96-kHz sample rate to maintain the competition with home theatre and the "quality" available in the consumer environment. The second camp responds that while doubling the sample rate from 48 kHz may indeed yield some minor "quality" improvement, the reality of pushing audio through small holes in the screen into a large acoustic environment such as a theatre means that there is no chance of hearing this "quality" improvement. More so, 96 kHz would burden every piece of equipment with twice the DSP hardware and the cost thereof for no audible reason. (Note: "Quality" is placed in quotes because the word is indefinable in this context.)

As of this writing no compromise has been reached. One concept is to add 96 kHz as an option. Such an addition requires careful analysis in the handling of multiple formats. Will content producers need to create two masters and maintain dual inventory, one for the 48-kHz-equipped theatres and another for those equipped for 96 kHz? This may not be acceptable due to the additional time and money required, depending on the approach to the two masters. The industry continues to look for solutions to gain consensus. The following language has been proposed:

Irrespective of the associated image frame rate or rates, the delivered audio sample rate contained within the digital cinema package (DCP) shall be either forty-eight thousand samples per second per channel, commonly expressed as 48.000 kHz, or ninety-six thousand samples per second per channel, commonly expressed as 96.000 kHz.

A theatre playout system shall have the capability of performing sample rate conversion as needed.

This compromise requires the input to accept 48 kHz or 96 kHz but allows for downsampling or upsampling for processing and subsequent outputs in either 48 kHz or 96 kHz.

Also under discussion in SMPTE is Digital Cinema Channel Mapping and Labeling. This document's intent is to standardize what channels are called and the link between that name and the channel number for channels in use today. The document also assigns names (called *labels*) to channels that have been proposed for use in the future. Key features as taken from the draft document are as follows:

Definition of Terms

Left   *A loudspeaker position behind the screen to the far left edge, horizontally, of the screen center as viewed from the seating area.*

Center   *A loudspeaker position behind the screen corresponding to the horizontal center of the screen as viewed from the seating area.*

Right   *A loudspeaker position behind the screen to the far right edge, horizontally, of the screen center as viewed from the seating area.*

LFE Screen   *A band-limited low-frequency-only loudspeaker position at the screen end of the room.*

Left Surround   *An array of loudspeakers positioned along the left side of the room starting approximately one-third of the distance from the screen to the back wall.*

Right Surround   *An array of loudspeakers positioned along the right side of the room starting approximately one-third of the distance from the screen to the back wall.*

Center Surround   *A loudspeaker(s) position on the back wall of the room centered horizontally.*

Left Center   *A loudspeaker position mid-way between the center of the screen and the left edge of the screen.*

Right Center   *A loudspeaker position mid-way between the center of the screen and the right edge of the screen.*

LFE 2   *A band-limited low-frequency-only loudspeaker.*

Vertical Height Front   *A loudspeaker(s) position at the vertical top of the screen. A single channel would be at the center of the screen horizontally. Dual channels may be positioned at the vertical top of the screen and in the left center and right center horizontal positions. Tri-channel may be positioned at the vertical top of the screen in the left, center, and right horizontal positions.*

Top Center Surround   *A loudspeaker position in the center of the seating area in both the horizontal and vertical planes directly above the seating area.*

Left Wide   *A loudspeaker position outside the screen area far left front in the room.*

Right Wide   *A loudspeaker position outside the screen area far right front in the room.*

Rear Surround Left   *A loudspeaker position on the back wall of the room to the left horizontally.*

Rear Surround Right   *A loudspeaker position on the back wall of the room to the right horizontally.*

Left Surround Direct *A loudspeaker position on the left wall for localization as opposed to the diffuse array.*

Right Surround Direct *A loudspeaker position on the right wall for localization as opposed to the diffuse array.*

Hearing Impaired *A dedicated audio channel optimizing dialog intelligibility for the hearing impaired.*

Narration *A dedicated narration channel describing the film's events for the visually impaired.*

Lt/Rt *Lt/Rt stands for left total and right total and is used to convey that four channels of audio have been matrix encoded into two channels. Subsequent decode would yield the four channels.*

Mono *A single audio channel reproduced through the center speaker position.*

Dialog Centric Mix *A mix in which the dialog is predominant and dynamic range compression may be employed.*

CHANNEL MAPS AND LABELS: LEGACY CHANNELS

Channel numbers listed refer to the input side of the digital cinema system. Digital audio via AES carriage is not mandated; however, if used, the pairings are specified. Labels apply to both input and output throughout the audio chain. The channel maps and label tables in Figures 7.7–7.15 are titled by the number of channels and as such are not format names.

AES Pair #	Channel #	Label / Name	Description
1	1	L/Left	Far left screen loudspeaker
1	2	R/Right	Far right screen loudspeaker
2	3	C/Center	Center screen loudspeaker
2	4	LFE/Screen	Screen Low Frequency Effects subwoofer loudspeakers
3	5	Ls/Left Surround	Left wall surround loudspeakers
3	6	Rs/Right Surround	Right wall surround loudspeakers
4	7	Lc/Left Center	Mid left to center screen loudspeaker
4	8	Rc/Right Center	Mid right to center screen loudspeaker
5	9	Cs/ Center Surround	Rear wall surround loudspeakers
5	10		Unused/User defined
6	11		Unused/User defined
6	12		Unused/User defined
7	13		Unused/User defined
7	14		Unused/User defined
8	15		Unused/User defined
8	16		Unused/User defined

FIGURE 7.7   Nine channel.

AES Pair #	Channel #	Label / Name	Description
1	1	L/Left	Far left screen loudspeaker
1	2	R/Right	Far right screen loudspeaker
2	3	C/Center	Center screen loudspeaker
2	4	LFE/Screen	Screen Low Frequency Effects subwoofer loudspeakers
3	5	Ls/Left Surround	Left wall surround loudspeakers
3	6	Rs/Right Surround	Right wall surround loudspeakers
4	7	Lc/Left Center	Mid left to center screen loudspeaker
4	8	Rc/Right Center	Mid right to center screen loudspeaker
5	9		Unused/User defined
5	10		Unused/User defined
6	11		Unused/User defined
6	12		Unused/User defined
7	13		Unused/User defined
7	14		Unused/User defined
8	15		Unused/User defined
8	16		Unused/User defined

FIGURE   Eight channel.

7.8

AES Pair #	Channel #	Label / Name	Description
1	1	L/Left	Far left screen loudspeaker
1	2	R/Right	Far right screen loudspeaker
2	3	C/Center	Center screen loudspeaker
2	4	LFE/Screen	Screen Low Frequency Effects subwoofer loudspeakers
3	5	Ls/Left Surround	Left wall surround loudspeakers
3	6	Rs/Right Surround	Right wall surround loudspeakers
4	7		Unused/User defined
4	8		Unused/User defined
5	9	Cs/Center Surround	Rear wall surround loudspeakers
5	10		Unused/User defined
6	11		Unused/User defined
6	12		Unused/User defined
7	13		Unused/User defined
7	14		Unused/User defined
8	15		Unused/User defined
8	16		Unused/User defined

FIGURE   Seven channel.

7.9

AES Pair #	Channel #	Label / Name	Description
1	1	L/Left	Far left screen loudspeaker
1	2	R/Right	Far right screen loudspeaker
2	3	C/Center	Center screen loudspeaker
2	4	LFE/Screen	Screen Low Frequency Effects subwoofer loudspeakers
3	5	Ls/Left Surround	Left wall surround loudspeakers
3	6	Rs/Right Surround	Right wall surround loudspeakers
4	7		Unused/User defined
4	8		Unused/User defined
5	9		Unused/User defined
5	10		Unused/User defined
6	11		Unused/User defined
6	12		Unused/User defined
7	13		Unused/User defined
7	14		Unused/User defined
8	15		Unused/User defined
8	16		Unused/User defined

**FIGURE
7.10**   Six channel.

AES Pair #	Channel #	Label / Name	Description
1	1	L/Left	Far left screen loudspeaker
1	2	R/Right	Far right screen loudspeaker
2	3	C/Center	Center screen loudspeaker
2	4		Unused/User defined
3	5	S/Surround	Mono Surround to all surround loudspeakers
3	3		Unused/User defined
4	7		Unused/User defined
4	8		Unused/User defined
5	9		Unused/User defined
5	10		Unused/User defined
6	11		Unused/User defined
6	12		Unused/User defined
7	13		Unused/User defined
7	14		Unused/User defined
8	15		Unused/User defined
8	16		Unused/User defined

**FIGURE
7.11**   Four channel.

AES Pair #	Channel #	Label / Name	Description
1	1	Lt	Matrix encoded left
1	2	Rt	Matrix encoded right
2	3		Unused/User defined
2	4		Unused/User defined
3	5		Unused/User defined
3	6		Unused/User defined
4	7		Unused/User defined
4	8		Unused/User defined
5	9		Unused/User defined
5	10		Unused/User defined
6	11		Unused/User defined
6	12		Unused/User defined
7	13		Unused/User defined
7	14		Unused/User defined
8	15		Unused/User defined
8	16		Unused/User defined

FIGURE   Two channel.

7.12

AES Pair #	Channel #	Label / Name	Description
1	1		Unused/User defined
1	2		Unused/User defined
2	3	Mono	Single channel center channel
2	4		Unused/User defined
3	5		Unused/User defined
3	6		Unused/User defined
4	7		Unused/User defined
4	8		Unused/User defined
5	9		Unused/User defined
5	10		Unused/User defined
6	11		Unused/User defined
6	12		Unused/User defined
7	13		Unused/User defined
7	14		Unused/User defined
8	15		Unused/User defined
8	16		Unused/User defined

FIGURE   One channel.

7.13

Name	Label	Description
Vertical Height Left	Vhl	Far left top of screen loudspeaker
Vertical Height	Vhc	Center top of screen loudspeaker
Vertical Height Right	Vhr	Far right top of screen loudspeaker
Top Center Surround	Ts	Center of the theatre ceiling loudspeakers
Left Wide	Lw	Outside the screen, front left loudspeaker
Right Wide	Rw	Outside the screen, front right loudspeaker
Left Surround Direct	Lsd	Left surround single loudspeaker for localized directionality
Right Surround	Rsd	Right surround single loudspeaker for localized directionality
LFE 2	Lfe2	Low frequency effects subwoofer style loudspeaker
Rear Surround Left	Rls	Rear wall left loudspeaker/s
Rear Surround Right	Rrs	Rear wall right loudspeaker/s

FIGURE 7.14   Labels: non-legacy channels.

POTENTIALS

One of the more exciting sections of the Audio Characteristics document and the subsequent references in Channel Mapping and labeling is the one that discusses the availability of additional channels of audio beyond the 5.1, 6.1, 7.1, and 9.1 channels of audio we have today. Many suggestions and proposals have been put forward on where to place these channels in the theatre, but only one has been used commercially and that in only one theatre. Certainly it cannot be said what will end up being used and what will be discarded; however; a discussion of pros and cons is in order.

First is the one new channel that has been used, the *top center surround* (Ts), or as it is known in the industry, "the voice of God." This channel is mounted in the center of the theatre in the ceiling over the audience. The experiments and the single film to use this channel have shown it is very effective for conveying a sense of audio space. Helicopters hovering directly over your head, sounds panning from the screen directly over your head to the back wall, and pans laterally across the theatre are all very impressive with the top center surround. This channel also improves the immersive character of the surrounds. The potential drawback to this channel is in its

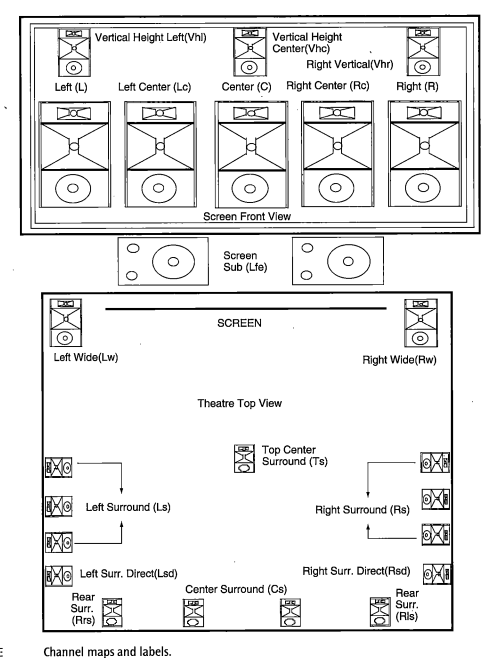

mounting and implementation in the theatre because the speaker(s) might be difficult for theatre personnel to maintain. Speakers positioned over the seating area also have increased liability issues.

The next additional channel is the vertical height channel. The present large screen Imax format utilizes this channel. In the IMAX format this is a single channel mounted center screen at the top of the screen. Although the human ear is not as sensitive in the vertical plane as in the horizontal, with large screen pans and placement at the top of the screen it can be fairly effective.

Most advocates for vertical height in Digital Cinema envision two vertical height channels, but opinions vary in their placement. One scheme is to place a left vertical height (Vhl) speaker at the top of the screen halfway between the left and center speakers and a right vertical height speaker (Vhr) halfway between the right and center speakers. A second scheme would use the top of the screen above the left and right speakers, respectively. Yet a third scheme would place these speakers at the top of the screen but outside the screen boundaries left and right. Some experiments have taken place with vertical height speakers at the top of the screen in the left, center, and right positions. The ultimate value of these schemes is generally unclear and more experimentation will be required.

Another proposal calls for turning the present single rear wall channel into a stereo pair—i.e., rear surround left (Rls) and rear surround right (Rrs). This would allow more discrete placement of sounds and smoother panning across the rear wall and hence panning around the theatre in general. Many theatres currently use multiple speakers for the rear channel, which would simplify installation.

It is suggested that an additional LFE channel would be advantageous, especially if it were located in the back of the theatre. Although low-frequency sounds lack much directionality, some feeling of location may be garnered with this approach as well as additional headroom for low-frequency effects. Another potential solution would put the extreme low frequency from the surround channels into the rear LFE channel, as most surround systems are limited in low-frequency response.

For the sake of argument, assume that the vertical height left and right, top center surround, rear surround left and right, and LFE2 just discussed are creatively useful and economically viable and can be implemented, thereby adding five channels to the existing channel counts. Assuming the nine-channel legacy possibility (left, center, right, left extra, right extra, left surround, right surround, center surround, and sub), we have therefore filled all 16 channels. So although 16 channels seem to be a lot, they will be filled quite easily.

At the current time, the audio committees in SMPTE have two other audio documents nearly ready for balloting: Digital Cinema Audio Physical and Electrical Interfaces and Digital Cinema Audio LFE Characteristics. Digital Cinema Audio Physical and Electrical Interfaces describes the types of connectors to be employed and pin designations for audio inputs and outputs for both analog and digital signals. Digital Cinema Audio LFE Characteristics defines the frequency response and roll-off slope for the subwoofer channel so that all manufacturers will be the same. Neither implementation nor filter design is specified; however, output parameters are defined so that filter design can be accomplished according to each manufacturer's design philosophy.

As time goes on, audio committees will need to tackle the downmixing of audio, wherein the film has more channels than the theatre. The audio processor will mix the channels that the theatre doesn't have into the channels the theatre does have, and do so in an intelligent way. It has been proposed that this downmix could be dynamic in nature and that the original mixing team could determine how this downmix works on a frame-by-frame basis if need be. Static downmix parameters could be available as well. Potentially the opposite, or upmixing, may also be needed, for example, to upmix a 5.1 channel mix in a theatre that has an 8.1 channel system.

These two features are examples of activities that will require data that will control the process. These types of data are called *metadata*. Audio metadata are the descriptive information about the audio and the control of the audio parameters. Digital Cinema audio will require audio metadata and, because of that, the metadata must be defined and specified so that all processors will understand the incoming metadata and respond consistently. In the work done so far on metadata, 13 audio parameters have been identified. However, no work has begun on the specification for either makeup or carriage of these metadata. Figure 7.16 shows examples of audio parameters.

Looking at Parameter 8 in more detail, a possible implementation of the channel assignment parameter could consist of a 32-bit channel assignment word where the presence of a 0 or 1 in a bit location indicates the presence of the specified audio channel in the audio data file. Channel assignment bit

Parameter 1.
Parameter name: Audio Data Format
Description: Provides an indication of the format of the audio data including compression type.

Parameter 2.
Parameter name: Number of audio channels
Description: Indicates the number of output audio channels contained within the audio data.

Parameter 3.
Parameter name: Audio Data Sample Rate
Description: Indicates the playback sample rate of the audio data. For compressed audio data formats this will indicate the playback sample rate of the decompressed audio data.

Parameter 4.
Parameter name: Audio Block Size of Formatted Data as Transported
Description: Block size information for the decoding of audio data. For audio data that has a fixed frame length the block alignment is equal to the length of the frame in bytes. For PCM audio data, this value must be equal to (Number of channels* (Bits per Sample (round to nearest byte))).

Parameter 5.
Parameter name: Bits per Sample
Description: Specifies the number of bits of data used to represent each sample of each channel. For multiple audio channels, the number of bits per sample is the same for each audio channel. Note: This data parameter may not be used/appropriate for compressed audio data formats.

Parameter 6.
Parameter name: Audio Data Program Title
Description: Provides descriptive information about the title of the audio data program material in extended ASCII format that is readable by distributors and exhibitors.

Parameter 7.
Parameter name: Audio Data Program Descriptive Information
Description: Provides descriptive information about the audio data program material in extended ASCII format that is readable by distributors and exhibitors.

Parameter 8.
Parameter name: Channel Assignment
Description: Provides channel assignment information by linking the channel number to predefined speaker locations and defines the order in which the channel audio data appears in the audio data file.

Parameter 9.
Parameter name: Channel Downmix Information
Description: Provides channel downmix information so that multi-channel audio data can be configured to meet the channel spatial locations present in a presentation theatre. It is assumed that 5.1 channels is the minimum allowed theatre channel configuration where the 5.1 channels correspond to FL, FR, FC, BL, BR and LFE.
Dynamic Downmix (dynamic mix) information can be conveyed by updating the Channel Downmix Information throughout the audio data.

FIGURE Audio parameters.

7.16

(Continued)

```
Parameter 10.
Parameter name:        Time Alignment Information
Description:           Provides time alignment information of the audio data referenced to
                       the start of the program. This may be a value that contains the
                       sample count of the first sample of the audio data in the current file
                       relative to the start of the program. The sample count is related to the
                       number of samples per second as defined in the Audio Data Sample
                       Rate parameter.
Parameter 11.
Parameter name:        Program Level Information
Description:           Contains content specific measurements of the audio that can be
                       used to match the levels of program material within the theatre
                       environment.
Parameter 12.
Parameter name:        Dynamic Range Compression Information
Description:           Contains parameters for controlling the dynamic range compression
                       of the audio material within the theatre playback environment.
Parameter 13.
Parameter name:        Image Frame Rate
Description:           Contains the image playback frame rate for use in audio data
                       alignment.
```

FIGURE   Audio parameters. *(Cont'd)*

7.16

locations could be related to spatial locations (taken from the channel mapping document) as shown in Figure 7.17.

THE REALITY

Other audio standards will be necessary in areas such as synchronization, security encryption, loudness control, dynamic range control, watermarking, branching for versioning, play lists and potential audio editing. From a systems standpoint, definitions will be necessary for data interchange of audio coding even if a generic PCM coding is employed. It is quite possible that some of these areas, such as loudness and dynamic range, may not become standardized and manufacturers will then use their capabilities to differentiate themselves from one another. The biggest potential negative of this standardization process is that the standardization stymies innovation. Manufacturers may feel that doing anything other than a cost-effective

Bit	Location	Bit	Location	Bit	Location
0	Left- L	11	Top Center Surround- Ts	22	TBD
1	Right- R	12	Vertical Height Left- Vhl	23	TBD
2	Center- C	13	Vertical Height Center- Vhc	24	TBD
3	Low Freq. Effects- Lfe	14	Vertical Height Right- Vhr	25	TBD
4	Left Surround- Ls	15	Left Wide- Lw	26	TBD
5	Right Surround- Rs	16	Right Wide- Rw	27	TBD
6	Left of Center- Lc	17	Left Surround Direct- Lsd	28	TBD
7	Right of Center- Rc	18	Right Surround Direct- Rsd	29	TBD
8	Center Surround- Cs	19	Low Freq. Effects 2- Lfe2	30	TBD
9	Rear Surround Left- Rls	20	Hearing Impaired- HI	31	TBD
10	Rear Surround Right- Rrs	21	Narration for the Visually Impaired- VI	32	TBD

FIGURE
7.17

Spatial locations.

implementation of the standard is not necessary or profitable. With such a relatively clean sheet of paper for audio in Digital Cinema, the hope and surely the plan are to build the innovation into the standard and therefore have the benefit of a standard with innovative engineering. History will plot the success of these standards endeavors.

Although work does continue on specifying and quantifying audio for Digital Cinema, progress will be slow, until a workable business model for Digital Cinema emerges and DCI issues a full specification. Some interaction exists between all the involved organizations, but no real progress will be made until a final specification from DCI is reality.

The improvements and additional features that will be in audio signals for Digital Cinema will offer the moviegoer an enhanced reality, delivered in a more consistent manner and specifically processed for a particular environment. We are heading into a new era of audio in the cinema.

8 — Digital Cinema Distribution

Darcy Antonellis
Warner Bros. Entertainment, Inc.

Digital Cinema brings with it the promise of transforming the traditional methods of distributing filmed entertainment that have been utilized for decades. Why alter this traditional process? After all, in analog form, film distribution has changed for the better over the years. Release printing processes have shown great technological improvements. Improvements in film stock, high-speed printing, chemical processing and consistency, printing element preparation, and cleaning are just some significant enhancements made to expedite the processing of film prior to its distribution.

Along with those innovations, land and air transportation have likewise seen significant improvements over the past several decades. These improvements have benefited the film industry by providing faster delivery of release prints to theaters on a worldwide basis. What formerly took weeks now takes days. Release prints can be dubbed, subtitled, and distributed to multiple countries worldwide on an expedited basis. These developments have provided the foundation to support revised theatrical release strategies and the rollout of worldwide *day & date*[1] methodologies.

But even while making processes faster, the improvements over the past several decades have not materially changed the inherent workflow and distribution practices associated with filmed entertainment. With the advent of Digital Cinema, the fundamentals of distribution to theaters may introduce a profound new paradigm shift in filmed entertainment.

---

[1]*Day & date*: the entertainment industry term for releasing a feature on the same day in foreign territories as the North American release date, which typically is the first release date. Logistics challenges have always been associated with implementing a day & date strategy due to local territory needs.

The use of both unicast and multicast systems via satellite, terrestrial broadband, or a combination of both, which have been used for decades for television product, provide an ideal platform for Digital Cinema distribution. Many of the processes around distribution scheduling, conditional access to receivers, file management both from central site and at client side (in this case, at each individual exhibitor location), and back-channel reporting are applicable to Digital Cinema delivery requirements. Figure 8.1 shows a typical satellite distribution scheme used for such applications.

This chapter will describe and discuss the attributes and challenges associated with Digital Cinema distribution. The major components of Digital Cinema distribution include content preparation (both from film-based elements as well as digital elements), the transport mechanism from distribution center to exhibitor, security protocols implemented on several levels both at the asset and transport levels, exhibitor-side receiver and reporting components, asset management, and archival systems.

DIGITAL DISTRIBUTION FUNCTIONAL AREAS

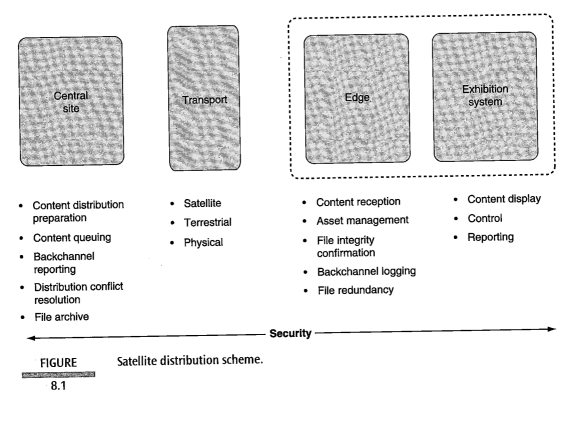

Central site	Transport	Edge	Exhibition system
• Content distribution preparation	• Satellite	• Content reception	• Content display
• Content queuing	• Terrestrial	• Asset management	• Control
• Backchannel reporting	• Physical	• File integrity confirmation	• Reporting
• Distribution conflict resolution		• Backchannel logging	
• File archive		• File redundancy	

← ——————————— Security ——————————— →

FIGURE   Satellite distribution scheme.

8.1

Unlike core display technologies that were developed specifically to provide the basis for Digital Cinema to become reality, distribution of file-based content is today used extensively for a variety of business applications and outlets. Also, the growth of broadband access and the expanded use of the Internet provide perfect resources to support Digital Cinema distribution. The development of compression technologies currently used for other distribution outlets provides methods to support large file distribution.

Because of preexisting processes and systems used predominantly within the television industry for years, this chapter will frequently draw parallels to such systems to provide the reader with additional references to further understand the use of applied technologies to support business needs. Finally, a case study is provided that details digital content delivery testing conducted by Warner Bros.

CONTENT PREPARATION

Content preparation typically begins via one of two ways, by compressing and encoding the feature film using the interpositive as the master source or by compressing and encoding with the use of a digital intermediate master source file. In either case, the compression and encoding protocols are coupled to the related server and display system(s) intended to be used within the exhibitor's location. While significant work has been done in preparation for setting standards—namely, through entities such as SMPTE and ISO—content providers must still encode to specific server/display systems.

The most significant challenges with respect to content preparation reside within the compression and colorimetry components of feature film preparation. As the creative community increases its use of the digital mastering process, the existing practice of employing interpositives as the reference for Digital Cinema version creation is no longer appropriate. The Digital Cinema paradigm redefines quality based on continuing improvements in resolution capture and display capabilities. Also, tools most commonly available within the video domain that can be used to manipulate the look and feel of the feature film are replacing those processes that are purely photochemically based.

DELIVERY

Transport mechanisms can take several forms and can be combined to successfully provide customized last-mile connectivity while not diminishing the capabilities of long-haul, high-bandwidth carrier options. Since Digital Cinema can take advantage of "just-in-time" delivery options, data rates and bandwidth allocations can also be customized to optimize any network configuration. Where days are required to deliver film release prints in physical form, digital delivery can be customized by urgency of delivery. Using Internet protocol (IP) over MPEG or DVB transport mechanisms, the file can be segmented and distributed on a packet basis in streaming or broadcast form or opportunistically. The use of opportunistic data available within a transport stream provides exciting options for digital delivery. It allows for the file to be sent in a store and forward fashion using available bandwidth over time and thus requiring no incremental, additional bandwidth allocations. The file delivery mechanism is complete only when all packets are received and confirmed via checksum.

However, while not currently used, methods of delivery using progressive download models are technically feasible for late deliveries of features. In this case the feature could actually begin while the balance of the file is still being transmitted with portions continuously cached at the exhibitor server. One can argue that due to Digital Cinema file sizes (today typically greater than 50 GB), certain challenges regarding packet delivery consistency and error correction can be reasonably managed, especially using current store and forward technologies. The use of terrestrial secure dedicated fiber, virtual private networks, broadband cable, or ADSL capacity can be tailored to suit delivery and budget constraints. In most cases and even in large markets, it would be acceptable for delivery of a feature film to take several hours (e.g., overnight) to be successfully sent and confirmed back to the hosting server from the distribution center. Again, as the reference has always been delivery within days, the new paradigm will measure delivery within hours and ultimately minutes.

Above all, distribution of Digital Cinema files brings with it opportunities to implement two critical components of content protection and piracy countermeasures: migration to "just-in-time" delivery and introduction of advanced security protocols intended to protect the file from piracy during the distribution process.

Delivery of feature films just prior to their scheduled exhibition provides embedded security improvements by virtue of eliminating the entire traditional physical distribution process in which release prints typically pass from printing labs, to distribution depots, to shipping entities, and finally to exhibitors. Due to dependencies on traditional shipping methods that are affected by factors such as weather and transportation organizations, the process of getting feature films to theaters on time today is less a science and more of a conservative planning exercise.

SECURITY

In the area of security and security protocols, the advantages of distributing files versus release prints are significant. However, there continues to be an ongoing debate as to whether or not Digital Cinema brings with it options for better, more robust security. After all, one could argue that one print shipped traditionally has significantly less global exposure than the distribution of a feature in file format over potentially public networks. This view tends to be based more around comfort associated with traditional methods and less on technological evaluation.

Security should be approached as a multilayer, multidimensional activity addressing storage, transport, and content security. The state in which content resides on a local server can be considered one component whose keys are managed discretely from other types of authentication needed for that transport.

Whether via satellite or terrestrial, some form of conditional access can be applied to provide basic addressing from source to destination. Additionally, encryption applied to data packets is used to protect both *essence* (visual and aural content) and *metadata* (a pre-defined and encoded data set of key attributes associated with the content). Encrypted packets whose keys are managed discretely are then distributed via a protected transport stream, thereby providing dual content protection. Options for applying multiple layers along with key management, as well as the use of watermarking and forensics tracking, are discussed in greater detail in this chapter.

Once received at the exhibitor location, the digital file, called the *Digital Cinema Package* (DCP), is typically stored locally within the theater system. The package contains essence and metadata. The metadata attributes can be passive descriptors or active enablers to trigger functionality within the exhibitor display system.

The metadata can include instructions regarding release window, authorized play period, and other contract terms to provide media management at discrete locations of multiple files. Once the picture has played its engagement, it is technically possible, if contract terms so provide, that deletion procedures could be automatically scheduled within the exhibitor display system or done remotely via the host distribution system and scheduling application.

Back-channel reporting plays a key role in file management between the host and client. It can be established via a variety of methods but most commonly is done via the Internet. The back channel provides messaging back to the host that includes file delivery confirmation, file format integrity, and information regarding file movement from the caching server to playout system. In some cases this could be accomplished by a singular system but as multiple content sources are delivered (the challenges of which will be described later) at different times and speeds, some form of cataloging and offloading from the caching server to the exhibitor display system(s) is prudent. This helps to maintain discrete transmission and display environments and reduce errors associated with data corruption issues, problems that may occur with the distribution link that can affect the display system, and storage contention issues within the caching server handling multiple features.

DIGITAL ASSET MANAGEMENT

Digital Asset Management (DAM) is another key component of Digital Cinema distribution. Massive files with numerous pieces of interstitial material and data quickly become difficult to catalog and track. While digital distribution has developed relatively rapidly, applications suited for file management from a scheduling, distribution, and archival perspective are limited in availability and adequate functionality needed to support Digital Cinema once fully deployed.

Of critical importance is the establishment of metadata standards. A significant amount of work has already taken place, and metadata for the purpose of describing the image itself from reference display system to theater display system have already been preliminarily defined through SMPTE. Elementary metadata identifying the values necessary to support interchange are mapped and must be carried between systems to successfully display the original file.

While discussions remain ongoing, it is possible to include metadata fields that could be populated by, and link to, exhibitor box office data. By virtue of creating both a digital distribution link and required back channel for file management and reporting, metadata also provide a pathway back from the exhibitor to the distributor. This link could provide real-time data ranging from, but not limited to, exhibition date, time, complex, screening room, and box office receipts associated with exhibition times. Also, it could confirm specific activities like date/time stamp of actual playing of the file (feature) and discrepancies associated with the digital display system like file playout discontinuity or security breaches associated with non-authorized attempts to access the file. System monitoring of the display's current state is available and can be captured as data reported back to a distribution central site via the reporting back channel.

DIGITAL ARCHIVING

As part of the move to Digital Cinema, a digital archiving strategy for digital masters must be considered. As with digital asset management, much work remains to effectively manage Digital Cinema masters. Several factors have to be considered including the native resolution of the original source material and its form. An uncompressed feature film of roughly 2 hours in length mastered at 4K resolution requires approximately 8 GB of storage. In compressed form for display, the file size drops down to between 90 GB and 300 GB for a 3-hour feature film. These numbers will continue to change as compression algorithms continue to improve.

Today, industry practice is to physically archive the original production elements (e.g., 35mm film original camera negative, including unused outtakes) and their intermediate elements (e.g., chemically processed interpositives, internegatives, answer and check prints). These elements are stored in humidity- and temperature-controlled environments to inhibit fading and deterioration. This practice not only preserves cinema's heritage for future generations, it also can yield economic benefits by making future re-releases possible. For example, outtakes provide bonus materials for DVD.

With Digital Cinema, this archival methodology will change. The retention of the *Digital Cinema Distribution Master* (DCDM) is essential to support creation of subsequent distribution outlet master creation. For example, the DCDM can be used to generate high-definition and standard-definition versions to support home video and television outlets. Figure 8.2 shows the process used to create the DCDM at Warner Bros.

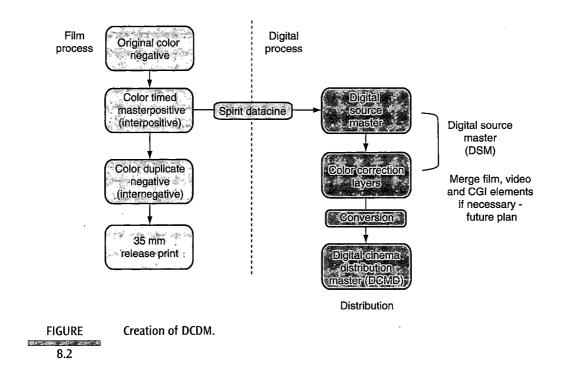

FIGURE   Creation of DCDM.

8.2

SYSTEM OVERVIEW

Distribution Options

Distribution of Digital Cinema feature files can be accomplished via three primary methods: through the use of optical media (typically DVD), digital storage media (tape or HDD technology), and digital distribution (both via satellite or terrestrial).

While this chapter is intended to focus on digital distribution using Internet protocol over a variety of transports, it is important to briefly discuss the first two methods currently used to distribute Digital Cinema. DVD (whether replicated/stamped or DVD-R) and digital tape are today most widely used to distribute digitally prepared features to exhibitors. The DCDM is the source used to create these multiple copies. Local ingest is still required to upload the feature onto the display's server system (see Figure 8.3).

However, using optical media or digital storage media still requires physical distribution as the mechanism to transport the feature from dis-

DIGITAL CINEMA PROCESSING OVERVIEW
EXHIBITING THE DIGITAL FORM

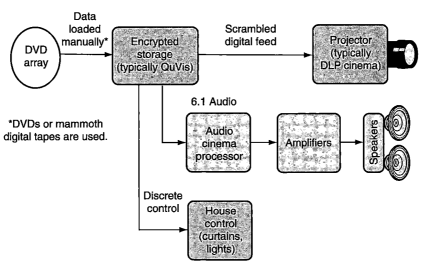

Sample ingest process to Digital Cinema display system.

8.3

tributor to exhibitor. The economic benefits are limited to reduced fees associated with smaller assets to be shipped versus those associated with shipping roughly 45 pounds of film per print to each exhibitor. A typical feature requires 10 to 15 DVDs, while high-density digital tape, disc, or hard drive typically requires one singular cassette or unit to store the feature.

Moreover, there are greater savings associated with shipping DVDs or tape on a rush basis versus a film print, primarily based upon the payload differences in the medium used. These methods are still dependent on transport agents and carriers to move the feature from point to point.

Digital distribution is widely viewed as the logical platform of the future to support Digital Cinema from a mass market perspective. There are several options currently available and more are anticipated as bandwidth access, compression improvements, and intelligent switching networks make moving large files more reliable. Likewise, the option of streaming a feature over terrestrial public networks continues to be developed and has been tested[2]

[2]SHD Digital Cinema Distribution over a Global High-Speed Network: Internet2, Yamaguchi, Shirai, Fujii, Fujii: NTT Network Innovation Laboratories, August 2003.

across Internet2, the next generation high-speed network. This option provides the capability to move large, high-resolution files direct to display systems within the exhibitor location. The challenges associated with this model include reliability across the network to ensure minimal packet loss and re-transmission needs as well as adaptive buffering systems that would manage data transmission fluctuations that would interrupt playback. In most cases, the use of store and forward systems is possible for non-broadcast, non-real-time exhibitor requirements. Streaming can become a viable option as reliable high-capacity connectivity makes its way into exhibitor locations regardless of geography.

Store and Forward methodology, coupled with the use of new transmission optimization tools that improve the *Quality of Service* (QoS) of IP-based networks, can be used very effectively to distribute Digital Cinema files. Since packet losses less than 1.0% can interrupt streaming delivery, transmission tools that compensate for packet loss and latency issues associated with buffering of data are critical. These tools, together with enhanced *Forward Error Correction* (FEC) and the ability to send the Digital Cinema file in a non-broadcast fashion, provide acceptable reliability for network transmission schemes and allow for the use of opportunistic data transmission models to be leveraged at compelling cost-effective rates.

In either case (via streaming or store and forward), the issue of last-mile connectivity is affected by exhibitor location and broadband access. The use of satellite or terrestrial delivery coupled with last-mile options, business rationale, and cost considerations will drive architectural decisions for delivery on an individual basis. For example, rural locations may be perfectly suited for satellite delivery via the use of a low-cost receive only (RO) system mounted on the exhibitor's premises (see GDMX Case Study later in this chapter). In more urban areas where satellite reception as well as dish installation options are limited, the use of commercial long-haul fiber networks coupled with last-mile broadband providers may be more appropriate. In all cases, network and content security is crucial and are discussed in the section *Case Study: Warner Bros. Entertainment Inc.: Proof of Concept.*

System Components

The basic system architecture needed to support Digital Cinema distribution can be described in the context of satellite delivery requirements versus terrestrial network delivery requirements. Subsets of these architectures can be combined where satellite is used for the long-haul portion of delivery to a central aggregation site and a wide area network (WAN) is used for depot-type delivery and is attached to last-mile broadband providers into exhibitor locations.

The transport component illustrated earlier in Figure 8.1 present a high-level view of typical architectures that support Digital Cinema distribution. These assume that standard transmission protocols are maintained, whether MPEG-based transports that are DVB-compliant or IP-based transports that utilize some form of TCP/IP or UDP/IP. Enhancement tools are not standardized for networks and continue to improve, leaving selection up to the distributor or manager of the network.

It is important to understand that the transport platform is completely independent of the display system codecs used. This means that different compression schemes can be successfully utilized for the feature and the transport. The compressed DCDM can be subsequently wrapped utilizing another compression scheme for transport. An example is the use of wavelet-based compression algorithms for Digital Cinema file creation, while MPEG transports are used as the carrier compression scheme on which the file rides.

File Attributes

A Digital Cinema file is roughly similar in structure to a video-on-demand file, with the content resident as well as descriptions about the content and instruction sets that enable specific functions within the VOD environment. As stated earlier, a Digital Cinema package (DCP) contains the content asset itself (the essence), which includes visual and aural content, and metadata, which contains attributes about the file.

The DCP as defined by SMPTE[3] (although still in draft form as of this writing) includes the image structure supporting various resolutions, along with color encoding, and white and brightness reference coordinates that are unique to different display systems at this time. These references support 1.3, 2.0, and 8.0 megapixels at 24 fps resolution systems.

---

[3]SMPTE Draft DC28.101-2883B Rev. 7.4 2004-1-29.

Additionally, file formats supporting interstitial elements such as sub-title streams are included. Audio files are maintained discretely from visual files. The entire structure is intended to provide a standard for the DCDM package that would be transportable between different vendor systems.

Included in the package is a metadata set critical to defining both passive and active attributes of the file. In metadata terms, the composition or self-contained Digital Cinema asset includes various descriptors about the asset(s) themselves. XML-based asset descriptors include, but are not limited to, feature title, trailer information, ratings, feature version (e.g., English vs. French), first and last frame information (equivalent to start-of-message and end-of-message information in the video domain), and playlist information that directs file activation on a timed sequential basis. Known within the SMPTE draft[4] as "reel structure," it enables file management and playlist sequencing.

Digital Distribution Functional Areas

The use of satellite and terrestrial broadband technology has been previously described (see Figure 8.1). This section talks more specifically about the core systems needed to support digital distribution regardless of the transport selected.

Central Site

The central site can be defined as the distribution hub, network operations center, or master control. All describe its function relative to existing distribution models. Typically its role is to aggregate, schedule, distribute, archive, and report on file distribution across a distributed network. Whether through the use of multicast scheduling or point-to-point delivery, the central site *pitches*[5] content to edge servers located remotely at exhibitor locations. The edge servers *catch* the content, decode and store it locally for dissemination to a local server assigned to a specific display system or onto a RAID array that serves multiple streams to displays using SAN and routing

---

[4]SMPTE DC28 Application Specification for Digital Cinema Packaging (AS-DCP) -Proposed SMPTE 000X 2004-02-11.
[5]"pitcher/catcher": generic terminology typically associated with video-on-demand systems; refers to store and forward method of delivery of file from source to destination.

technology and eliminates the need for a 1:1 architecture. Back-channel reporting to the central site confirms file delivery and file integrity at the edge server. The central site provides distribution reporting that includes network performance (retransmission requirements), delivery completions, deliveries queued and awaiting delivery, delivery failures, and edge server status.

One of the challenges with management of Digital Cinema distribution (as with video-on-demand) is remote management of edge server storage. Caching contention issues must be assumed during the design phase and automated offline storage should be considered. One solution is to provide that the central site management application can purge the caching server of dated files not locally purged and move them offline so other files can be delivered. Absent such functionality, contention issues around delivery of files from multiple distributors are possible.

Edge Server (Exhibitor Location)

The client side (edge server) architecture for file reception includes the following components used to support satellite and terrestrial network reception. For satellite reception, an integrated receiver/decoder (IRD) is required to receive the downlinked satellite signal and decode the MPEG stream. The decoded stream is likely to have two layers of content protection applied, which will be discussed later, as well as some form of conditional access used to authorize the decoding (but not decrypting) process between receiver and decoder. Akin to set-top-box authorization, conditional access is intended to restrict delivery of multicast feeds to selected receivers. In this way, only those exhibitors who have contracted to receive a specific feature are authorized to do so. For delivery to the edge server via terrestrial networks, TCP connection and high-speed switching appliances attached to the decoder are required.

Once received, the file remains in encrypted form until, again via a public and private key methodology, the file is authorized for playout via the display system. In cases where the exhibitor is using a local (staging) server in each auditorium and transferring the file between caching server and staging server, the file remains in encrypted form. From an architectural perspective, at no time should the file be in the clear. Decryption should only occur within the cinema display system.

With respect to redundancy, SAN technology coupled with RAID array features provides solutions in the area of storage and file redundancy. Although traditionally used for IT-based business applications, the use of

RAID arrays for redundancy in motion picture production- and distribution-related applications has become common. They allow an environment to be protected via a one-for-many scenario versus the traditional 1:1, primary and backup, device-to-device methodology. Using networking, a standby system with mirrored content can back up multiple systems.

Back-Channel Reporting

Back-channel reporting provides feedback to the central site via an Internet or dial-up connection between the edge server, running a file management application, and the central site scheduling application. It confirms file receipt and integrity and notifies the central site of storage contention issues and re-transmission requirements due to network failures. For security purposes, the back channel provides valuable feedback confirming the presence of authorized devices and deletion of expired files.

Enhanced functionality can extend beyond the local reception environment into the exhibitor scheduling and ticketing systems. While technically capable, this functionality is left more to business decisions and contractual agreements between distributors and exhibitors.

Security

As discussed previously, security of Digital Cinema files through the distribution process and while locally stored at the exhibitor until playout is of critical importance. Growing illegal file-sharing and piracy escalation worldwide, plus the availability of a pristine digital copy on the Internet that can be used as a master source for illegal packaged goods manufacturing, make protecting the digital file essential to rolling out Digital Cinema on a large scale.

The need for security while the movie is being shown is being approached on several fronts that include active measures for protecting the feature as well passive measures that aid in identifying the feature at any point in time. From a distribution perspective, the file, once compressed, is encrypted using a form of a generally accepted military-grade encryption algorithm. As of this writing, AES 128 bit encryption is generally accepted but no firm standards have been established as encryption development

---

[6]SMPTE DC28 AS-DCP Track File Essence Encryption–Proposed SMPTE 000X 2004-03-01.

Case Study: Warner Bros. Entertainment Inc. : Proof-of-Concept

221

continues. SMPTE has drafted a specification[6] that utilizes AES with encrypted KLV triplets for track files to be uniquely encrypted.

In conclusion, this chapter described three layers of content protection: the content package itself (decrypted only on playout), the transport path itself (decrypted only on reception,) and authentication of the reception device via conditional access that confirms device identification.

CASE STUDY: WARNER BROS. ENTERTAINMENT INC. : PROOF-OF-CONCEPT

By Ken Long – Manager, GDMX

The advent of the *Digital Video Broadcasting* (DVB) standard, which has allowed a standard protocol for the integration of *Internet Protocol* (IP) data into a broadcaster's existing digital satellite bit stream, has made the distribution of Digital Cinema content over satellite possible and practical. This method inserts IP data into the broadcast transport stream, multiplexed with one or more real-time audio/video content streams or other protocol data encapsulated as MPEG content. The result is a single transport bit stream that contains each individual data stream multiplexed serially, identifiable by a *program identifier* (PID) that determines each 188-byte packet as being part of a given content stream. The receiver/decoder is then programmed to recognize the PID of a particular content stream it is interested in decoding.

The basis for transmitting a digital feature film via satellite is the same as for transmitting other computer files over multicast IP networks. However, Digital Cinema content presents a unique challenge. Because the files are very large, it is quite common to find breakpoints resident in the software used to process those files that go unnoticed with smaller data sets but caused by overruns and other types of failures when presented with 50 to 100 GB datasets. Also, because of the high value of the content, adequate electronic means to protect it from unauthorized downlinking, copying, or exhibition must be thoroughly implemented. Finally, because even a minor error or break-up of the image during theatrical presentation is unacceptable, methods must be used to ensure the perfectly reliable delivery of the content, even given potentially unfavorable conditions at the downlink site or the unavailability of a back channel for retransmission requests (however, this reliability can be achieved through the use of unique encoding technologies).

Security of the digital files during their transmission and storage is of great concern. The advances in the bandwidth of home Internet connections, the compression efficiency of modern codecs, the popularity of peer-to-peer file-sharing software, and the speed with which a digital version of a film can traverse the Internet all represent threats. So everything possible must be done to protect the files from anything but legitimate exhibition in the designated theater. Thus the use of a secure encryption technology remains critical. If left unencrypted, the media would be vulnerable to theft not only at the theater, but also by anyone in the footprint of the satellite transmission.

For the case study described here, the entire process for the successful multicast distribution of Digital Cinema content consisted of three major phases: the digital encoding of the film content and the packaging and encryption of the asset, the satellite transmission itself, and finally the decryption, unpackaging, verification, and delivery of the digital asset to the playout device.

To accomplish these tasks, we configured a rack with a receiver PC that consisted of a Broadlogic PCI-based DVB integrated receiver/decoder card, a DSL connection, a backup dial-up modem, and all of the Linux-based software necessary to run the system. The rack also contained a network-attached RAID array for storing the media files, a QuVis QuBit ST Digital Cinema Server as well as audio digital-to-analog converters and an *uninterruptible power supply* (UPS).

Phase 1: Asset Creation

The first phase included the creation of the asset to be transmitted. The choices of bit rate and codec will depend on the target resolution and quality for projection (1K, 2K, 4K), as well as the type of playout device being used. Since we were using a QuBit server for playout, our files were compressed using the QuBit Media Format version 1 (QMF1) at a *maximum data rate* (MDR) of 30 MB/s and a 51-dB SNR. However, it should be noted that the transmission system developed is not dependent on a particular playout device and can work with anything capable of accepting an external bit stream.

Once the files have been encoded and/or compressed for the playout device, they need to be encrypted. We chose the 256-bit key length and block size variant of the Rijndael block cipher for this task. This algorithm (as of

Case Study: Warner Bros. Entertainment Inc. : Proof-of-Concept

223

this writing) is recognized as extremely secure and difficult to attack by the Computer Security Division of the National Institute of Standards and Technology (NIST) and was chosen as the cipher of choice for federal agencies to use when protecting sensitive classified information.

However, because we want to transmit this content to a number of different theaters but be able to differentiate between them when distributing keys, a public-key cipher is necessary. For this the *Diffie–Hellman* (DH) key agreement protocol was chosen. This is implemented by creating a public/private-key pair for each receiver intended to go to a particular cinema. The public keys are stored at the uplink, and the private key is placed on a medium that cannot be copied, such as a smart card. Thus the fixed Rijndael session key can be encrypted using the DH method, once for each cinema downlink. In this way, the presence of the smart card would be required for successful decryption. If the smartcard were to be found missing, the public key would be revoked at the uplink and no further content would be decryptable by that card.

Once encrypted, the feature film must be split up into manageable sections. Through testing, it was found that splitting the encoded media into 15-GB sections made for much more efficient memory utilization during the metacontent creation process. To split the files, Eugene Roshal's RAR Archiver software was used in uncompressed mode. One advantage of using the RAR Archiver was that 32-bit CRC values are calculated during the split operation, which will allow the confirmation of data integrity during reconstruction of the segments on the downlink side. A second advantage is that split archives can be further scrambled with another password that can be sent via the back channel only to a particular network address. This provides some confirmation of the physical location of the receiver device (location verification will be discussed later).

Once the feature clip has been encrypted with the public keys of each cinema downlink and then broken up in segments, they are ready for transmission.

Phase 2: Transmission

The transmission phase begins by scheduling the encrypted and segmented assets to be transmitted. As discussed previously, this involves generating a metacontent stream using a delivery optimization application. There are several commercially available. The algorithm allows an arbitrary length input to be converted to an infinite stream of 1-KB metacontent packets. Each metacontent packet is a representation of the entire input data set. The complete construction of the output stream requires the collection of only a certain number of these packets, with no regard for which specific packets are collected. This means that the unpredictable nature of packet loss is negated. Each client will receive at its optimum rate regardless of its percent of loss. Clients with higher loss will simply take longer to collect the required amount of metacontent to construct the entire package. Even sites with loss approaching 100% would eventually receive a complete file (although transmission times would become prohibitively lengthy for excessive packet loss). Traditional methods of error prediction and correction, such as forward error correction (FEC), require one to predict the maximum loss correctable and then be forced to incur the maximum penalty across all receivers, regardless of their individual loss, in order to compensate for the total loss budget. Metacontent also negates the need for methods utilizing back channels (Internet or dial-up) for any type of automatic repeat request (ARQ) method or error correction.

However, a back channel is still utilized for the reporting of the transmission status, as well as to authenticate the location of the receiver. Since the physical location of the downlink cannot be controlled to any greater extent than the footprint of a transponder or a spot beam, a method to more accurately check the location of the receiver prior to starting decryption is desirable. This can be accomplished by examining the source IP address for Internet back channels or the *automatic number identification* (ANI) of the source phone for dial-up back channels (the latter is preferable due to its greater difficulty of being faked.) This back channel can be used to deliver the first key needed to reassemble the segments, even before the smartcard is consulted for the DH key agreement phase and streaming decryption for output to the play out device.

Once the segments have been received at the downlink and the metacontent completely decoded, it is time to apply the decryption keys and prepare the asset for playout.

Phase 3: Asset Reconstruction and Delivery to Playout Device

The final phase finishes the process of delivery by loading (via the back channel) the keys needed for building up the complete feature film from the

Case Study: Warner Bros. Entertainment Inc. : Proof-of-Concept

225

15-GB segments. Since the RAR Archiver was used to split the encrypted feature into segments, it is used again to put them back together. During this phase, CRC values are checked, and a layer of scrambling is applied. This provides for a step in which the proper key is delivered to the receiver via the back channel only once certain requirements are met. For example, it could be used to enforce a start time (by delivering the key via the back channel immediately before the first permissible showing) as well as using IP addresses or telephone numbers to narrow down the physical location of the receiver.

The result is a file that can be streamed through a block-cipher decryption (in this case Rijndael 256) as it is being delivered to the playout device. This would likely need to be accelerated in hardware for high-bit-rate codecs. However, since at the current time the QuBit does not support streaming the media from an external source for playback, it was necessary to load the entire feature clip onto the QuBit first. This method is considerably less desirable from a security standpoint since it allows an unencrypted version of the film to sit on a disc, but as the technology in playout devices improves, this deficiency in the current generation will be corrected.

The end result is a feature-length digital film capable of being delivered without error to any number of cinema downlinks regardless of transmission packet loss. Each site is positively verified via the back channel with playback permission granted by a conditional access smartcard system.

9 Projection

Matt Cowan and Loren Nielsen
Entertainment Technology Consultants

Digital projection is one of the key drivers for Digital Cinema implementation. It is the most visible and most expensive component of the delivery chain. For Digital Cinema to be successful, the technology must transparently deliver the story to the screen. Cinema storytelling often uses dark areas of the image to develop the story, and as a result, color and dynamic performance, especially near black, are very important.

This chapter discusses requirements for the image. Picture performance dimensions include contrast, brightness, resolution, image size, color fidelity, motion management, and aspect ratios. Repeatability and stability are also important. In each of these dimensions, film sets a benchmark standard that must be met or exceeded by digital technology.

Several technologies have contended for this application space. DLP Cinema™ technology (from Texas Instruments) has been deployed in theatres for almost 5 years and is delivering acceptable performance on a day-to-day basis. Liquid-crystal-based technologies (from JVC and soon from Sony) have had less success in achieving performance and stability for this application.

The projector is one of the key elements in delivering the creative vision to the movie screen. Its performance requirements are driven by a combination of creative needs and the effects of the viewing environment. This chapter first examines the theatre viewing conditions and follows with a discussion of the required projector attributes.

VIEWING CHARACTERISTICS OF THE THEATRE

This section examines the viewing geometry, screen conditions, and lighting conditions within the theatre.

Theatre geometry

There is no standard design for a movie theatre, but there are some trends worth understanding. The presentation format is generally one of two different formats: flat, sometimes referred to as academy wide screen, has an aspect ratio of 1.85:1. CinemaScope (or Scope) has an aspect ratio of 2.39:1.

Theatre dimensions are often expressed as ratios. For example, projection throw distance is referenced to the screen width. Seating distance from the screen is expressed as a ratio to the screen height. These ratios are affected by the fact that there are different screen heights or widths for the Scope and flat formats. As an example, consider a theatre with the following geometry:

◆ Screen width—40′ for Scope and flat
◆ Screen height—16.7′ Scope, 21.6′ flat
◆ Projection distance—80′
◆ Projection throw ratio: 2:1, Scope and flat

A seat 40′ back from the screen is 2.4 screen heights back for Scope and 1.9 screen heights for flat.

Common Height

In traditional cinemas, the screen width is adjusted between Scope and flat formats. The screen height remains constant during this adjustment. For a Scope presentation, the side screen masking is pulled out to accommodate the 2.39:1 presentation aspect ratio. For flat, the masking is moved in to the 1.85:1 aspect ratio. In a common height theatre, the Scope presentation therefore has the largest screen size.

Common Width

Many newer cinemas are designed with a common width for Scope and flat. Top and bottom masking on the screen is moved up and down to accommodate the two aspect ratios. In a common width theatre, the Scope presentation has less screen area than a flat presentation. These two alternatives are shown in Figure 9.1.

Theatre Layout

Newer cinemas are designed with the projection booth behind the back wall of the theatre. The distance from the projector to the screen is approximately twice the width of the projection screen (see Figure 9.2). Usually the front row of seats is closer than one screen height in Scope presentation format. (Note that these are very rough rules of thumb; every theatre is different, and some are vastly different.)

The seating location of the viewers is critical to how much resolution is required to satisfy them. The closer they are, the more resolution they will require.

Theatre Contrast

Conditions within the auditorium affect the look of a projected image on screen. The theatre contributes stray lighting from aisle and exit lights that illuminate the screen. Light is also scattered back to the screen from the walls

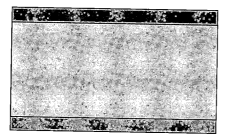

Common width screen configuration

Common height screen configuration

FIGURE 9.1 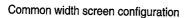 Changing the screen format in the theatre. Common width used in many modern designs uses top and bottom masking to convert from flat (1.85:1) to Scope (2.39:1). Common height uses side masking to convert.

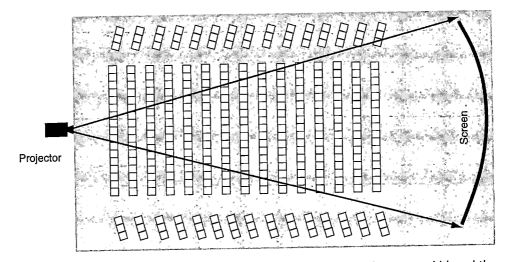

Projector

FIGURE

9.2

"Typical" theatre layout, with projection throw distance twice the screen width and the first row of seats at 0.8 screen heights back.

and seats. These stray sources of screen illumination compete with the projected image, resulting in degraded image quality. The degradation in image quality takes the form of lower-contrast images, reduced depth, and milky blacks. SMPTE has several specifications describing theatre performance.[1] These were written for film presentation and are being updated for digital projection.

PROJECTION SYSTEM PERFORMANCE PARAMETERS AND MEASUREMENT METHODS

The projector should be considered as part of a total visual system, starting with the source material and ending at the viewer's retina. The overall performance is dependent on each contributor to the system. It is possible to identify and isolate most of the factors that contribute to overall picture performance. This section addresses the principal projector performance parameters, what they mean, and how they are measured.

Screen Brightness

The screen brightness is very important for cinema. Screen brightness is the image brightness or luminance as seen by the audience. SMPTE

---

[1] SMPTE 196M.

specifies[2] that the screen luminance shall be 16 ftL (foot Lamberts) or 55 cd/m^2 open gate. This equates to 14 ftL (48 cd/m^2) with clear film in the gate. Current practice in Digital Cinema uses 12 ftL for peak projected white, which provides an approximate visual match to a film print running through a projector set at 16 ftL open gate. Experiments are ongoing to evaluate whether increasing the Digital Cinema setting to 14 ftL (48 cd/m^2) improves the visual match to projected film. The gating factor is the ability to achieve this brightness on very large screens with digital projectors. It should be noted that while SMPTE specifies screen brightness for a projected image, common practice in the cinema is to operate the projector with considerably less brightness than the 16 ftL specified.

The human visual system is very adaptive. In a movie theatre, the filmmaker is able to present convincing images of bright sunlight using a brightness level that is less than 1% of the brightness in the actual scene.

This is done by creating brightness and color relationships on the screen that persuade the viewer that it is bright sun. It is interesting to note that the human visual system, in spite if its highly adaptive nature, will see color relationships differently depending on the brightness of the image. This is especially true of the brightness range experienced in cinema. An image displayed at 6 ftL will look flat and desaturated compared to the same image at 12 ftL.

Luminance and Illuminance

Luminance is the *brightness* of an object. It is a reflective measurement determined by looking directly at the object. *Illuminance* is the light that comes from a light source that is used to *illuminate* an object. For Digital Cinema projection, luminance is the measure of how bright the screen is, and illuminance is the measure of how much light is coming from the projector and falling on the screen. The screen luminance, or brightness, is determined by the amount of light falling on the screen (illuminance) and the reflectivity of the screen. The screen reflectivity is called *screen gain*.

Screen brightness is measured in candelas per square meter (cd/m^2) in the SI system, or foot Lamberts (ftL) in the American measurement system. To convert one to another: 1 ftL = 3.426 cd/m^2.

Projector light output is measured in *lumens*. Lumens are determined by integrating the *luminous flux*, or light coming out of the projection lens

---

[2] SMPTE 196M.

(measured in lux) over the total illuminated area (1 lux = 1 lumen/meter^2). ANSI defines a specification to calculate the useful lumens output of the projector by measuring 9 areas of the screen and integrating these measurements over the screen area (see Figure 9.3).

To calculate lumens:

$$Lumens = Average\_incident\_flux\ (lux) \times Screen\_area\ (square\_meters)$$

Screen Gain

As mentioned before, luminance or image brightness is a function of illumination and reflectivity. In the theatrical situation, reflectivity of the screen is referred to as *screen gain*.

Screen gain sounds as if it is a property where the screen reflects more light than falls on it. Obviously this is not possible. Unity gain (gain = 1) is compared to a *Lambertian reflector*, as illustrated in Figure 9.4. A Lambertian reflector reflects incident light equally in all directions. A higher gain will reflect the light preferentially on axis, giving a higher on-axis reflectivity than a Lambertian reflector. This is at the cost of reflecting less light off axis. A typical screen gain curve is illustrated in Figure 9.5.

A high-gain screen will provide less brightness to observers who are off axis than to those on axis, causing non-uniform image brightness through-

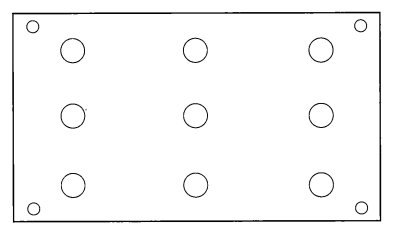

FIGURE

9.3
Diagram showing the 9 screen measurement locations for making a determination of the ANSI lumens from a projector. Note the additional 4 locations in the corner to measure screen uniformity.

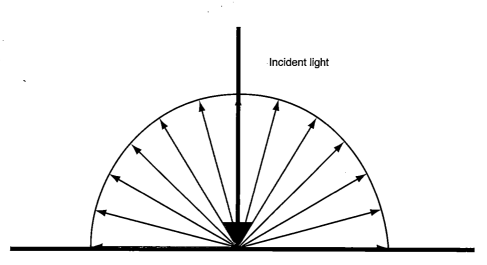

Screen

FIGURE
9.4

Lambertian reflector. Incident light hits the reflector and reflects equally in all directions, giving a uniform light distribution against screen angle. Note that this defines "gain = 1" for a screen. It is difficult to realize in practice, but it can be approximated by a piece of bright white paper.

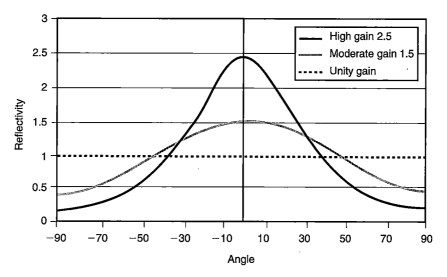

FIGURE
9.5

Plot illustrating the screen reflectivity against angle. Zero degrees represents the light reflected to the seat in the center of the auditorium, while higher angles represent the light reflected to seats off center. Note that a high-gain screen, while providing high brightness to the center seat, provides a dimmer image to the off-center seats.

out the auditorium. In extreme cases, "hot spotting" will occur, where the direct reflection of the projected image will be sufficiently brighter that the viewer will see a hot spot.

Screen gain design is a science and an art that attempt to maximize the reflection from the screen while maintaining coverage over a wide angle. Tied to the art and science is the use of screen curvature, which will focus the screen gain optimally over the seating array.

Image Brightness

Image brightness luminance is measured in cd/m², sometimes called *nits*. It is a measure of the reflected light, representing the image brightness that an audience will see.

Brightness should be measured from several positions in the theatre and averaged. Currently SMPTE is drafting documents that will provide a standardized practice for screen brightness measurement in the theatre, which is likely to be similar to the procedure for film, SMPTE 196M.

In designing a projection system, the on-axis screen brightness may be calculated approximately by the following:

$$Screen\_Brightness \approx \frac{Screen\_gain \times Lumens}{Screen\_area}$$

Tied to image brightness is the brightness distribution. Over time, it has become accepted that the most pleasing cinema images are brightest in the center and have a slight luminance fall off toward the edges. The optimal variance is between 15% and 25%, which is not noticeable visually but subtly draws the attention toward the center of the screen and reduces the effects of flicker in peripheral vision.

Importance of Image Brightness

The human visual system's perception of color changes with varying image brightness. As images become darker, the perception tends to become bluer and less colorful. This effect is apparent at the typical screen brightness levels seen in theatres. The perceived color and color relationships will be different for the same presentation made at 14 ftL (48 cd/m²) or at 7 ftL (24 cd/m²).

This effect can be seen by projecting an image and adjusting the brightness. To maintain color relationships, it is important that the image be projected at the luminance for which it was created.

Contrast Considerations

Contrast puts depth and drama into the picture. A low-contrast system in effect adds some light to the dark areas of the image, making the image appear milky and one-dimensional. Detail is diminished. For conveying artistic intent, contrast is one of the most important attributes of projector performance.

Contrast is specified in four different ways, resulting from four different measurement conditions: *off-to-on, ANSI* (checkerboard), *local area,* and *in situ.* For example, the same projection device may measure 2000:1 contrast off-to-on, 550:1 ANSI contrast, and 200:1 in situ contrast. This stresses the importance of understanding how contrast is measured to determine the contrast performance of the projector.

Off-to-On Contrast

Off-to-on contrast, sometimes called *sequential,* expresses the projector's ability to achieve absolute black. It is measured by comparing the ratio of the "full on" white light output to the "full off" light output. In other words, the luminance of a maximum brightness white field is compared to a minimum brightness black field. Digital projection systems are currently achieving close to 2000:1 sequential contrast. This is very comparable to film print performance.

Sequential contrast ratio is the one that best defines the suitability of a projector for cinema application. This is because the cinema medium is dark and relies on providing good image dynamics near black. A high-sequential-contrast system will provide good definition in this area, while a low-contrast system will wash out the image and lose details near black.

ANSI (Checkerboard) Contrast

ANSI contrast (sometimes called *simultaneous* contrast) compares the contrast between black and white squares in a 16-square checkerboard pattern (see Figure 9.6). This measurement is useful for determining the quality of the optical system in terms of flare. A system with low ANSI contrast will scatter more light from the white squares to the dark squares. The average light level of this pattern is much higher than most film frames, so this test is quite demanding and perhaps of limited utility in relation to how cinema images will look.

In practice, ANSI checkerboard contrast is difficult to measure. In a normal viewing system, it is measuring not only the effect of the scatter of light in the projection optics (which is intended), but also scattering through the port glass, the screen, and the room. Because projector manufacturers have no control over the environment external to the projector, they eliminate extraneous influences and make ANSI measurements by projecting into a black void and measuring the incident illumination where a screen would be, as opposed to measuring reflected light from a screen. While this is a valid way to make a measurement, it bears little relation to the performance in an actual installation. Typical ANSI contrast numbers for Digital Cinema projectors are between 450:1 and 600:1.

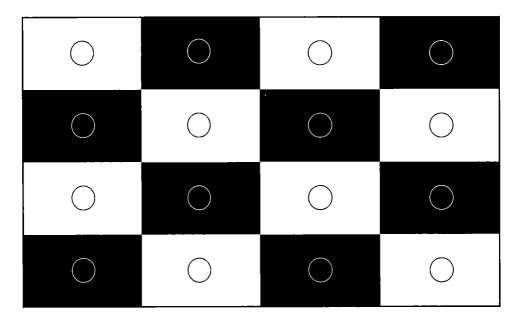

FIGURE 9.6   ANSI checkerboard contrast pattern showing eight white and eight black squares. Measuring location is the center of each square.

Local Area Contrast

Local area contrast defines the ability to maintain adequate contrast between small objects in the projected image. At the most extreme level, this can be measured on a pixel-by-pixel basis, using an alternating pattern of pixel-on and pixel-off. Local area contrast is important for maintaining detail in an image. Digital projectors generally provide higher local area contrast performance than film is capable of achieving.

In Situ Contrast

It is more useful to know how well the projection system (including effects of the auditorium) is performing than the isolated projector. In situ contrast measurements are made by measuring the actual contrast achieved in a working theatre. These measurements will account for the back scatter in the auditorium and sources of stray light. It provides a more accurate prediction of how the projected image will perform in an actual theatre system, and the resulting measurement provides a strong clue to how well the overall system will preserve image dynamics (see Figure 9.7 in the Color Plate section).

A very good theatre system is capable of providing approximately 200:1 in situ contrast, using an ANSI checkerboard contrast pattern.

Resolution

In a digital system, resolution is often confused with pixel count in the projection device. In fact, resolution is a more complex concept. From a human perceptual point of view, image detail and sharpness are what we see and experience in the image. Resolution plays a key role in this, but a more important factor is the ability to achieve high contrast on finer details. This performance is best described by a 2-D graph called *Modulation Transfer Function,* or MTF (see Figure 9.8).

Modulation Transfer Function

Modulation transfer function describes a system's ability to preserve image contrast at varying resolutions. Human perception values detail and sharpness more than resolution. A single resolution specification does not provide much information on the actual detail in the image. More important is how much

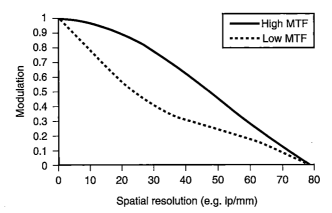

MODULATION TRANSFER FUNCTION

FIGURE

9.8

Plot showing the modulation of two different systems. Note that each system has the same limiting resolution (80 lp/mm) but very different response in the resolution between 10 and 60 lp/mm. The high-MTF system will have higher contrast in most detail in the image, resulting in a sharper overall picture.

modulation is available at mid-resolution. Detail and sharpness can generally be determined by a function of the area under the MTF curve. Consider the MTF curve in Figure 9.9.

On the horizontal axis, the MTF curve displays the spatial resolution of the system. This is typically measured in line pairs per millimeter (lp/mm) or lines per picture height (lph) and is a measure of the spatial resolution being characterized. The vertical axis shows the system response. In generating these curves, it is assumed that the system is being driven by a sine wave, which goes from fully on (1) to fully off (0). The resulting curve shows the degradation that occurs through the electronic and optical systems associated with the projector.

Spatial information contained in the image is presented to the viewer on both dimensions of the MTF curve. Information in the image can have both resolution and contrast at the detail level in the image. A measure of the amount of information a system can deliver can be approximated by the area under the MTF curve. This indicates that it is as important to preserve contrast at mid-resolution as it is to preserve high resolution. In fact, high resolution that substantially degrades contrast is of little visual value in the image.

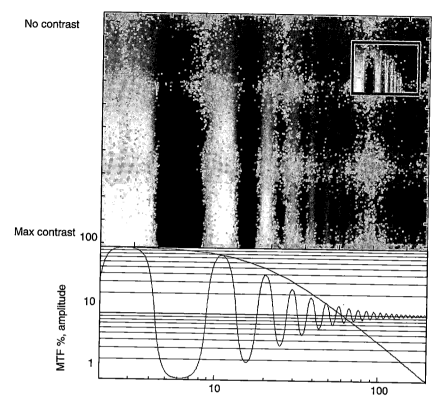

FIGURE 9.9 Plot showing the modulation of two different systems. Note that each system has the same limiting resolution (80 lp/mm) but very different response in the resolution between 10 and 60 lp/mm. The high-MTF system will have higher contrast in most detail in the image, resulting in a sharper overall picture.

Limiting Resolution

Limiting resolution is the finest detail that can be visually observed when the system is given an input that has full modulation (white = 1, black = 0), representing the finest detail that is possible to display. For a human viewer, limiting resolution occurs when the modulation drops to about 3%. Limiting resolution can be determined from the MTF curve by observing where the MTF curve crosses the 3% modulation level.

Some projector technologies, (e.g., DLP Cinema™) preserve high contrast at a pixel-to-pixel level, while LCD-based projector technologies show reduced contrast at the same resolution. This may give DLP projectors a higher limiting resolution than an LCD projector for the same number of pixels.

Pixelization and Aliasing

Closely tied to resolution is the pixel structure that makes up digital projectors. The imaging devices in digital projectors are generally made of distinct *picture elements* (pixels) that are used to make up an image. These elements are small colored dots that when viewed in totality result in an image. In current Digital Cinema technology, the image is made from 2048 horizontal picture elements. From a normal theatrical viewing distance (e.g., two picture heights), these picture elements blend together to give the appearance of a smooth image. If the viewer is too close to the screen, then pixelization and aliasing may be seen.

Pixelization describes a visible overlaid texture that is not part of the original image. The image often appears to be made up of individual colored squares, like a mosaic. Pixelization can be reduced or eliminated by increasing the number of pixels on the screen, by increasing the viewing distance, or by slightly defocusing the image. Some technologies (e.g., DLP Cinema™) are more prone to pixelization because the display structure has a noticeable black line around each pixel.

Aliasing describes a visible condition where a diagonal straight line in the image appears to have a fine stair-step texture to it. This occurs because the structure of the display is not fine enough to smooth the edges of lines. To minimize the appearance of aliasing, digital filtering may be applied at the input of the projector to reduce the high spatial frequencies in the image. This causes a slight blurring of the image but reduces the pixelization resulting from aliasing.

COLOR

Within projection systems, color is produced by mixing three primary colors together to produce the desired hue and saturation. There are practical limitations to the ability to show color. Projector designers endeavor to show the widest color range possible while maintaining high brightness on the screen.

Any color can be uniquely defined by three values. This drives a fundamental aspect of current projector architectures. They are designed to accept three independent input values (in current practice *RGB,* or red, green, and blue) to define the color desired.

Color Primaries and Color Gamut

In conventional digital projection systems, color is reproduced by using the three input values (*RGB*) to drive the three color channels in the projector. The three color channels correspond to specific primary colors. These three colors then define the boundaries of the color performance of the system.

Color science states that given three color primaries, any color can be produced that lies within the boundaries of the straight line joining the primaries. This area is called the *color gamut* (see Figure 9.10 in the Color Plate section).

In television, the gamut is well defined by ITU standards,[3] and the entire system is limited to performance dictated by this color gamut. This was defined when the NTSC analog broadcast standard was created, and compromises were made in the color gamut, in particular to allow higher brightness and longer life of the phosphors that make color in CRT displays. The result is that television has a smaller color gamut than film, in particular in the areas of yellow and cyan. Yellow drives rich skin tones, and cyan drives water and sky.

Therefore, in Digital Cinema, a color gamut wider than that for television is required to display film-like color. Current digital projector technology is based on the xenon lamp, which allows a much wider color gamut than television. The color gamut available is close to that of a film print. It is expected that wider gamuts will be available in the future with the implementation of alternative illumination sources, such as lasers. This drives a requirement that the Digital Cinema system support wider color gamuts for the future.

Current state-of-the-art performance for Digital Cinema projection is defined by the triangle outlined for DLP Cinema™ in Figure 9.10 in the color plate section. These are the color coordinates employed by Texas Instruments in their projector technology designed for cinema application, and these coordinates are being recommended to SMPTE as the baseline values for a reference projector.

---

[3] ITU BT.601 and ITU BT. 709.

White Point

White forms a vital part of the creative palette. A cinematographer will alter the color of white to set a mood—e.g., warm, cool, or edgy.

White point is critical to the cinematographer from two points of view. Firstly, the white point for projection must be close enough to neutral for the cinematographer to successfully overlay his color. Think of this as the watercolor artist painting on the white canvas. Secondly, it must be consistent from installation to installation. This ensures that the cinematographer's work appears the same on every screen. Yet the color of white is subject to surprisingly wide variation. In practice, there are three separate but related white points to be managed in the Digital Cinema system.

Encoding White Point

This is the white that is assumed by the encoding. Typically it is the color that is expected to be produced when the three input channels are equal (i.e., RGB). This ensures that the color that is "baked in" to the input signal is faithfully reproduced. This value is a requirement of standardization.

Display White Point

This is the color where the display is most efficient. In fact, the actual physical color of the display's white point is not particularly important, provided the display knows the white point of the encoded signal and is capable of performing a transformation to compensate for this color.

Creative White Point

This is the color that the cinematographer wishes to make white. For example, an early evening scene may have a yellower (warmer) white point, while a mid-day scene may have a bluer (cooler) white point. The choice of white points is dependent on the creative intent and cannot be designed or standardized. What is important is that the creative white point be available within the operational parameters.

In projector design, an optimized white point is a function of efficiency. The projector starts with a white light source—currently short arc xenon. It optically splits this source into red, green, and blue color channels. Each channel is modulated by the incoming coded *RGB* signal. As we saw earlier, colors are created by combining *R*, *G*, and *B*. White is also made by a combination of *R*, *G*, and *B*. The brightest possible white is available if all three-color channels are fully turned on. This fact drives an engineering decision to make the red, green, and blue primaries such that the combination of each channel fully turned on makes the correct color of white, referred to as the *native white point* of the projector. If a white different from the native white is desired, the projector is required to reduce the luminance of one or two of the component colors. This means that the different white will inevitably be dimmer than the native white.

Color and Luminance Management

Impact of Correct Color on Image Quality

Cinematography has been described as painting with light.[4] The projector and cinema screen represent the final canvas on which the painting is displayed. Color nuances are important to tell a story: mood is set and tension developed through subtle changes in color. For this reason, the projector must faithfully reproduce the intended color and color relationships.

It should be noted that at the time of writing, film represents the dominant display medium for cinema viewers. The creative and technical experts in the film industry know how to achieve the desired look of the picture using film attributes. As such, film is the standard against which digital is being compared. This means that in mastering, the digital image must be capable of representing the look and feel of the film image. This requirement has presented some technical challenges in the past.

This challenge is further compounded when projection technologies evolve. The current alternative projection technologies for Digital Cinema are dominated by Texas Instruments' DLP Cinema™ system. It uses a xenon lamp for illumination and has physical *RGB* primaries for displaying color. It is widely expected that other projection technologies will be introduced that have different inherent color characteristics—e.g., laser illumination. While this will give an expanded palette for painting, it creates a situation in which images from the same source content will appear quite different on the screen. This would be an unacceptable outcome.

This eventuality is being addressed with color management systems in the projectors. As discussed in Chapter Four of this book, the Digital Cinema data file will be converted to *X'Y'Z'* color coordinates, which allows all colors humanly visible to be coded. It is the responsibility of the projector to ingest these data and then display the intended color. Refer to the color gamut diagram in Figure 9.10 in the Color Plate section. It can be seen that there are humanly visible colors that are outside the gamut of current projector technologies. The future projector will be required to gracefully map these outside colors into its color gamut. This process is known as *appearance modeling* or *gamut mapping*.

Strategies for gamut mapping for Digital Cinema are currently being discussed and developed, and it is expected that SMPTE will document Recommended Practices to accomplish this process.

Color Calibration

To ensure that the intended color is shown on screen, it is necessary to calibrate the projection system. Note here that the projection system consists of not only the projector but also the port glass and screen. Each of these adds some coloration to the final image. Additionally, there will always be manufacturing tolerance in color from projector to projector.

As stated earlier, the color primaries for digital projectors are created by splitting white light into red, green, and blue components. Splitting is performed by dichroic mirrors, which are tuned to pass or reflect certain colors. These mirrors are not exact in their characteristics, so there will be variation from projector to projector in the exact color of red, green, and blue primaries. Compare CRTs, where the colors of red, green, and blue are dependent on the optical emission properties of phosphors, which are highly repeatable.

An effective calibration system should measure the color of reflected light from the screen and adjust the output properties of the projector to accommodate system variances. This ensures that the viewer sees the intended colors in the image reflected from the screen.

A simple and very accurate calibration system has been implemented in DLP Cinema™ projectors. While technically complex, it is operationally quite simple, requiring only the measurement of red, green, blue, and white colored targets. The projector does the calculations and adjustments internally.

---

[4] See, for example, John Alton, *Painting With Light*, (Berkeley: University of California Press, May 1995).

Color Space Matching with Film

To achieve a match with film, the digital projector must take on some of the characteristics of film. Because film is a subtractive system, it produces bright and deep secondary colors (yellow, cyan, and magenta). On the other hand, digital systems are additive and produce bright and saturated red, green, and blue. The result is a fundamental mismatch in the shape of the respective color spaces.

This mismatch must be corrected for the color relationships to work. There are two approaches to color management for matching the look of film. The first is to make the matching corrections in mastering, and the second puts the matching capabilities in the projector. In either case, the color space must be transformed from the scanned image characteristics to the digitally projected characteristics. Color corrector manufacturers are in the early stages of addressing this issue in their mastering hardware, and only limited tests have been performed using 3-D *look-up tables*, or *LUTs*, to test the concept.

The current generation of Texas Instruments' DLP Cinema™ projectors has implemented a color management system called *P7*. By setting the P7 parameters correctly, it is possible to achieve a good match to the color characteristics of film.

P7 profiles allow the independent targeting of seven target colors: red, green, blue, magenta, yellow, cyan, and white. The chromaticity and brightness of each color point may be independently set. The P7v2 profile was developed to allow the output of color correctors to more easily match the color properties of film, giving brighter secondary colors.

In current practice, this has allowed the film to be easily mastered for digital release. Most films in current digital distribution use the P7v2 color profile. Proposals under current consideration will put the color management in the color corrector.

Gamma Coding and Bit Depth Requirements

The luminance of each color must be displayed with sufficient precision to ensure that the viewer cannot distinguish steps in a smoothly shaded object. (The visible appearance of these steps are sometimes called "contouring.") This becomes an issue of matching the displayed image to perception of the human visual system.

The characteristic of the human visual system is such that the luminance difference it sees is proportional to the brightness of the image it is viewing. At the brightness level used for cinema (48 cd/m^2 full white), the perception curve follows a power law of approximately 2.6. The perceptible step near black of a 2000:1 contrast ratio theatre projector is about 1/100 of the luminance level near black.

It follows that the system must be capable of smallest luminance step at the dark end of the range of about 1/200,000 of peak white. This would require almost 18 bits to encode the data. However, it is possible to encode the luminance of each of the *RGB* functions such that the coding provides finer gradations at low luminance than at high luminance. This is done by applying an inverse power-law encoding on the luminance, thereby significantly reducing the number of bits required to encode the luminance of the image, with no perceptible loss in perceived image quality.

Recent tests have demonstrated that under optimum conditions the viewer requires between 11 and 12 bits using power-law 2.6 encoding to avoid contouring artifacts. As a result, the input bit depth required for projector design is 12 bits. (It should be noted that these tests were performed with a noise-free image. Introduction of small amounts of noise, such as film grain, can reduce the practical bit depth requirements by 2 to 3 bits.)

MOTION MANAGEMENT

Different projection technologies present motion differently, depending on how the image is created and projected onto the screen. When 35mm film is projected at the standard speed of 24 fps using a two-bladed shutter, the projector flashes each frame twice within 1/24th second before the next frame is moved into position, with equal time given to the black screen produced when the shutter closes. This gives a fairly crisp rendition of motion but introduces an artifact known as *retrograde motion*. This causes a juddering, where an object in motion will appear to judder back and forth as it moves across the screen.

Digital projectors use a different approach to motion. They build each frame in its entirety in a memory buffer and then display it for the entire frame time, with no black time between frames. This puts the image on the screen without a shutter in place. As a result, an object in motion will appear slightly soft, but the distinctive two-image judder will not exist.

DLP Cinema™ technology uses digital modulation to create its image; the light to the screen is either on or off. The duration of the on time during the frame creates the intensity of the color. During motion where the eye tracks across the screen, an artifact occurs where edges may appear to separate into multiple edges. This is slight but nevertheless noticeable. Digital modulation has no residual effects from frame to frame.

LCD technologies are inherently analog and provide uniform modulation for the entire frame time. They have a drawback that the actual switching time of the liquid crystal is slow, which causes a lag or ghost trail to appear behind moving images. As liquid crystals get faster, this trail becomes less noticeable, but there can be a mushy appearance to motion.

ASPECT RATIOS SIZING AND LENSING

Image aspect ratio is an important part of the visual presentation. Digital Cinema is presented using the same on-screen aspect ratio as the equivalent film product. The dominant aspect ratios for theatrical release in the United States are 2.39:1 (Scope) and 1.85:1 (flat). See Figures 9.11A and B.

Projection technology can respond in three fundamentally different ways to achieve the correct aspect ratio: electronic masking, anamorphic lenses, or electronic scaling in the projector.

Electronic Masking

The projection modulator is an array of pixels, with its own aspect ratio, designed by engineering considerations. The correct aspect ratio of the image can be created by electronically masking the area of the modulator that is outside the desired aspect. This may be thought of as an electronic equivalent to the aperture plate used in film projectors.

In the DLP Cinema™ projector, where the modulator is 2048×1080 pixels (and the pixels are square), its "native" aspect ratio is 1.89:1. To achieve a flat (1.85:1) aspect ratio, the modulator is electronically masked to 1998

A

B

FIGURE

9.11

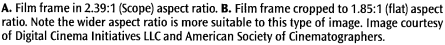

A. Film frame in 2.39:1 (Scope) aspect ratio. **B.** Film frame cropped to 1.85:1 (flat) aspect ratio. Note the wider aspect ratio is more suitable to this type of image. Image courtesy of Digital Cinema Initiatives LLC and American Society of Cinematographers.

pixels wide × 1080 pixels high. To achieve Scope aspect ratio (2.39:1), the full width is used and the display is electronically masked to 853 pixels high.

This electronic masking will also correct trapezoidal distortion caused by projecting down toward the screen, as shown in Figure 9.12 in the Color Plate section.

Anamorphic Lenses

In the current projector formats, electronic masking as described above for Scope reduces the usable pixels by 21%. It would be desirable to use more pixels not only to improve the overall image content but also to make the image brighter. This can be done by using an anamorphic lens to stretch the image horizontally to make it 2.39:1. The anamorphic factor is 1.27:1 for this lens. In projection systems using a 2048×1080 imaging device (e.g., DLP Cinema™), the anamorphic lens is provided as an option for Scope. It should be noted that using an anamorphic lens elongates the pixels as projected on the screen.

Electronic Scaling in the Projector

Digital projectors have the ability to scale the image electronically to make the source material fill the imager array. This allows them to take source formats that may be smaller or larger than the native imager and resize them. The projector will also resize to accommodate the anamorphic lens.

Sizing and Lenses

To achieve the correct image size, the magnification of the lens must be designed to accommodate the screen width and throw distance. In 35mm projectors, this has been accommodated by creating a catalog of fixed focal lenses that vary over a wide range of magnifications, ensuring that a correct lens will be available. Digital Cinema systems are providing zoom lenses to ensure that the image size is correct on the screen.

CONVERGENCE AND REGISTRATION

As we saw earlier, the colored image is made from images coming from separate red, green, and blue modulators. These images must be aligned to ensure that the pixels overlay as exactly as possible.

Misconvergence will appear as a colored fringe on a sharp contrast edge. For example, a vertical white line on a black background may have a green fringe on the left side and a magenta fringe on the right side. This indicates misregistration of the green channel.

Misconvergence is usually measured in pixels and can generally be determined by measuring it on a high-contrast pattern on the screen. Each manufacturer has its own specification for acceptable misconvergence. It usually defines a central zone of the image requiring a tight registration and an outside zone with looser requirements.

MECHANICAL ISSUES

Digital projectors are designed to have a form factor similar to that of film projectors. They use a similar lamphouse and power supply and are expected to be installed behind the same port. The power level of the xenon lamp is similar to that of a film projector, so it requires the same type of ventilation system.

Setup and Maintenance

At installation, the digital projector must be set up and calibrated. The setup issues are relatively straightforward.

◆ Mechanical and optical. The projector is located behind the port window and optically aligned to the screen. This requires the correct lensing, usually a zoom lens. The projector is unlikely to be directly on axis with the screen. This will cause some keystone distortion. Some of this may be removed through offsetting the lens. The balance will be removed by setting electronic masking to make the projected image square.

◆ Color. Color calibration is required to ensure that the projector is performing to its required specification. In the case of DLP Cinema™ technology, the projector's primary colors are measured and input back to the projector, which then calculates the required corrections automatically.

◆ Light level. The lamp should be adjusted to output 48 cd/m² on a full white image.

Setup in this manner will ensure that the projector is delivering accurate color and the image is optimally aligned with the screen.

The need for maintenance is an often-asked question. Digital projectors have no moving parts other than cooling fans. They are inherently reliable, but there is routine maintenance to be carried out.

◆ Lamp. As in a film projector, the lamp loses efficiency as it is used. To maintain optimal performance, the light output must be adjusted periodically to sustain specified brightness. This period is on the order of weeks. After 1000 to 2000 hours, the lamp will no longer output sufficient light for the screen and must be replaced.

◆ Dust and dirt filters. Periodically, the air filter must be changed. In addition, the optics may need to be cleaned to maintain optimum performance. Several versions of DLP Cinema™ projectors have sealed optical systems, substantially reducing the need for cleaning.

◆ Convergence. The alignment of the modulators may periodically drift and require touch-up. This should be done annually.

IMAGE QUALITY: THE REFERENCE PROJECTOR

Projection is about the image, not the hardware. Optimal image quality is achieved by optimized interaction of all the factors discussed up to now. Some of these factors are particularly important to the overall image.

◆ Contrast is the most important driver of image quality. The ability to achieve good solid blacks affects the ability to build punch or impact into a picture.

◆ Gamma, or transfer function, carries the dynamic information in the image.

◆ Color management ensures that the best color possible is presented to the screen.

◆ Pixel count, or resolution, ensures that the information in the source image can be viewed on the projector.

The mastering process for Digital Cinema involves a creative step in which the color, brightness, and dynamics of the image are set by an artist viewing an image created by a digital reference projector. The image is approved as it appears on this projector and embodies the *creative intent.*

One of the promises of Digital Cinema is that the image as viewed on the digital reference projector in the mastering suite will be delivered to each and every digital screen around the world. This requires that the projectors installed in movie theatres are set up to have identical characteristics to the reference projector used in mastering. This will ensure that the quality of image approved in mastering is delivered to digital screens in local movie theatres, even if projector technology differs. Currently SMPTE is drafting documents to describe the reference projector characteristics.

PROJECTION SYSTEM DATA INTERFACES

Current Digital Cinema architectures demand that the projector receive the picture as an uncompressed data stream. (There are some Digital Cinema models that provide for the compressed data to be decompressed inside the projector, but at some point, the image data are streamed in real time into the imaging chain of the projector.) To handle these data rates, bandwidths of up to 10 Gbits/sec are required.

Tests have shown that the Digital Cinema system will require 12-bit precision per color channel for uncompressed projector data. Using three-color primaries, this drives the requirement for 36 bits per pixel. Figure 9.13 shows the data rates required to stream image data into the projector at 12 bits per color and at 24 and 48 fps. Current system implementations are using less bandwidth because the color is subsampled and there are only 10 bits per color component.

TEST MATERIALS

Projector performance should be tested objectively to understand the numbers that are driving the performance envelope. The parameters identified earlier are the key ones to be measured. Such testing is not sufficient to ensure that a filmic image will result, however. The projector must also be tested using real motion images to ensure that, in combination, the performance package will work. Subjective tests will identify problems such as motion rendition or color depth problems where skin tones don't look real.

	Frame rate (per second)	
Resolution	24	48
2K x 1K	251	502
4K x 2K	1003	2007

FIGURE
9.13

Data rates in megabytes required to support 24 fps and 48 fps. Note that doubling the resolution quadruples the data rate. The data interfaces needed to carry the bandwidth required for Digital Cinema have not been resolved at time of writing but represent one of the ongoing challenges for its implementation.

Subjective testing is usually done with several experienced viewers. Test material is chosen to exercise the overall performance of the system. The material should be known to the observers to avoid confusing image difficulties that are caused by the material, not the projector under observation.

Standard Evaluation Material, called *StEM*, has been produced by DCI and the American Society of Cinematographers (ASC) and is available for non-commercial use.[5]

CANDIDATE PROJECTION TECHNOLOGIES

A number of candidate projection technologies have been demonstrated for Digital Cinema. To date, only one has entered the marketplace as a product: DLP Cinema™.

DLP Cinema™

DLP Cinema™ is a technology developed by Texas Instruments for high performance projection applications. The projector has a three-channel RGB configuration as discussed earlier. It uses a reflective modulator in each channel to vary the amount of each color mixed on the screen.

The modulation is done using mirrors to switch the light on and off, to control the absolute amount of light that arrives at the screen. This is known as pulse width modulation. To achieve a dark pixel, the light is on for only a small fraction of the frame time. To achieve a bright pixel, it is on for a large part of the screen time (see Figure 9.14 in the Color Plate section). This yields light processing that is digital all the way to the retina, where it is integrated into an analog light value.

The advantage of digital light processing is that it is very stable and uniform across the screen. The modulator has only two positions: on or off. Light levels are accurately controlled at the screen and not subject to temperature or bias level differences on the modulator (see Figure 9.15).

---

[5]See www.dcimovies.com/ and click on StEMAcce.pdf.

DLP CINEMA™ PERFORMANCE

	TI 2K Chip Based
Technology	DLP Cinema™
Resolution	2048 x 1080
Contrast ratio	>2000:1
ANSI contrast	>500:1
Light output	>25,000 ;umens
Color management	Color management engine targets exact colorimetry

FIGURE 9.15   Basic performance parameters of DLP Cinema™ technology. DLP produces a slightly different look to the image in motion, due to the rapid switching of the mirrors. These can appear as a texture visible when the eye is tracking across the screen.

Additionally DLP Cinema™ technology has image management systems integrated with it to manage subtitles, link encryption, and image color and dynamics.

DLP Cinema™ has received substantial traction in the market. It has been operating in theatres for 5 years in demonstration and the first stage of deployment. It has shown itself to be stable and reliable.

D-ILA

LCOS (Liquid Crystal on Silicon) is a liquid-crystal-based modulator technology. It is manufactured by creating a pixel and driving structure directly in silicon and using it to drive a liquid crystal structure that is built directly over the silicon. The drive structure activates the liquid crystal to modulate the light. The technology is reflective.

LCOS is attractive because it is inherently inexpensive to manufacture and scales up to accommodate large arrays. 4K LCOS displays have been demonstrated. LCOS has colorimetry capabilities similar to DLP in both color primaries and white point. The pixel structure in LCOS is interesting because it has very little dead area around the pixel, so the pixels tend to blend together at the edges. This is especially true with a bright image, where the pixel edges spill over to adjacent pixels (due to electric field fringing), causing a smoothing effect.

The main drawback of LCOS is that it is liquid crystal based. Liquid-crystal-based displays are inherently non-uniform and require periodic setup to correct display uniformity. Additionally, liquid crystals will drift with temperature, resulting in hue shifts in colors near black, in turn causing black areas to take on unwanted color. Liquid crystal also has relatively slow relaxation time, which will leave slight trails on high-contrast objects that move, providing a different feel to the motion. This phenomenon appears to be inherent to the technology.

LCOS technology has been offered to the market by JVC, under the trade name *D-ILA*, and Sony has announced a product named *SXRD*, with its own type of LCOS. While the JVC product has been installed in some post production and digital preview applications, no cinema projector suitable for screens of 15 meters and wider has yet been offered into the marketplace. At this time, it is not clear whether the Sony product will fare any better. Performance comparisons are shown in Figure 9.16.

Laser Technology

Laser-based projectors have been demonstrated in various forms for many years. Lasers are an attractive light source for cinema because of their efficiency. They can be adapted to DLP image modulators or can be used on alternative modulators. One such modulator is the *grating light valve* (GLV), which is a diffractive modulator with inherently very high contrast ratio and

CHARACTERISTICS OF LCOS PROJECTOR FROM JVC AND SONY

	JVC QX1	Sony prototype
Technology	LCOS - DILA	LCOS - SXRD
Resolution	2048 x 1080	4096 x 2160
Contrast ratio	>2000:1	2000:1
ANSI contrast	>400:1	
Light output	>12,000 lumens	Up to 10,000 lumens
Color management	Based on physical primaries	

FIGURE 9.16   Comparison of basic LCOS performance for JVC and Sony products.

is very fast. It is a line scan device, so the image is swept from top to bottom or from left to right on the screen, one line at a time.

Laser technology has some potential difficulties that have not been adequately addressed. Practical lasers for cinema will be solid state. These will require approximately 20 watts each of red, green, and blue to achieve adequate brightness for a 50-foot screen. The state of the art of solid-state lasers is presently not sufficiently developed to deliver reliable devices at close to these power levels.

There is also concern about how laser-based colors will look. Serious questions about speckle and color perception of monochromatic sources have been raised, which need to be answered.

REFERENCES AND RESOURCES

SMPTE 196M, Society of Motion Picture and Television Engineers specification

ITU-R Recommendation BT.601, International Telecommunication Union

ITU-R Recommendation BT.709, International Telecommunication Union

Charles Poynton, 1996. *A Technical Introduction to Digital Video* (New York: John Wiley and Sons).

WWW.DLPCinema.com -TI website describing their approach to Digital Cinema projection

John Alton, 1995. *Painting with Light* (Berkeley: University of California Press.)

10 Theatre Systems*

Michael Karagosian
Karagosian MacCalla Partners

The idea of using digital systems to project images in theatres[1] has inspired a
wide range of system approaches. Those from the telecommunications
industry think of the system as network centric. Those from the broadcast
industry think in terms of delivering streams of content. Those in the computer industry think in terms of information technology (IT) architectures.

But the requirements of the cinema are unique, imposing a special set
of constraints on systems and operations. In the traditional analog film
world, content arrives from a variety of sources to the theatre. Feature *trailers* (or previews) come from various distributors. Then there are policy
trailers, promotional trailers, advertisements, and of course, the feature
film itself. Movies arrive in several canisters, requiring in-theatre splicing in
order to mount on modern platter systems. All of these elements conform
to industry standards that govern the width of the film, the size and placement of sprocket holes, the placement of audio tracks, and the placement of
the image. Adherence to industry standards permits these separate elements to be spliced together to *build* a complete *show*.

In U.S. theatres, a show typically runs on a *platter*, providing a continuous
feed of film to a single projector. Projectionists in other countries prefer to use
two projectors, requiring that a *changeover* take place as one reel ends and a
new reel is begun. In the digital world, the platter is analogous to a *server*, and a

---

[1] Called *cinemas* outside North America.

single projector is used. Although rapidly giving way to the "little port" small electronic projector, typical systems also incorporate a slide projector for *pre-show* entertainment. Then there are *house controls*, such as auditorium architectural dimmers and possibly screen curtains and masking, that need to be operated, and other *performance controls* such as sound format selection.

A device called an *automation controller* orchestrates the many events that take place in the projection booth, as well as monitor faults. Upon receiving a start command, the typical automation controller ramps down the house lights, starts the film projector, opens the projector *douser* after the projector comes up to speed, selects the correct sound format, and shuts down the slide projector. It may perform these steps as a series of timed events, but often it bases them on *cues* that are tagged to the film itself and sensed upon playback. If the automation controller senses that the film tension in the projector is low or nonexistent, indicating that the film was threaded wrongly or is simply broken, it will not let the projector start; or if the projector is already in operation, it will shut it down.

When a *show* must be moved from one screen system to another, the platter itself is physically moved: spliced film, automation cues, and all. In a matter of minutes, a skilled operator can move a show from one screen system to another, thread the film onto the new projector, and be ready to start. No re-building of the show or re-insertion of automation cues is required. Cinema operators take pride in having the ability to move a platter show in less than 15 minutes.

All of these operations, at a minimum, must be duplicated in the Digital Cinema system. The Digital Cinema must allow a *show* to be built with digital content that arrives from a variety of sources. The show must include the means to store *performance controls*. The show must be portable, so it can move from screen-to-screen in relatively short order. The system must provide a means to monitor overall operation. Digital systems not only need to duplicate these services, but should also improve upon them to add value to the approach.

The introduction of digital systems poses new challenges to theatre operation. Digital content requires digital security, which has no parallel in film systems. Theatre owners want Digital Cinema systems to marry with their back office operations in order to automate show scheduling, for system monitoring, and for efficient data gathering.

This chapter reviews the basic principles of system interoperability, the user requirements put forth by stakeholders, the several approaches to Digital Cinema system design undertaken by manufacturers, and the challenges that remain.

SYSTEM INTEROPERABILITY

Interoperability is necessary where business requirements demand that competitive products coexist in a "plug and play" environment. A successful strategy of interoperability most readily works at natural business boundaries. Manufacturers embrace interoperability when it extends beyond the boundary of their product, inviting healthy competition and bringing confidence to the marketplace. Manufacturers tend to resist interoperability when it is asked to apply inside the boundary of their product, because they see this as inviting competition in unattractive ways. Thus, to plan for practical interoperability, one must first look at traditional product boundaries and services offered in the marketplace.

Digital Cinema borrows many concepts from existing product areas. From the broadcast and IT markets, it borrows the server, the digital equivalent of the film platter. The Digital Cinema projector has evolved from those used in the staging and rental markets. Most efforts toward interoperability in Digital Cinema have focused on the content interface into the server, or media block, and the interface between server and projector. However, a deeper study shows that a much broader and more extensive view of interoperability is required.

At a system level, a rollout of Digital Cinema presents considerable demands on interoperability. It is unlikely in a Digital Cinema rollout scenario that all screens in a cinema complex, and indeed, all screens in a circuit, will be changed out at one time. In fact, the process of rolling out Digital Cinema is expected to take many years. The challenge is therefore to create a digital projection infrastructure within the complex in year one such that systems with possibly different specifications purchased in year 5, or even year 10, can "plug in" without major impact. Without system-level interoperability, it will be difficult to bring confidence to the marketplace and accelerate the rollout. Following this objective, system-level interoperability was described by NATO in its Theatre Systems Operations and Controls report dated April, 2003, as illustrated in Figure 10.1.

Interoperability, as described here, outlines the four business domains that meet in the projection booth: *delivery, presentation, back office,* and *security.* Of these, only delivery and presentation exist in film systems today.

The digital *delivery system* must deliver a well-defined *Digital Cinema package* (DCP). It must also provide a means to confirm delivery of the content files to the theatre.

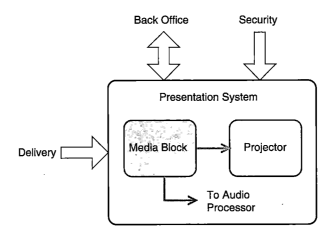

The *security system* must deliver security keys such that the presentation system can decrypt the desired content. Most stakeholders assume that a *security manager* device will be present in the projection booth, serving as a bank for content security keys. Content security keys can be delivered to the bank, while the bank provides copies of these keys to the presentation systems that request them.

The *back-office system*, in its most complete form, gives the exhibitor the ability to automatically generate *show schedules* and *show play lists*. A show schedule is a list of show times, and a show play list is a list of the various content elements of the show, including the order in which they play. Both schedule and show play lists must work with presentation systems of any make or manufacture. The back-office system will also gather information about the content played, security keys exchanged, and the health of the equipment.

The *presentation system* is the core of the Digital Cinema system. The presentation system includes both *projector* and *media block*. (See the section *Media Block Architectures* for more information.) The model as shown does not address storage, as storage system design is dependent upon the media block architecture.

Note that the interoperability diagram does not identify the input to the projector as a significant point of system-level interoperability. Following traditional product boundaries, and to ensure product simplicity and security, projector manufacturers may prefer to include the media block in their presentation systems.

USER REQUIREMENTS

User requirements for Digital Cinema have been published by exhibitor organizations around the world. In late 2001, a joint statement by international exhibitor organizations was published providing general user requirements for Digital Cinema. In February 2002, NATO published a more detailed list of user requirements. Both sets of user requirements are instructive and are presented in Figure 10.2.

MEDIA BLOCK ARCHITECTURES

Few items have caused more misunderstanding and confusion among engineers in Digital Cinema than the concept of a *server*. To a broadcaster, a server outputs a synchronous stream of content. To an information technologist, the server outputs either asynchronous or isochronous data. To facilitate meaningful conversations among experts of both camps, the term *media block* was coined in late 2002. The media block provides the essential signal processing functions of the system. The input to the conceptual media block is independent of transmission type, accepting synchronous or isochronous data, or possibly files. The output of a media block characteristically is a synchronous stream.

The media block functional diagram for Digital Cinema is illustrated in Figure 10.3. Signal processing that would be performed in the media block for both image and audio might include decryption, decompression, and fingerprinting. Other functions are possible, and may be required, such as color space conversion if the content is distributed in a color space other than that of the projector. Resizing may also be necessary, as the resolution of the projector's imaging device may be different from that of the image data itself, or the screen masking design may require image resizing to create the best on-screen fit using the available optical path. If the image is distributed in an interlace format, then a format transformation from interlace to progressive may be required. In the case of the DLP Cinema™ projector, the projection technology most commonly used in Digital Cinema applications at the time of this writing, the projector already has the functions of color space conversion, resizing, and interlace-to-progressive transformation internally implemented.

THE NATIONAL ASSOCIATION
OF THEATRE OWNERS

DIGITAL CINEMA USER REQUIREMENTS
February 22, 2002

On December 12, 2001, Exhibitor Associations around the world presented their concerns and
requirements below regarding Digital Cinema Systems, listed below.

International Exhibitor Associations Concerns for Digital Cinema

Our Goal:

♦ To encourage the development of fully interoperable, competitive products that can be
   maintained at relatively low cost, in the manner of today's film projection systems. We need to
   accomplish thiswhile providing a minimum digital presentation quality that exceeds that of film,
   and that meets thequality needs of the creative community. To achieve this goal, international
   cooperation is needed.

We Need:

♦ Minimum presentation standards for image projection, including color gamut, contrast ratio,
   and pixel count.

♦ International standards for digital image and audio data representation, storage, and play out.

♦ System support for more than one method of movie data delivery (e.g., physical, satellite
   transmission, fiber, etc.)

♦ International acceptance of a single encryption algorithm.

♦ Rules for digital rights expression and for electronic methods of exhibitor authorization that
   duplicate the current rights and facilities existing in 35mm technology.

♦ International acceptance of a single image compression algorithm.

♦ International standard for a single audio compression, if implemented.

♦ International standards for electronic interfaces, networks, and protocols used on all
   equipment, including secure interfaces.

In addition, the National Association of Theatre Owners has compiled the following set of User
Requirements for Digital Cinema, listed on the following pages.

(Cont'd)

FIGURE   NATO Digital Cinema user requirements.

10.2

NATO DIGITAL CINEMA USER REQUIREMENTS   Feb 22, 2002

Overall

1. The system architecture shall insure the lowest cost of ownership.

2. Normal maintenance procedures shall not compromise the security of valued content.

3. The system shall make use of, wherever possible, existing and established standards to govern system interfaces and processes.

4. Content shall be playable with uniform results on different makes and technologies of playback and projection equipment.

5. In order to promote product competition, proprietary technologies shall be standardized and fairly licensed.

Content Packaging

6. Digital content shall be packaged for efficient store and forward distribution, so as to minimize the use of the facility's data storage.

7. The system shall allow the Exhibitor to have full discretion over presentation of ads, trailers, and features.

8. Exhibitors request the ability to select language, rating version, etc.

Distribution

9. The system shall employ "single inventory" distribution of content, such that the same set of digital files can play with uniform results on different makes of equipment.

10. Content shall be distributed such that completeness and integrity of data is validated automatically upon receipt, and can be validated manually after receipt.

11. Digital content that is encrypted prior to distribution shall retain the original encryption throughout the distribution process.

Content Protection

12. The mechanisms and processes that support content protection shall not interfere with normal business operation within the facility.

13. The content protection and right management system shall support a policy of "No Dark Screen". When a facility is authorized to play content, then usage of that content may be logged in an audit trail by the exhibitor, and no effort is made to prevent the content from playing within that facility.

14. Content decryption keys or licenses shall be delivered to exhibition sites based on the identity of the facility, and not on the identity of specific projection equipment.

15. Keys or licenses shall be delivered to the facility in a non-repudiate manner.

(Cont'd)

NATO DIGITAL CINEMA USER REQUIREMENTS   **Feb 22, 2002**

16. Content shall only be decrypted, whether of the original encryption or a link encryption, in components that pass an authentication process, where authentication is defined as a secure process that determines the legitimate nature of the component. (E.g., "I am a projector".)

17. Digital image streams or files shall not be available in clear text form in unprotected components, networks, or links of the playback system.

18. It is desired that playback systems provide either an image or audio watermark that encodes sufficient information for forensic evaluation.

Encryption
19. Cryptographic content security shall be based upon strong, established, tested, non-proprietary encryption algorithms.

20. If decryption algorithms and link encryption algorithms are to be renewable, they shall be renewable without obsolescence of hardware.

Audit Logs
21. Audit logs shall be securely retained by the exhibitor.

22. Audit logs, or portions of audit logs, shall only be available to the exhibitor and by parties who have contracted with the exhibitor for access. Parties who have contracted for access shall only have access to data that is material to that party.

Control and Monitoring
23. The system shall have networked supervisory controls and monitoring that can be remotely accessed by means of secure networks.

(cont'd from previous page)

Three distinct media block architectures for Digital Cinema systems have been either implemented or proposed. These are the *Broadcast Model*, the *Datacentric Model*, and the *Preprocessing Model*, which are explored below.

Broadcast Model

The broadcast model gets it name by following the server architecture of the broadcast industry. In the broadcast industry, the server, or media block, is the image-rendering device. The output of the broadcast server is essentially what consumers view in their homes, after transmission over air, satellite, or cable. Thus, the output of the server is a stream. To say that this class of

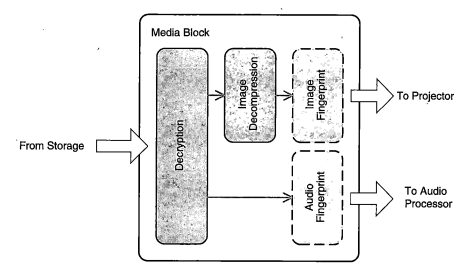

FIGURE

10.3

Media block functional diagram for Digital Cinema.

product is limited to broadcast applications would be wrong, however, as it is also popular in post production applications.

In early implementations of Digital Cinema, the broadcast model seemed a logical system architecture to pursue. Professional broadcast-style products having the desired image quality and interfaces were readily available. Several companies embraced this model and developed products targeted for cinema use.

A broadcast model media block stores content, decompresses the image and audio data, and *pushes* a synchronous audio stream to the cinema audio processor and a synchronous image stream to the projector. Image data are transmitted to the projector using either the single-link SMPTE 292M or the dual-link SMPTE 372M interface, also known as single-link or dual-link HD-SDI (high-definition serial data interface), respectively. The push nature of the media block requires it to be the synchronization point for image and audio.

Early media blocks and projectors employed the HD-SDI interface while transporting streaming data over the link in the clear. In 2001, Texas Instruments (TI), developer and manufacturer of DLP Cinema™, introduced CineLink™ link encryption for SMPTE 292M, providing a layer of protection that was sufficient to "keep honest people honest." TI's link encryption has since been incorporated by most media block manufacturers.

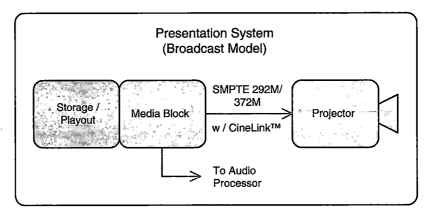

FIGURE

10.4

Broadcast style media block in a Digital Cinema system.

The block diagram in Figure 10.4 depicts the broadcast style media block in a Digital Cinema system.

As of this writing, broadcast-style Digital Cinema media blocks have been produced by Avica Technology Corporation, EVS Broadcast Equipment SA, GDC Technology Limited, and QuVis, Inc. The common characteristic of these products is their self-contained storage.

Self-contained storage, however, is not necessarily an advantage in the cinema. In the cinema environment, moving a show from one screen system to the next requires a transfer of all show-related files. A 2–3-hour movie having an image resolution of 1920×1080 pixels, 4:2:0 color representation, and 8-bit color depth could require 100 GB of storage. With sustained high-speed hard drive transfer rates of 50 MB/sec, moving 100 GB of data from one screen system to the next will take over 30 minutes to complete, regardless of the speed of the network.

Images having 12-bit color depth, 4:4:4 color representation, and 4K resolution—as required by stakeholders—require a transfer rate for real-time operation that is beyond that of a single hard drive. To achieve a high transfer rate, an arrayed storage technique must be used. However, it is unlikely that a practical storage method can transport a movie over a network faster than 2× real-time. In a 4K world, a 2-hour movie would *at best* require 1 hour to transfer between screen systems. (To understand the network bandwidth required, note that 12-bit/color, 4K 4:4:4 data at 24 fps with 10:1 compression will require 200 Mb/sec of network bandwidth for real-time transmission.) Compare this to the 15 minutes that exhibitors achieve when manually transferring a film-based movie from one screen to the next. As systems progress to higher image resolution and color bit depth, the large transfer time required of the broadcast model media block becomes a major disadvantage of this approach.

Datacentric Model

The datacentric model borrows its approach from the IT industry. The media block is separated from storage, so that off-the-shelf IT storage solutions can be applied. These storage systems do not stream synchronous data, but instead transport data isochronously over a network when requested to do so. The isochronous image and audio data are requested, or *pulled*, by the media block, which then operates on the data, performing the functions of data decryption, image decompression, and fingerprinting.

While the input to the datacentric media block is isochronous in nature, the output of the media block is synchronous, usually an HD-SDI link that feeds the projector. The prime advantage of using a datacentric model is that large off-the-shelf redundant storage arrays with fast data transfer capabilities can be employed. These large arrays can feed multiple screen systems when high-speed data transports are used. Figure 10.5 depicts the datacentric server in a Digital Cinema system.

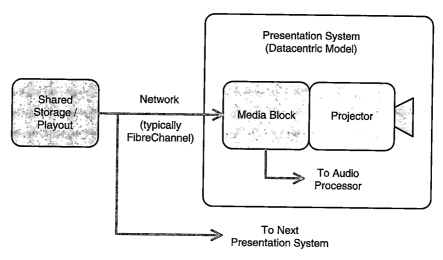

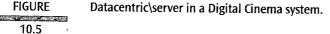

FIGURE
10.5

Datacentric\server in a Digital Cinema system.

There are several advantages to using the datacentric technique. Network data transported to the media block retain their original encryption and compression, minimizing the bandwidth requirement in the link. By mounting or integrating the media block inside the secure projector housing, the original encryption is maintained right up to the projector, while also eliminating the need for link encryption. The use of *storage area network* (SAN) centralized storage allows movies and other show elements to be rescheduled on the fly, without requiring time-consuming data transfers between screen systems. This is possible because movie files remain in the central storage array, while the networked data streams are electronically switched to the desired media block and projector according to the programmed schedule. However, if the multiplex contains a large number of screens, a very high-bandwidth SAN will be required, posing the primary challenge to the datacentric model.

In 2000, QUALCOMM Incorporated introduced the first datacentric media block to the marketplace with their QDEC 1000 decoder module. The QUALCOMM team, with significant leadership by Steve Morley and the late John Ratzel, recognized the functional advantage that centralized IT-style data storage and serving would bring to Digital Cinema. QUALCOMM's system employed a third-party FibreChannel-based SAN, reducing their hardware development to the QDEC 1000 decoder module. QUALCOMM's system allows for up to six 2K decoders from one central storage/server array, and multiple storage arrays can be modularly added to support any size multiplex.

In 2001, Grass Valley Group also introduced a Digital Cinema server that incorporated three datacentric media blocks. Introduced as part of their Profile® XP Media Platform line, the product incorporated internal SAN storage using a FibreChannel network. Grass Valley's design, however, did not allow the decoder electronics to be installed inside the projector and instead bundled decoder and storage in the same box, requiring link encryption to secure the SMPTE 292M link to the projector. In 2003, GDC Technology also introduced a datacentric server architecture, based on a centralized SAN with network-connected decoders at or near their projectors.

Preprocessing Model

The potentially limited lifespan of encryption and compression algorithms could present a major problem for Digital Cinema. Film has enjoyed a

100-year lifetime, enabling users today to readily view preserved content created in the early days of the technology. Will a user 100 years from now be able to do the same with content produced for today's Digital Cinema systems? The answer could very well be "no."

This was one of several problems that led to an alternative processing model suggested by Mike Tinker of Sarnoff Laboratories in 2002. The Sarnoff model attempts to solve the problem of technology obsolescence and the high cost of specialized signal processing by introducing a preprocessing stage in the cinema signal processing chain. The concept would allow content in any format, of any resolution, having any encryption and compressed by any algorithm, to be decrypted, decoded, color space transformed, and resized for the target projector. All signal processing would be performed by means of off-the-shelf CPUs running renewable software. Figure 10.6 illustrates the concept.

The preprocessing model does not require real-time processing for the preprocessing stage. Low-cost computers can be incorporated to perform signal processing tasks in software, in advance of show time, storing an uncompressed, or lightly compressed, intermediate file whose resolution and color space are transformed to match those of the target projector. It is the intermediate file that the media block sends to the projector at show time.

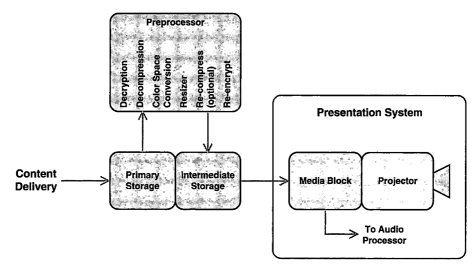

FIGURE 10.6 Preprocessing stage in the cinema signal-processing chain.

The strength of this idea is that it takes advantage of the availability of ever-changing and ever-more-powerful computer technologies to solve what is destined to become an ever-increasing problem of technology obsolescence. It relies upon software, not hardware, to carry out all signal-processing functions, allowing users to renew the signal processing algorithms when necessary.

But a weakness is that it forces decryption of the original encrypted content in the preprocessing stage, requiring re-encryption when storing the intermediate file and thus possibly introducing a point of attack in the security chain. It also requires a higher transfer rate of the intermediate storage system than would be required if the original compression was retained, regardless of which server model is followed. Higher transfer rates require more expensive storage solutions. The larger file size of the intermediate file also burdens the movement of content in the case of the broadcast server and reduces the number of screens that can be serviced by a SAN in the IT model.

The concept of software-based signal processing is attractive to the industry from the viewpoint of renewability. As more powerful CPUs are developed, it is inevitable that software-based signal processing will find its way into Digital Cinema systems.

OPERATIONS AND MAINTENANCE

The business of the exhibitor can be compared to that of a merchandiser. Products are sampled in advance; products are ordered (in the case of cinema, they are rented); products are displayed; the relative success of sales may affect product placement within the merchandiser's shop; and any event that could impede the sale of products, such as those that may occur with equipment and personnel, must be dealt with in a responsive manner. To be effective, the operational performance of the system must fit the needs of the business, making theatre operations an important element to understand and appreciate.

WORKFLOW

Operational requirements have evolved through the use of film systems, and while some requirements may be demanding for digital systems, others are not. Upon receipt of a feature film, a show must be capable of being built within an hour. Once built, a show must be capable of being moved from one screen to the next in 15 minutes without having to rebuild the show. The technology must allow multiple feature films to be received by the theatre and loaded into the system within a matter of hours. Equipment must be replaceable and operational within a show period. These requirements are not necessarily exact, but high system performance in these areas is important to the exhibitor.

While it is important to meet the minimum performance expectations set by film systems, Digital Cinema also has the potential to bring new operational tools into the theatre environment. These include the electronic creation of show schedules and show play lists, and the ability for maintenance personnel to remotely monitor system status and performance over private networks. In general, Digital Cinema systems have the ability to integrate with exhibitor back-office information systems that film systems simply do not. Interoperability between back-office information systems, the presentation system, the delivery system, and the security system brings an important new element to cinema operations.

The workflow of the cinema begins with the booking of the movie. A movie may be booked for a particular screen 6 months or more in advance by the exhibitor's central office. Over time, agreements are made as to trailers, advertisements, and public service announcements. As the opening date moves near, all elements of the show are identified. Once the content of the show is firmed up, it is possible for the exhibitor to create a *show play list* along with the *schedule* for these shows and to transmit this list to the intended venue. Even if the complete show is not yet determined, a schedule and partial show play list can be created centrally, sent to the theatre, and edited by the theatre management as the final details become known.

Building a show through an electronic process is expected to create efficiencies that could lower operational costs for the exhibitor. This is one of the few operational advantages that Digital Cinema promises to create for the exhibitor.

PERFORMANCE CONTROLS

As explained earlier, a show is currently built by splicing together the various show elements onto a single *platter*. These elements include policy trailers, advertisements, movie trailers, as well as the individual reels of the feature film.

Tags are physically added to the film print to trigger *performance controls* through *automation systems. House controls*, a subclass of performance controls, include the activation of electrical and electromechanical functions such as house lighting dimmers and movable screen masking. Although it would be desirable, there are no standards in the film-based systems industry for triggering performance controls. Cinema owners create their own standards by requiring automation systems of the make of their choosing to be installed throughout each cinema complex, if not the entire chain. Unfortunately, this is the only way film-based shows achieve interoperability among screens within the complex.

Performance controls are required to perform functions in addition to house controls, such as selecting the sound format at the cinema audio processor, as well as operating an alternative image source, typically a slide projector or an electronic advertisement projector. The performance control functions required of one theatre complex may not be the same as those of another, due to different policies, different equipment makes, and alterations in equipment configurations. Thus, the commands for performance controls need to be both portable and configurable by the exhibitor.

Portability and configurability can be achieved by placing triggers or time-valued performance control commands in the *show play list*. These commands may be triggered by the presence of time-valued event markers in the content-owner-created *composition play list*, or there may be time-valued performance control commands in the exhibitor-created show play list itself.

SHOW PLAY LISTS AND SCHEDULES

The show play list is a list of the various content elements of the show, commanding the order in which they play (see Figure 10.7). An individual content element may be a policy trailer, or an advertisement, or a movie trailer, or a feature film. Content elements are identified by pointing to their *composition play lists*. A *show schedule* is also created to command when shows are played. Both schedules and show play lists can be created by cinema owner central offices as well as local cinema managers, making them tools of the theatre back-office information system. To be interoperable, they must work with presentation systems of any make or manufacture.

```
Show Play List

time              action
00:00:00:00       House Lights  50%
00:00:00:00       Start Ad System
00:00:00:00       Set Audio Format to Stereo
00:10:00:00       House Lights 25%
00:10:00:00       Stop Ad System
00:10:00:00       Start Policy Trailer A
00:11:00:00       Start Logo Trailer B
00:12:00:00       House Lights  0%
00:12:00:00       Start Feature Movie
01:47:00:00       House  Lights 25%  [credits]
01:52:00:00       House Lights 100% [end of movie]
```

FIGURE

10.7

Show play list.

TIME-CODE

The *show play list* may also allow the inclusion of time-valued or content-valued time-code generator seed values. The purpose is to seed a local time-code generator with the desired value at particular points in the show, allowing external time-code-driven devices to operate consistently from show to show. Time-code generators, and time-code-driven equipment, are not considered to be a requirement of ordinary motion picture shows. Certain time-code-driven audio equipment, however, may be useful in some screening rooms and when implementing foreign language tracks. Time-code capability will likely be required of specialty shows, where additional effects or a time-code-driven show element, such as external audio or lighting, could be required.

SUPERVISORY CONTROLS AND MONITORING

The role of film-based automation systems has been described in terms of performance controls. Automation systems, however, also serve a supervisory function in film-based systems, monitoring for film breakage and other critical system parameters, stopping the projector or shutting down the lamphouse if a potentially damaging problem exists.

Remote supervisory monitoring of the cinema system is a feature that will be useful to operations engineers. In a multivendor environment, a standard approach is required to enable interoperability of networked monitoring agents. SNMP, which stands for *Simple Network Management Protocol*, is widely discussed for Digital Cinema. The SNMP standard is governed by the IETF (Internet Engineering Task Force) and is widely deployed on networked equipment found in the entertainment industry. The standard allows the manufacturer to define a *management information base* (MIB), which is the tool for specifying the behavior of device-specific monitor and control points. The MIB can be submitted to the IETF for publication with the standard where it is identified with the particular product for which it is intended, or it can simply be implemented ad hoc.

SNMP manager software can be used to monitor SNMP agents both locally in the theatre and remotely. While a variety of implementations are possible, it is expected that secure, private, wide area networks will be used to enable remote communication to these systems.

LOGGING SHOW OPERATIONS

Integration with theatre back-office information systems will lead to the creation of detailed logs of digital projection system operations. The back-office system will be capable of creating reports tailored to the requirements of the exhibitor. If desired and agreed to by the parties involved, such reports may be shared with business partners. In some cases, the authenticity of logs may need to be demonstrated. Such data may be digitally signed so that users may verify the data's authenticity.

PIRACY PROTECTION AND SECURITY

The threat of movie piracy has grown with the availability of portable video camcorders. While studios and exhibitors are financially damaged by piracy that occurs prior to opening night of a new feature film, piracy prevention in the theatre is important. A guiding plan for piracy protection has not been agreed to by exhibitors and studios at the time of this writing. In discussion are piracy prevention tools such as encryption of content, asymmetrical encryption of security keys that permits use of the key only in a specific theatre complex, increased projection booth security, forensic marking of image and/or audio by the distributor, forensic marking of image and/or audio at presentation time, camcorder jamming (should such technology become available), encryption of all links over which content travels, monitoring of equipment security certificates in the projection booth, and auditing of security key usage and the possibility of sharing that and other data with business partners.

The art of security is the abstraction of trust, shifting the issue of trust from those who are not trusted, into the hands of those who are trusted with highly valued content. In today's business environment, the exhibitor is trusted. High-quality 35mm prints of first-release motion pictures are entrusted into the hands of exhibitors daily and are delivered to the exhibitor by trusted companies. As electronic content can be vulnerable to unauthorized duplication, it is prudent to encrypt it. By encrypting the content, trust is shifted to the holder of the security key. So that security keys are not transmitted in the clear, they also are encrypted, using the public key of the exhibitor. This shifts trust to the exhibitor's environment. Within the exhibitor's environment, steps will be taken to ensure that the security key is not exposed in the clear and thereby not vulnerable to theft.

As explained in the above scenario, there are no inherent impacts to business through the introduction of encryption into the exhibition environment. Just as the exhibitor is trusted today with film prints, the exhibitor can be trusted to handle the security key. However, it is possible to create security implementations that impact the business relationship as well as business operations. Many of the implementations being discussed today cross these boundaries. Such security implementations restrict the movement of content by requiring that keys be delivered (and thus married) to projectors, and/or introduce extensive digital rights management that forces the exhibitor into rigid business arrangements that today are somewhat flexible. The potential electronic revocation of security keys in the midst of a movie run and the potential electronic revocation of security certificates contained within equipment are also major issues. Security certificates, should they be introduced, would seriously undermine confidence in this new technology if a very expensive projector could be rendered useless by simply revoking its certificate.

Key Management Methodology

Key management is the area of security most discussed to date. As previously noted, the method for managing security keys has the potential to negatively affect business operations, requiring much attention as to how this task is performed. An electronic key to decrypt content may be accompanied by rules enforced through digital rights management. These rules, for instance, may require that a movie play on a certain screen with certain equipment, restricting the movement of content. Such restrictions could negatively impact an exhibitor's ability to maximize the commercial potential of all films by not allowing the exhibitor to react to audience preferences. Restricted movement of both content and equipment can also negatively impact an exhibitor's response time when equipment failure occurs. An example where electronic rules could interfere with community standards is with the selection of movie trailers that accompany a feature film. In some communities, the content of a particular trailer may not be considered appropriate for the intended audience. For instance, a trailer depicting violence that might accompany a movie targeted for young audiences. Other electronic rules could force the sharing of business data, such as a list of accompanying trailers and ads that the exhibitor may not wish to divulge. The potential introduction of electronic rules that affect business operations and community standards is a serious concern to exhibitors.

The management of security keys will be governed by a *security manager* (SM). The SM is a device within the projection booth serving as a bank for content security keys. (See the section on *Interoperability.*) The bank receives content security keys from outside sources, by means of a private wide area network or simply through a physical device, such as a smart card. The bank provides copies of these keys to the presentation systems that request them. Exhibitors would like only one SM in the projection booth, as opposed to a scheme that has been proposed where each movie distributor could require its own individual device with no limits as to the number of security managers in the booth. Multiple SMs will lead to a situation reminiscent of film-based digital audio in the 1990s, where exhibitors were forced to buy equipment that was of a different make but otherwise functionally identical to what they already had in order to play a movie.

The SM introduces an important new business element into the projection booth. Its operation, however, along with each of the security-related issues raised in this section, are without agreed-upon solutions at the time of writing. Even when agreements are eventually in place, the immaturity of the SM as a business element makes it vulnerable to changes in requirements. Interoperability between the SM, presentation system, and back-office system is very important to reduce the impact of change and obsolescence.

CONTENT DELIVERY

Electronic delivery of content to the theatres can be achieved in one of several ways. The three basic methods available are delivery on a physical media, delivery over air waves, and delivery over physical transmission mediums. To encourage competition, stakeholders have not placed restrictions on delivery mechanisms, asking that systems be designed such that any combination of transport methods can be supported.

Practical business operation, however, demands that all systems are capable of at least one common delivery medium. Exhibitors have requested a "lowest common denominator" physical delivery medium, which could be as simple as a USB or Firewire drive that all systems accept. In this way, should electronic delivery methods such as satellite or fiber fail, or should such methods not be available or desired in particular locations, distributors will have only to support one type of physical delivery mechanism, increasing the likelihood that the physical medium is available from the distributor when needed in an emergency.

PUTTING A POINT TO IT

This chapter has presented user requirements, server architectures, operational requirements, piracy prevention, delivery mechanisms, and many of the issues surrounding these topics for implementation of theatre systems. At the time of this writing, some areas, such as piracy protection, require much more discussion to light the path forward. Certain areas, such as system operations, require more development before stakeholder needs are met. Other areas, such as image quality, require new products to be developed to meet emerging industry standards.

But simply solving the technical challenges is not enough to launch the largest transition in the history of motion picture exhibition. While studios stand to benefit from Digital Cinema through cost savings incurred with electronic distribution, and while manufacturers stand to benefit from sales of new equipment, exhibitors will experience no new revenue flow from the transition, while absorbing the risks of maintaining and competing with new technology. Balancing this equation is the most significant challenge that lies ahead for Digital Cinema.

11

An International Perspective

Peter Wilson
Snell and Wilcox Ltd.
Patrick Von Sychowski
Screen Digest

EUROPE

Background—Cinema and Economics

Existing cinema in Europe is very diverse. Cinemas are operated by a variety
of owners: US-owned majors, large networks assisted by the European Union
(e.g., Europa Cinema), large European multiplex operators, local governments, family businesses, and charitable organizations. Some are quite profitable while others could not possibly operate without subsidy from another
source. Facilities vary from 1500-seat auditoriums in prime locations to temporary accommodation in a village hall that might seat only 50 people. Any
implementation of Digital Cinema must reflect this diversity of interest. It is
politically unacceptable in Europe to disadvantage minority communities.

   Distributors again stretch from the US majors to small family concerns.
There is a political imperative in most countries to encourage the screening of
locally produced films. Digital Cinema systems offer a potential advantage
when distributing movies with small print and marketing budgets. The systems will be required to facilitate the screening of programs produced in a
wide range of technologies.

Exhibition

There is a wide range of cinemas in Europe built in a large variety of designs
over a long period of time. The basic categories can be described as art

house, mainstream, crossover (both art house and mainstream content), and community.

Art House

These cinemas normally show culturally important, ethnic, historic, or local films. They are often subsidized by local government, central government, or European community programs. They are considered to be essential to preserve cultural identity and encourage local film production. The movies shown may not always have a high commercial value.

Mainstream

These cinemas typically show the latest blockbusters. They may be in private family ownership, and new cinemas in the main will be built only if there is a guaranteed *minimum catchment area* (the gross number of people in the area divided by the number of screens. The usual metric is 20,000+ people per screen to justify its build.). The majority are multiplexes owned by multinationals.

Crossover

These cinemas combine both mainstream blockbuster presentation with art house classics at different screening times. With film this is a labor-intensive process, as the films may need to be changed on an almost daily basis. Digital Cinema with its inherent flexibility may encourage more cinemas to be multitype, thereby improving revenue flow.

Community

These cinemas may be permanent or temporary. They may be in remote locations with very small communities. Distribution and cost of equipment are key issues.

Screen Sizes

Screen sizes in Europe vary from as little as 3 meters across to as much as 15 meters. A significantly different lamp power is needed to service small vs.

large screens. A significant challenge is the matching of the projection technology in a cost-effective way to the differing earnings potential of the various sized installations.

Temporary Venues

It is quite common in local communities for the central social venue to be multipurpose: it may be a cinema, theatre, sports hall, or exhibition center with retractable stadium seating. The projection equipment will certainly be multipurpose and possibly used for Saturday night satellite football.

Health and Safety Requirements

The health and safety requirements are not yet harmonized across Europe although Brussels bureaucrats are trying hard. In fact, local government departments can have significantly different requirements for seating arrangements, fire exits, wheelchair access, fire escape sign brightness position, and safety light brightness. As the local governmental body will invariably license the venue, they will also set the parameters for the auditorium. This will significantly affect the cost and performance of the projection system. For example, achieving a contrast ratio of 2000:1 will be totally impractical if the equivalent open gate screen brightness is the standard 12 ftL and the local health and safety regulations cause a significant background screen wash by enforced positioning and brightness level of the safety lights. There is little in the way of current reference material available to help the screen operator negotiate the best setup for his or her auditorium.

Standards for Venues

France is believed unique in having the CST (Commission Supérieure Technique de l'Image et du Son) as a regulatory body established by legislation. The CST has the authority to set and enforce the design standards for cinema auditoria. The CST has adopted an additional standard for Digital Cinema presentation. France is particularly concerned about low-grade pirate Digital Cinema installations.

A significant part of the preparations for Digital Cinema should be a set of recommended practices for the auditorium, and if seating positions and viewing angles will be substantially different from before, a set of guidelines for production, whether on film or digital, will be required. For example, television production techniques are very different from cinema primarily due to the different viewing angles. As resolution increases and cinemas pack in more seats close to the screen, the average viewing angle changes, thereby the pace and style of production will change if those new seats are to be accommodated.

Distribution

Distribution in Europe is a combination of mainstream operations, concentrating on blockbusters, and a hugely diverse independent sector distributing everything else. Each country has many film distributors offering a very wide variety of films.

Censors

Different censor requirements for different countries can be a substantial issue. A famous example was the requirement in the United Kingdom to remove 24 frames of *Star Wars Episode II* that contained a head butt scene. Why? The head butt is the favorite greeting method that a football hooligan uses when meeting a fan from a rival team, and the censors believe film should not encourage violence!

Dubbing

In many countries in Europe it is customary to dub a film into the local language. This must be arranged by the local distributor. Digital Cinema allows for several dialogue languages to be carried in the same transport wrapper.

Subtitles

In some European countries it is common to screen movies in the original language but with subtitles. This can be difficult to manage; Belgium, for example, has four languages in general use, although currently only two are commonly used for cinema release. However, if Digital Cinema resulted in more screens in the German- and Walloon-speaking sections of the country, there might well be a drive for these languages. The technical flexibility of Digital Cinema can solve many of these issues. However, the current structure of distribution may have to change significantly to reap the full benefits a file-based system with multiple versions embedded in the same bit stream can offer.

Audio Descriptor Language

There is now a growing movement to facilitate audio descriptions of movies to enhance the blind or partially sighted in their enjoyment.

Alternative Content

Several operators in Europe offer live *alternative content*—e.g., concerts or sports. VTHR in France, for example, has for many years offered alternative content to French regional centers. This may be high-brow opera from the Paris or Lyon Opera house or Sunday night wrestling. UCI in the United Kingdom recently offered soccer on the big screen.

Government and Technology Initiatives

Each government within the European Union has its own way of allocating development resources to technical projects such as Digital Cinema. The United Kingdom government in particular is keen to promote research and development into the required technologies for Digital Cinema. In addition, the governments of the United Kingdom and soon Italy also support test bed facilities similar to the Digital Cinema Laboratory[1] in Hollywood.

EC Initiatives

Media Plus

The Media Plus department within the EC government was formed to promote European culture in the media. They have several successful programs

---

[1] See etcenter.org/dcl.asp

assisting film, television production, film distribution, and exhibition. For example, the Europa Cinema group benefits largely from Media Plus assistance. Media Plus is also now exploring plans to support pilot Digital Cinema chains across Europe.

Framework 5 (Outgoing Research Project Framework)

The MetaVision project is described as follows: "The MetaVision project aims to ensure that European originated archives, films, and new productions can co-exist, integrate, and be interoperable with all the world's major current and planned systems (at both Standard and High Definition). It also aims to ensure that the equipment and systems are available specifically tailored to meet the technical, geographical, and linguistic interfaces and maintain the independence and cultural flair that makes European programme-making unique."[2]

Framework 6 (Incoming Research Project Framework)

Following the very successful Framework 5 technology initiative, the EC is now awarding projects for Framework 6. Framework 6 projects tend to be quite large and are often known as integrated projects. A typical project to cover Digital Cinema would bring together the exponents of the key technologies to make a Digital Cinema chain. It would work as follows: a lead company would contract to do the project administration, supported by companies and institutions that develop the key technology. Currently there are several Digital Cinema submissions to the Framework 6 board for approval.

In addition to the successful MetaVision project, there is a new project called METACAMERA that will develop a high spatial and temporal resolution camera to facilitate digital production and a follow-on compression system for distribution.

EUREKA

EUREKA is a long-standing European program for developing technology. It is coordinated by a Europewide body and funding is allocated on a national level. ITEA (Information Technology for European Advancement) runs

---

[2]www.ist-metavision.com

underneath the EUREKA umbrella and project number 00005 is set out to define production, distribution, and display standards.

European Digital Cinema Forum (EDCF)

EDCF is currently a voluntary body that aims to function as a network for European cooperation to:

◆ Identify key issues, gather information, and create models to encourage private investments and public support schemes.

◆ Liaise with other relevant bodies to assist in the establishment of appropriate worldwide standards for E-Cinema and D-Cinema. *E-Cinema* describes systems for large-screen presentations other than first-run film programs. They can be used for sports events, cultural events, and perhaps cine clubs. They may use standard or high-definition TV images and television color space. E-Cinema systems tend to be implemented with lower-cost equipment.

◆ Coordinate and establish European user requirements for standards for all parts of the E- and D-cinema chains through content, commercial, and technical modules.

◆ Initiate and coordinate R&D relevant to European Digital Cinema.

◆ Stimulate European production with a broad scope of quality content for E- and D-cinema.

Initially supported by institutions from France, the United Kingdom, and Sweden, the EDCF is now a formal organization set up under Dutch law with subscription-paying members from all across Europe. The board will be democratically elected.

LOCAL INITIATIVES

Belgium

Kinepolis

Kinepolis is a Belgian cinema operator with cinemas in Belgium, France, Spain, Switzerland, and Poland. They represent 85,000 seats with 24 million cinemagoers in 2003. Kinepolis is making a significant investment in digital projectors for digital movies, digital commercials, and other events. An initial order of 10 DLP cinema projectors has been placed.

Euro 1080 Event Channel

As an example of alternative content distribution, Euro 1080 broadcasts the first European HD channel in conjunction with Alfacam (a Belgian production facilities company), which relays live events such as rock concerts and football (in the United States, soccer) to the digital screens mentioned above.

France

CST

The CST (Commission Supérieure Technique de l'Image et du Son) is a government institution with regulatory authority. The CST for many years has set the design and operational standards for French cinemas and regularly inspects cinemas for conformance to its standards. The CST recently added to its web site a Digital Cinema supplement that specifies the requirements of Digital Cinema based on their existing celluloid standards.[3]

Video Transmission en Haute Resolution (VHTR)

VTHR is really the pioneer in large screen presentation. In operation since the early 1990s, it regularly transmits large-screen (non-Hollywood) presentations like classical concerts or opera performances all across France. One of the most popular programs is Sunday night wrestling. VTHR was set up to satisfy the need for large-screen entertainment in small communities across France.

Italy

The Italian Ministry of Culture is supporting the creation of a Digital Cinema laboratory and test facilities at the famous Cinecittà studio site.

---

[3]www.cst.fr

The Italian Ministry of Communications is also active in the issues of standardization of Digital Cinema. Together these activities are part of a new Moving Image Center.

Sweden

Folkets Hus Och Parker (FHP)

FHP owns a significant number of community venues in Sweden. Many of these are in small communities and have existing celluloid presentation capability. FHP have always suffered from availability problems with release prints. As Sweden is not a major market in Europe, the number of prints available is often limited. This can lead to a significant delay in receiving a film in a small community, which has a negative impact on any marketing operation for the film. As a result, in 2000 FHP decided to mount a Digital Cinema trial to see if digital distribution would yield more immediate availability within the distribution system. Pilot trials in 2002/2003 have been very successful. FHP now has 12 Digital Cinemas across Sweden, some in conventional cinema buildings and some in meeting halls. Initial benefits are increased availability and flexibility (it is very easy to change the movie according to different time slots). Alternative content is also facilitated.

UK

Digital Test Bed @ the National Film Theatre

The UK Department of Trade and Industry (DTI), in conjunction with the British Film Institute (under the UK Film Council as part of the Department of Culture and Media and Sport), has set up a *Digital Test Bed* (DTB) facility at the National Film Theatre. This facility has a fixed laboratory with a provision to bring in equipment for testing and experimentation as required. The intention is to work closely with the test labs in other parts of the world such as the Digital Cinema Laboratory in Hollywood and a planned Italian Test Bed at Cinecittà. The DTB has hosted several very valuable informational events, including a workshop for projectionists. In the near future it is intended to work toward international standards.

DTI/DCMS Group on Future Applications: "Electronic Film, Production, and Distribution"

The UK Department of Trade and Industry and the UK Department for Culture, Media and Sport formed a joint study group in 2000 to look into the emerging electronic and Digital Cinema area. This committee meets four times per year and has approximately 50 representatives from all the major sectors related to celluloid presentation and future digital presentation.

UK Film Council

Fund for Digital Production   The UK Film Council has a fund for promoting digital production. This fund sponsors short digital movies. Any format can be used from DV to HD.

Film Council Digital Screen Network (DSN)   The Film Council has also announced a cinema development fund called the *Digital Screen Network* that has allotted a significant amount of money (£13 million, or approximately $23.13 million) to promote the digitization of cinemas. As of May 2004, 14 companies had passed the pre-qualification stage and will be invited to tender to build and operate the Digital Screen Network of approximately 250 screens.

The driver behind both of these initiatives is the promotion of UK talent into the world arena by facilitating the making and presentation of specialized film that will reap the benefit of digital distribution. Until now, restricted print and distribution budgets have hampered local talent.

Electronic Theatre

This project was funded by the UK Department of Trade and Industry to evaluate the possibility of widening the sphere of cultural events by recording at the originating venue and then relaying via a variety of technologies to large screens in selected destination venues. For example, *Les Miserables* and *The Barber of Seville* were both relayed from live stages to remote audiences.

Arts Alliance

In the United Kingdom, the Arts Alliance (www.artsalliance.com, a private venture capital company) owns more than 100 independent screens under the City Screen label. Several of the City Screen venues already have digital capability. The Arts Alliance is putting together a pioneer consortium to operate a number of their screens digitally. If this is successful, they will look to a more comprehensive rollout.

EUROPEWIDE SPONSORED PROJECTS

E-Screen

E-Screen is an EC project, led by Elsacom (Italy) with the support of the European Space Agency, to set up the first multilanguage network for Digital Cinema. It was started in 2002 and has a network of film theatres using a satellite distribution network. There are currently eight screens in five countries. UCI Cinemas, *Screen Digest*[4] and Cinecittà are project partners. The next stage will offer a turnkey post production, multilingual mastering, encryption, encoding, and delivery system in conjunction with Marina Studios, Cinea, and Qubo.

European Docuzone

This project is an extension of the very successful Dutch Docuzone Program. The Dutch program will be extended to several other countries in Europe. The target is 175 screens. The equipment installed will be Digital Cinema grade with a mixture of DLP 1.3K and 2K projectors, as appropriate to the venue.

Theatre Heritage and Advancing Learning and International Access to Culture (THALIA)

THALIA is an 18-month project that began in January 2003. It is organized into six work packages, covering technology, business planning, investment sources, dissemination of results, quality assurance, and management. THALIA is the market validation phase of a new service to extend the cultural heritage of Europe's performing arts. The idea is to acquire the best of live theatre, and cultural and educational events and distribute them via a new network of electronic theatres for showing on large screens with high-quality sound. The service draws on recent developments in digital distribution and projection.

---

[4]www.screendigest.com

D-Cinema Europa Network (DCEN)

Initiated in 2002 by the Association Européenne pour la Diffusion du cinema Numérique[5] under the Media Plus program, DCEN aims at creating a network of digitally equipped theatres around Europe. These theatres are all part of the Europa Cinema network.

ORPHEUS

Initiated in April 2003 within the framework of the EC Media Plus Program, ORPHEUS is focused on the production, distribution, and exhibition of a set of alternative programs, focused on cultural features: four operas in HDTV and two digitally restored classic movies. The partners are Elsacom S.p.A., UCI, Cinecittà Holdings, BBC OpusArte, La Compagnie, and Lyric Theatre of Barcelona. The territorial coverage will include nine EU territories. The project's goal is to validate the distribution of alternative content and the ongoing definition of relevant business and operational models of doing so. Distribution will start by spring 2004.

E-CINEMA LIVE

T-systems has set up an E-Cinema distribution system called E-Cinema Live. Events so far have been a Bon Jovi concert, *The Barber of Seville*, a Melissa Etheridge DVD promotion, and an Elton John concert.

Commercials

There are digital systems delivering commercials in many parts of Europe, predominantly in Finland, the United Kingdom, and Germany.

Technology in Europe

There is a long tradition of local and Europewide funding for research, both commercial and academic, in both the technological and creative industries. As described earlier, Framework 5 funded many successful projects including MetaVision. Framework 6 is now under way with larger integrated projects such as RACINE IP.

Within Europe there are specialist manufacturers and vendors for the distribution and presentation of digital movies, including projectors, scaling

---

[5]www.adn-cinema.com/

systems, compression systems, server systems, security systems, and audio systems. In addition, European companies also make telecine machines, film scanners, and film recorders. Europe also has a large pool of skilled computer graphic artists and special effects experts.

Related Work

Digital Video Broadcasting (DVB)

While the primary goal of DVB is to oversee the technology for direct broadcasting, it has also generated standards for data broadcasting that are used worldwide. These standards are appropriate for Digital Cinema distribution by satellite.

Media Exchange Format (MXF)

Europe played a significant part in the standardization of MXF as a file wrapping format for data transmission. The MXF group is currently evaluating special profile requirements particular to Digital Cinema.

Formats for Europe: 2K/4K

It is expected that Europe will initially adopt a mostly MPEG-2 distribution system, migrating to 2048×1080. Presentation will be 2048×1080 nominal until 4K becomes a commercial reality. It is expected that the major studios will release digital movies at 4K resolution in the future, so an elegant method will be needed to avoid obsolescence and ensure interoperability. It is expected that presentation in Europe will be at 1K (1280×1024), 2K (2048×1080), or 4K (4096×2160) depending on the individual venue.

Special Issues Arising

Some discussion has occurred about adopting 25 fps for capture and presentation with the possibility of 50 fps for special presentation. This leads to the general issue of frame rate. There are now stunning archive restorations appearing, the great majority of which are 24 fps. Unlike film, a Digital Cinema system could support several frame rates in addition to 24:

for example, 16 fps for films made in the silent era, 30 fps for masterpieces like *Oklahoma*, and 48 fps to support high-speed motion within a film.

There is also a movement toward adopting the Univisium 2:1 aspect ratio, which in film terms can be originated on 35mm film within 3 perfs. One of the contenders for 4K presentation is 4K×2K, whose 2K equivalent is 2K×1K, which fits very well with the Univisium format with simple horizontal cropping for 1.85:1 or vertical cropping for 2.40:1.

An important factor in Europe will be the ability to screen movies originating from a variety of sources including DV. Since it is envisaged that many of the venues will be multipurpose, alternative content will be a very important factor.

ASIA

Background—Cinema and Economics

Asia is the most diverse film and cinema territory anywhere in the world, to the point where grouping its many countries and markets together begins to strain the notion of a single region. It features the world's potentially largest cinema audience (China), the world's most prolific film industry (India), the world's highest ticket prices (Japan), the world's highest level of piracy (Malaysia), and many other regional and local unique characteristics.

It is perhaps not surprising then that the region has seen almost as many different digital paths to cinemas as the rest of the world put together. These include the highest possible technical end of 4K Digital Cinema in Japan, to the world's largest Digital Cinema network in China, the most widespread second tier digital network in India, as well as regional digital hot spots such as Singapore. All of this exists on top of filmmaking markets, types of economies, and sociopolitical environments that can be wildly varying even within a single country, let alone between neighboring states or countries on opposite ends of the continent (e.g., Iran and the Philippines).

With Asia continuing to attract international attention as a global economic power center, with focus recently shifting from Japan to China, cinema and Digital Cinema have proven no exception. If not quite dictating the digital agenda, the region has a stronger potential to influence digital developments than any other territory outside of the United States, including Europe.

Even if no homogenous approach is ever likely to emerge from the continent,[6] it is well worth studying in its many digital incarnations for clues to how Digital Cinema in the rest of the world, including both developed and developing nations, may develop.

Exhibition

Exhibition in Asia is not easy to characterize, not least because the number of cinemas cannot be reliably quantified and the very definition of what constitutes a cinema as opposed to other form of screening venue is often in doubt. Add to this the highest level of piracy anywhere in the world, centered mainly on Southeast Asia, but also rampant in China, India, and (if online P2P piracy is included) advanced territories such as Korea and Japan. There is more stratification of cinema venue and quality tiers than in other regions, with many layers in between the familiar first-run modern multiplexes, second-tier cinemas, and non-cinema screening venues.

Mainstream

The highest-end cinemas follow the traditional pattern of multi- and megaplexes, whether in developed countries such as Japan or developing nations like Thailand. With a premium price for a premium product (mainly Hollywood features, with a varying degree of successful local productions), these cinemas must conform to the norms and standards that are dominant in the United States and elsewhere. They are installed both by local and international operators, such as UCI, Warner Bros., and even Kodak.

Most of the digital installations in such venues tend to be limited one-off installations in countries such as Taiwan, Thailand, and Hong Kong that are best characterized as *showcase*. Some exhibitors have sought to embrace high-end Digital Cinema on a wider scale, notably Japan's T-Joy consortium (centered on Toei), but recently also Singapore's Eng Wah, who announced plans to build a 20-screen multiplex totally equipped with DLP 2K projectors. China's 100-screen test bed network is the largest such premium installation base in the region.

---

[6]While this section in theory covers the whole of the Asia-Pacific region, there has been next to no Digital Cinema development in either Australia or New Zealand, despite both being major regional film production centers. As such, there is little reference to either territory, other than to note that they are likely to follow closely developments in the US and Europe.

Second and Third Tiers

Even major film markets such as India and China tend to have relatively limited releases of films, with even the largest blockbuster typically only going out on a few hundred prints. This means that there is an extensive network throughout Asia of second- and third-tier cinemas that have to wait a long time for prints, but whose primary audience can typically only afford a ticket price of less than U.S. $.20 to $.30. This is most common in India, which has a large urban and rural base of what are called B- and C-cinemas. Yet these cinemas offer escapism to the most avid cinema-going populations in the world, for example in the Philippines.

It is therefore not surprising that low end E-Cinema operations have had the greatest impact in the shortest time in India, where the Mukt/Adlab/GDC network of low cost digital screens has grown to over 100 in less than a year, screening on average a new title in digital every second week, day and date with major urban multiplexes.

Other

Even though widespread disk piracy satisfies most of the audience demand not met by the above type of cinemas, there is still a significant range of other cinema venues. Because it is difficult to define precisely whether these constitute cinemas, the calculation of film screens in the region can vary by tens of thousands. A notable case in point is China's network of traveling 16mm projectors in poor inland regions, which are set for a digital upgrade as part of the effort to have 2,500 E-Cinema screens in place across the country in time for the 2008 Beijing Olympics.

Screen Sizes

Screen sizes vary tremendously across Asia, home to the most cinemas and screens (any way counted) anywhere in the world. These range from the many Imax cinemas, to large multiplex and single screen cinemas, down to the tiniest improvised screen for an ad hoc projection of a pirated or old 16mm copy. With 2K Digital Cinema projectors destined for multiplexes, a great range of projectors can be expected at all other screening venues, including HD, E-Cinema, SD, and simple video projectors.

Temporary Venues

Temporary screening venues play a larger part in Asia than in probably any other part of the world. These include mobile cinemas, but can also be considered to include makeshift "video cinemas" showing the latest pirated Hollywood blockbuster.

Health and Safety Requirements

Health and safety requirements vary significantly across the region.

Standards for Venues

Many Asian territories lay down various levels of strict requirements for cinemas, though these are mostly not related to technical specifications or performance but rather religious or socio-economic in nature.

Distribution

While Hollywood films often dominate, there are strong local distributors in most Asian territories who handle all manner of films. The greatest battle they face is not between foreign and domestic films, or the films of their rivals, but the battle to beat the pirates in supplying the film to audiences in a timely, convenient, and affordable manner. This is where most observers see digital distribution and exhibition as having the greatest potential for the exhibition industry.

Censors

Varying degrees of censorship range from total restriction (in North Korea), to import restrictions and restraints on subject matters of domestic films (China, Vietnam, and Burma), self-censorship on a range of taboo subjects and explicit gestures (India), to strong moral clampdowns (Singapore), and many other forms of political, moral, religious, economical, and social restrictions. As such, these territories will closely monitor what impact the introduction of digital technology in film distribution and projection is likely to have.

Dubbing

Several countries tend to dub imported films into local languages or dialects. There are no clear rules for where and how these traditions are to be found across Asian territories.

Subtitles

Subtitling is important, not only for imported foreign films (whether from Hollywood, Bollywood, Hong Kong, or elsewhere), but equally so for the many different ethnic and linguistic groups within any one country. These minority cinema audiences can account for tens if not hundreds of millions of cinema goers, potentially disenfranchised at the box office if films are only supplied in the dominant language of the country, be it Mandarin, Hindi, or anything else.

Alternative Content and Advertising

The screening of alternative content and digital advertising has been low-key to non-existent in most of Asia. This will change as preparations get underway for the Beijing 2008 Olympics, which is expected to be a showcase of HDTV and Digital Cinema technology and capability in China.

LATIN AMERICA

Background—Cinema and Economics

Latin America is a strong emerging cinema market, despite the financial crisis that much of the region suffered in the late 1990s. South America and to a lesser extent Central America (with the exception of Mexico) have seen major investment in the exhibition sector, with majors from North America and Australia all building multiplexes to cater to higher-quality demand from local middle classes. At the same time, many territories remain significantly under-screened and the majority of the populations are financially excluded from these better cinemas because of the high ticket prices.

There is limited state support for cinemas, other than informal screening venues, which tend to be financed by charitable institutions. Several Latin American countries have seen revivals of their domestic film industries, particularly Mexico, Brazil, and Argentina, with films that have become major art house hits in the U.S. and Europe. Yet overall the local film industries tend to be small, with little inter-American export of film and a primary reliance on Hollywood for popular content. The currency crisis has led to fewer prints being made of popular hits (domestic and Hollywood) and there is a significant level of piracy, if not as high as in some parts of Asia. Television and particularly *Telenovellas* remain the most popular form of mass entertainment.

While Mexico was the first country with a high-end Digital Cinema installation (in 2000), it is Brazil that has become the sole Latin American territory with a major Digital Cinema program, thanks to the efforts of post production major TeleImage.

Exhibition

Mainstream

Mainstream cinemas tend to be modern multiplexes in large cities, built in the last five to ten years. While there has been significant investment from overseas cinema operators (UCI, Hoyts, Village Roadshow, Cineplex, and many others), local operators have also tapped into the middle classes' demand for upscale screening venues, notably CineMex in Mexico and Ribeiro in Brazil. Most of the content in these cinemas tend to be Hollywood blockbusters, but with local productions in resurgence, there have at times been an even split between popular local films and Hollywood imports. In Brazil, TeleImage has worked with majors such as UCI to fit out new multiplexes with digital-only screens.

Second run

Second run cinemas tend to show the same content as the mainstream multiplexes, but at a later date and at a cheaper ticket price. These are found mainly in smaller cities and rural areas but also in less affluent parts of major metropolitan regions. The prints tend to be old and scratched, and overall exhibition quality, from seating to audio, leaves a lot to be desired. It is these venues that Brazil's Rain Network is targeting with its low-cost MPEG-4-based solution.

Other

This category encompasses everything from mobile screening venues (in Mexico a handful of these are even digital) to temporary screening venues in places such as schools, film clubs, prisons, universities, churches, and community centers, many using 16mm projectors. There is also a small number of art house cinemas, though their impact and importance on the overall cinema market is limited.

Screen Sizes

Screen sizes vary greatly depending on the cinema venue. There are still some surviving movie palaces from the Golden Age of Latin America film and cinema (1930s up to 1950s and the arrival of television) with screens 40 meters wide. Multiplexes and art house cinemas are similar to U.S. and West European screen sizes, as are Imax-type cinemas.

Temporary Venues

There is a great variety of temporary venues, as discussed above.

Health and Safety requirements

Modern multiplexes have health and safety regulations in line with those in Europe and U.S., though they tend to have little impact on Digital Cinema or E-Cinema deployments, mainly due to the small number of installations.

Standards for Venues

No Latin American country imposes regulations for the standards of venues, other than health and safety ones, such as fire exits, discussed above.

Distribution

Film distributors are generally affiliated with one or more of the Hollywood studios, often in partnership with a local player. TeleImage has been successful in dealing with all major distributors for both domestic, Hollywood, and art house/European films, in securing content for its digital network. It also often acts as co-producer, by virtue of its role as post production and completion major in Brazil. It has also managed to create digital distribution masters of mainstream Hollywood titles.

Censors

All Latin American countries have institutional film classification and censor offices, which must approve all cinema releases. While there is some restriction on sex, violence, and religious portrayal, the level of censorship is not greatly different from those of most European territories (with some notable exceptions such as Cuba).

Dubbing

Apart from children's films, most foreign films are shown in their original language. Attempts to move to dubbing of Hollywood films in Mexico met with a major industry backlash in 2003.

Subtitles

Subtitling is the preferred means of translating foreign films in Latin America. In Brazil (which is the only significant non-Spanish speaking country in Latin America), TeleImage had to resort to scanning release prints that had subtitles laser burnt into them previously, as there was no electronic subtitling option available to it in its first years of operation, and films could thus not be electronically "subtitled" in the projector or server.

Alternative Content and Advertising

TeleImage has been at the forefront of screening alternative content in its network of digital screens (seven as of early 2004). It has shown the World Cup in HDTV in 2002, as well as Formula One, pop and rock concerts, DVD launches, and special promotional and corporate events. The company also has its own sports rights and deals with Globo. It has funded the digital installations through ingenious sponsorship deals with technology companies such as Intel. Overall, the company has been one of the most noteworthy proponents and exploiters anywhere in the world of the full capabilities that Digital Cinema has to offer.

AFRICA & MIDDLE EAST

Background—Cinema and Economics

The majority of sub-Saharan Africa, North Africa, and the Middle East are under-developed cinema markets, with little external or internal investment in the cinema industry and minimal domestic film production and distribution. While there are incentives for adopting lower-end digital distribution and projection solutions, most countries are too poor to have even a sustainable E-Cinema network along the lines of India. Most common are public venues where VHS machines are connected to a television set, screening videos that more often than not are pirate copies, in what are best described as "video cinemas."

Exhibition

With the exception of a small number of upmarket cinemas in affluent Gulf Region states, the only two territories with any major cinema markets comparable to those in OECD countries are Israel and South Africa. Both of those countries have cinema operators who are active beyond their borders, with Ster Kinekor and International Theatres having invested in several European countries. Cinemas in the region split between modern, second-tier, and community networks.

Modern

Modern multiplexes are built in South Africa, Israel, and some larger cities in wealthier states to cater to the upper and middle classes. Apart from the first two territories, even these cinemas tend to get print copies long after the pirate version of the same film has been widely in circulation. Multiplex standards in South Africa and Israel are comparable to the best in North America and Europe, though also here they are not priorities in international distribution patterns.

Second Tier

These are cinemas for the masses, which tend to show old prints of everything from Hollywood films to Bollywood imports and some local releases. Ticket prices are cheap and the quality of standard varies, but is generally low.

Community

These are improvised cinemas in schools, churches, and other community venues. Some use 16mm projectors, others just a VHS and a television.

Screen Sizes

Screen sizes at modern multiplexes correspond to those of typical multiplexes in the West, with a limited number of large format (e.g., IMAX) screens as well.

Temporary Venues

While there are some outdoor cinemas, most of the temporary venues tend to come under the community cinemas heading, discussed previously.

Health and Safety Requirements

The few modern multiplexes tend to have stringent health and safety requirements, while second-tier and community cinemas have a poor record of complying with any existing health and safety requirements.

Standards for Venues

There are no mandated standards for cinema venues in Africa and the Middle East, other than separation of female and male patrons in Muslim countries. Modern multiplexes tend to follow SMPTE guidelines and a limited number have THX or Dolby certification.

Distribution

Distribution of Hollywood films is handled by local affiliates, who also tend to deal with any domestic distribution.

Censors

Censorship differs greatly among different countries in Africa and the Middle East, most of it directly connected to the local political situation and religious groups. The former is particularly sensitive, whether for majority or minority groups, with religious organizations acting as de facto film, media, and print censors. Widespread piracy, however, means that material that would not be approved by the powers that be still gets widely distributed and seen.

Dubbing

Dubbing is common in some countries, though often restricted to single voiceover.

Subtitles

Subtitling is common in both Israel and South Africa for local languages and is also used to a limited degree in other territories.

Alternative Content and Advertising

South Africa has been at the forefront in the region for alternative content, mainly thanks to the efforts of exhibitor Ster Kinekor, cinema advertiser

Cinemark, and technology integrator Spectrum Visual Networks. Having converted more than 50 screens to low-end digital for advertising, these have also been used to screen everything from sports matches to four film festivals on niche subjects (short films, gay and lesbian films, etc.) in its first year of operation. Israel and other territories have not pursued digital advertising and alternative content to the same extent.

Appendix

The DC28 Standard

Wendy Aylsworth
Chair, Digital Cinema Technology Committee, SMPTE DC28

The Society of Motion Picture and Television Engineers (SMPTE), www.smpte.org , exists to advance the engineering and technical aspects of the motion picture, television, and allied arts and sciences. This is accomplished through the dissemination of scientific information, education, and the publication of standards that further the interests of the general public in these arenas.

The Digital Cinema Technology Committee, DC28, was created in 2000 to develop and recommend an approach to D-cinema. An important goal was to ensure in the future the benefit of the past—a single distribution method that could be exhibited in any theater. Approximately 3 years were spent assessing the end-to-end aspects of picture mastering, compression, copy protection, transport, audio, theater systems, and projection. These assessments included the readiness of technology and the marketplace, as well as what standards would need to be developed by DC28 as opposed to standards in other SMPTE Technology Committees or other standards bodies that could be readily applied, such as wrappers, metadata, compression and transport. Following this initial phase, the committee was reorganized in 2003 into the current structure of three working groups responsible for the generation of a suite of engineering documents in the areas of mastering, distribution, and exhibition.

The Mastering Working Group is responsible for the development of engineering documents as they relate to all the forms of content, including picture, audio, subtitling, etc., that will be delivered to the world's exhibition theaters. The Distribution Working Group is responsible for the development of engineering documents as they relate to the compression, encryption, packaging, and transport of the mastered content. Their documents also include information on the proper composition and playout of the content, as well information related to regional geographic requirements for motion pictures. The Exhibition Working Group is responsible for the development of engineering documents as they relate to the reception, security, and uniform quality playout of the content, as well as the operational management of both the content and systems.

International participation in DC28 is critical to the goal of a worldwide standard. You can join in this groundbreaking work and partake in a significant piece of history by joining SMPTE at http://www.smpte.org/membership/. As of June 2004, about half of the necessary standards, recommended practices, and engineering guidelines have been drafted and have started going through the process of open standards review, revision, and balloting. Beyond the initial suite of standards, continuing work will be required to ensure interoperability among these evolving standards. International collaboration will be critical over the coming years to ensure these engineering documents form a solid foundation for the coming century of motion pictures.

Contributor Biographies

Darcy Antonellis, Executive Vice President, Distribution and Technology Operations, Warner Bros. Technical Operations Inc. and Senior Vice President, Worldwide Anti-Piracy Operations, Warner Bros. Entertainment Inc.

At Warner Bros., Darcy has been responsible for the studio's conversion to digital distribution including their recent migration to the next generation store and forward content delivery. Her newly appointed corporate position for Warner Bros. Entertainment Inc. encompasses worldwide oversight of the company's anti-piracy activities. She was elected a Fellow and Governor of SMPTE in 2003. In 2002, she was selected as one of *Broadcasting and Cable Magazine*'s top ten "Next Wave" female industry executives in the area of technology. She is a two-time Emmy winner for Technical Production for both the 1994 Lillehammer and 1998 Nagano Winter Olympics while working for CBS as Vice President of Olympics and Technical Operations.

Chris Carey, Senior Vice President, Studio New Technology, The Walt Disney Studios.

Chris is responsible for coordinating all of the technological strategies, standards, and policies for the studio across all of its production, manufacturing and distribution divisions. Previously, he was Senior Vice President and General Manager of Worldwide Post Production and Operations. In that capacity, Chris oversaw all creative and technical aspects of the DVD, Video, and Theatrical Distribution operations. Prior to that position he was Senior Vice President of Post Production Services, overseeing all aspects of Post Production within the studio.

Matt Cowan, Principal and Founder, Entertainment Technology Consultants.

Matt is a principal at Entertainment Technology Consultants, an organization specializing in the science and applications of Digital Cinema technology. He has over 20 years experience in the development and application of new products in the media and display fields. Matt was instrumental in developing the current mastering processes used in Digital Cinema, which introduced the use of the digital mastering theatre for color and dynamic range adjustment.

Richard Crudo, ASC, President, American Society of Cinematographers.

In addition to wide ranging commercial and television work, Richard has shot numerous independent and studio films. His first independent feature credit was in 1994 on a black-and-white film, *Federal Hill.* His other credits include *American Buffalo, The Low Life, American Pie, Music from Another Room, Bongwater, Outside Providence, Down to Earth, Out Cold, Bring It on Again, and Grind*

David Gray, Vice President, Production Services, Dolby Laboratories, Inc.

David joined Dolby Laboratories in 1980 as an applications engineer in the Los Angeles office and attained his current position of Vice President, Production Services in 1993. David received a Scientific and Engineering award from the Academy of Motion Picture Arts and Sciences in 1992 and was the 1994 recipient of the SMPTE Samuel L. Warner Award for contributions to motion picture sound. In 1998 he received the John A. Bonner Medal of Commendation for outstanding service and dedication in upholding the high standards of the Academy of Motion Picture Arts and Sciences.

Michael Karagosian, Partner, Karagosian MacCalla Partners (KMP).

Michael is advisor on Digital Cinema technology and policy issues to the National Association of Theatre Owners. He co-chaired the SMPTE DC28.7 Working Group on Theatre Systems, founded and chaired the DC28 Packaging Ad Hoc Group, and is secretary to the DC28.30 Working Group on Exhibition. As a partner in Karagosian MacCalla Partners, he advises the UK Film Council in their planned rollout of 250 Digital Cinema screens in 2004-2005. He designed the world's first 5.1 format cinema processor for Dolby Laboratories, and also the first THX-approved cinema processor. His DSP-based surround decoder is used today by studios such as Skywalker Sound, Industrial Light and Magic, and Pixar Animation Studios.

Glenn Kennel, Texas Instruments.

In a 20-year career with Kodak, Glenn developed digital products and processes for motion picture post production and display. As a consultant, he helped Digital Cinema Initiatives (DCI) draft the technical specifications for Digital Cinema. He recently joined the DLP Cinema™ group of Texas Instruments in a role that includes technology and business development. Glenn also chairs the SMPTE DC28 Color ad hoc group.

Bill Kinder, Pixar Animation Studios.

Bill leads Pixar's efforts in Digital Cinema, achieving the first ever digital theatrical release of a digitally produced film, *Toy Story 2.* Bill has innovated digital mastering methods at the studio since *A Bug's Life* DVD, the first ever created directly from a digital source. Most recently he produced the DVD for *Finding Nemo. Toy Story 2, A Bug's Life,* and *Finding Nemo* are all Pixar Animation Studio films presented by Walt Disney Pictures.

Bob Lambert, Senior Vice President, Worldwide Media Technology and Development, The Walt Disney Company.

Bob's New Technology & New Media group is responsible for identifying and developing new technologies and related new business opportunities that will have an impact on the entertainment industry in the years ahead, and for integrating these new media initiatives into company strategies and practices. Bob has been active in digital production, Digital Cinema, next generation media, and technical development for twenty years.

Loren Nielsen, Principal and Founder, Entertainment Technology Consultants.

Loren is co-founder of Entertainment Technology Consultants, where she focuses on technical issues around achieving theatrical-looking images using digital technologies. Her background incorporates over 15 years of management and marketing of start-up ventures in the technology and entertainment industries. She is in demand as a producer of high-quality presentations for the demonstration of new technology to the entertainment community and is active in the development of business models for Digital Cinema.

Charles Poynton, Color Scientist.

Charles is an independent contractor specializing in the physics, mathematics, and engineering of digital color imaging systems, including digital video, HDTV, and Digital Cinema (D-cinema). A Fellow of SMPTE, Charles was awarded the Society's prestigious David Sarnoff Gold Medal for his work to integrate video technology with computing and communications. He is the author of *Digital Video and HDTV: Algorithms and Interfaces.*

Robert Schumann, President, Cinea, Inc. A Subsidiary of Dolby Labs.

Robert has been involved with securing high-value movie content since 1994. He has worked extensively on closed and open security systems within multimedia playback systems. He holds four issued U.S. patents and has been a member of the SMPTE DC28 security standards groups since 2000. He founded Cinea, Inc. in 1999.

Leon Silverman, Executive Vice President, LaserPacific Media Corporation.

Leon joined Eastman Kodak when LaserPacific Media Corporation was acquired in 2003. In addition to his role at LaserPacific, he serves Kodak as the Director of Strategic Business Development and Entertainment Imaging Services, and a is Vice President of Entertainment Imaging.

Peter Symes, Manager, Advanced Technology, Thomson Broadcast & Media Solutions.

Peter has been working in the television industry since 1967. He is the Engineering Vice President of SMPTE and follows closely the development and standardization processes for Digital Cinema. Peter is the author of *Video Compression Demystified.*

Charles S. Swartz, Executive Director & CEO, Entertainment Technology Center at the University of Southern California.

Charles oversees efforts to further the entertainment industry through new technology. He assumed his current position at the Entertainment Technology Center in 2002, where he has refocused and recharged the research center. He serves in two positions for the Society of Motion Picture and Television Engineers (SMPTE): Governor representing the Hollywood Region and co-chair of the Hollywood education committee. In 1996, the *Los Angeles Business Journal* named Charles one of 100 technology leaders in Los Angeles. In 2004 he was named a Fellow of SMPTE.

Patrick Von Sychowski, Senior Analyst, *Screen Digest.*

Patrick pioneered the coverage of Digital Cinema research for *Screen Digest.* He is an adviser to several commercial and public Digital Cinema projects in Europe. Patrick is also the founder and editor of *Screen Digest's* E-Cinema Alert industry newsletter.

Peter Wilson, Vice President, Display Technologies, Snell and Wilcox Ltd.

Peter is a member of the management team at Hampshire, UK-based Snell and Wilcox Ltd. His responsibilities are Digital Cinema and Display Products. He has been involved with both film and television for over 25 years, many of these in a pioneering role. Peter has been in key roles furthering the cause of HDTV for 19 years, first for Sony and then for Snell and Wilcox. He was instrumental in setting up the world's first high-resolution Digital Cinema demonstration in 1988. Peter also facilitated the very first feature movie shot in HD, *Julia and Julia.*

Index

DATE DUE

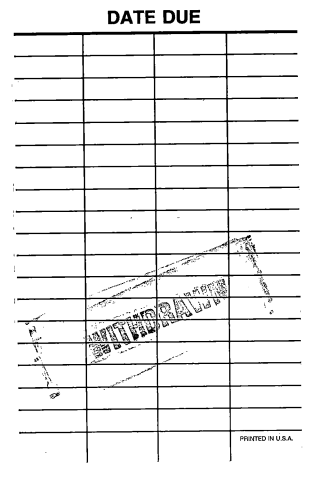